Metaphor
and the Poetry of
Williams, Pound, and Stevens

Metaphor
and the Poetry of
Williams, Pound, and Stevens

Suzanne Juhasz

Lewisburg
BUCKNELL UNIVERSITY PRESS

© 1974 by Associated University Presses, Inc.
Associated University Presses, Inc.
Cranbury, New Jersey 08512

Library of Congress Cataloging in Publication Data

Juhasz, Suzanne, 1942–
    Metaphor and the poetry of Williams, Pound, and
Stevens.

    Bibliography: p.
    1. Metaphor.   2. Williams, William Carlos,
1883–1963. 3. Pound, Ezra Loomis, 1885–1972. 4. Stevens,
Wallace, 1879–1955.   I. Title.
PS310.M4J8   811'.5'208   72-13393
    ISBN 0-8387-1243-6

For Jo and Joseph

Contents

7

Acknowledgments

I wish to thank the following publishers for having given me permission to quote from published works:

Jonathan Cape Ltd. for permission to quote from *The Poetry of Robert Frost,* edited by Edward Connery Lathem. Reprinted by permission of Jonathan Cape Ltd. on behalf of the Estate of Robert Frost.

Faber and Faber Limited for permission to quote from Ezra Pound, *Collected Shorter Poems,* 1926, and *The Cantos,* 1956. Reprinted by permission of Faber and Faber Ltd. Also for permission to quote from Wallace Stevens, *The Necessary Angel,* 1965, *Collected Poems,* 1954, and *Opus Posthumous,* 1957. Reprinted by permission of Faber and Faber Ltd.

Grove Press for permission to quote from H.D., *Selected Poems,* 1957. Reprinted by permission of Grove Press, Inc. Copyright © 1957 by Norman Holmes Pearson.

Harvard University Press for permission to quote from J. Hillis Miller, *Poets of Reality,* 1965. Reprinted by permission of the Belknap Press of Harvard University Press.

Holt, Rinehart and Winston, Inc. for permission to quote from *The Poetry of Robert Frost* edited by Edward Connery Lathem. Copyright 1916, (c) 1969 by Holt, Rinehart and Winston, Inc. Reprinted by permission of Holt, Rinehart and Winston, Inc.

Alfred A. Knopf, Inc., for permission to quote from Wallace Stevens, *The Necessary Angel,* 1965, *The Collected Poems of Wallace Stevens,* 1954, and *Opus Posthumous,* edited by Samuel French Morse, 1957.

MacGibbon & Kee Ltd. for permission to quote from William Carlos Williams, *The Collected Earlier Poems,* 1951, *Many Loves and Other Plays,* 1961, *Selected Essays,* 1954, *Pictures*

Metaphor
and the Poetry of
Williams, Pound, and Stevens

1
Metaphor and Imagism

Williams, Pound, Stevens, and the Imagist Movement

William Carlos Williams, Ezra Pound, and Wallace Stevens are modern poets whose use of metaphor is fundamental to the structure of their poetry. The essays in this book closely examine each poet's characteristic use of metaphor and the function it fulfills in his work, especially in long poems: Williams's "Asphodel, That Greeny Flower" and *Paterson*, Pound's *Cantos*, and Stevens's *Notes Towards a Supreme Fiction*.

In this chapter, after summarizing the function of metaphor in the work of each of the poets (the substance in brief ot the subsequent chapters), I concentrate upon the poets as a group: on what their practices and their theories have in common. I find in Imagism a source and common denominator for their shared ideas. Specifically, I see their emphasis upon metaphor as a structuring element in poetry as a means by which they have dealt with the problems raised by the Imagist aesthetic, which is at least in part their own.

Metaphor functions in Williams's poetry as the linguistic embodiment of the imagination. The imagination, for Williams, is that power which mediates between the mind and the world. It liberates both words and objects by transposing them into the medium of the imagination. Williams uses metaphor to define the relations that exist between the particular forms and objects in the world. He views these relations in terms of dualities, so that metaphor's primary function is to suggest the nature of dualities and, especially, to conjoin their elements: to bring them together as closely as possible for the purpose of revelation. Metaphor, as the agent of the imagination, can accomplish this movement toward unity, toward the reparation of what Williams sees as the essentially divorced condition of modern life.

In his earlier poetry Williams uses metaphor in this way to render fully the complexities inherent in a moment of perception. In his old age he applies new insight to his use of metaphor and comes to see that art, which presents objects elevated by the action of the imagination to a form of truth unavailable to them in their original form, is what we mean when we use the term *reality*. The ability of metaphor to conjoin dualities is what is real, and the separation of things into dualities is what is not real; it is art (the work of the imagination) that can achieve this vital reality.

In "Asphodel, That Greeny Flower," an important long poem of his old age, Williams builds a poem about love and the imagination around one figure only, the figure of the flower. Since all of the poem's metaphors originate from this one center, the pattern they create from their pronounced consistency in function and form, moving and developing through three books and a coda, controls the structure of the total poem.

Williams's major work, *Paterson,* is a much longer and less tightly structured poem than is "Asphodel," yet it, too, depends for its complex development upon a similar use of metaphor and the creation of pattern from these metaphors. Each of its first four books explores a specific duality: subjective-objective; artifact-artist; artistic form-natural form; perversion-virtue. Its fifth book, the book of the imagination, uses metaphor in the same way in order to describe the imagination's power to achieve harmony. In each book the duality is first presented at its simplest level, usually by means of an image of a concrete object. Metaphors, continually used in reference to this image, extend and develop its implications, thereby obliquely controlling the progression of the poem and linking its varied and assorted segments together.

Although Ezra Pound's theory and practice of metaphor differ in many respects from those of Williams, he, too, uses metaphor and the patterns that metaphors form to provide structure in *The Cantos*. Pound wishes to foster a direct and active response to poetry, rather than one that is intellectual and abstracting. Metaphor is a primary agent in provoking this kind of response. Individually, metaphors are the most compressed form of image, in that, since they are basically unparaphrasable, an understanding of them depends upon imaging rather than explanation. Pound's basic form for metaphor is the compound word, which selects concrete elements from a perception or experience and juxtaposes them to form a new and third entity: an image, in Pound's use of the term. The compound word omits any linguistic rendering of the relation between the two elements, for the hyphen is like an arrow, pointing to a relation that the reader must supply himself by an active recreation or image. In sequence, Pound's metaphors form patterns in accordance with the sound and rhythm patterns of words (*melopoeia*) rather than by logical or explicit connections. Melopoeia, too, requires a direct, moment-to-moment response from the reader.

In addition, metaphor is for Pound a linguistic agent—not of the imagination, as it is for Williams—but of the truth. Figurative language can effectively present the true lines of relation that exist between all the forces of existence. Literature should both call forth and also express action—especially emotional experience. Metaphor, because of its function as a linguistic agent of the truth, is the most powerful form in which verbal equations for human emotions can be achieved. In *The Cantos* gods and visions of the gods are so important because the gods themselves are outward manifestations of states of mind or mood; visions of them, expressed through myth, are those very moments when things internal are transformed, through art, into things external.

Pound has many styles in *The Cantos,* each one appropriate for rendering specific subject matter. Metaphor is especially suited to the gods and is used to express those visions of the gods which form one strand in the organizational structure of Pound's gargantuan work.

The primary function of metaphor in the poetry of Wallace Stevens is to effect a relation between the abstract and concrete elements of language that is indicative of the existing situation in human experience. All of Stevens's speculations about the nature of man and of the world revolve around the complexity of the relation between imagination and reality, a problem that he is continually approaching from new perspectives and points of view. In his theory he sometimes views metaphor as a solution to the problem and sometimes as a major obstacle to its solution. However, as he postulates these theories throughout his works of poetry, his use of metaphor remains consistent. Poems may talk about a world without metaphor, but they seem to need metaphor to express these ideas—that is, in order to be poems.

Notes Towards a Supreme Fiction is an example of Stevens's characteristic metaphoric technique as it is used to structure a long, major work. Series of metaphors exemplify or embody abstract statements that precede them. They move back and forth from abstract to concrete language, constantly creating relations between abstract and concrete phenomena. The metaphors are usually a series of parallel statements, phrases in apposition to one another and to the introductory statement that they also modify. Within each section the metaphors, because of this structure, define the concept in question by acting as a totality of what Stevens calls its complications or resemblances. This form extends from smaller to larger structures of the work. It compasses the relation of the ten sections in each part of the poem to their titles, which are also statements of concepts ("It Must Be Abstract," "It Must Change," "It Must Give Pleasure"), and the relation of the three parts to the title of the total work, *Notes Towards a Supreme Fiction.*

For each of the poets, although his use will display many variations, there is a characteristic form of metaphor. For Williams a characteristic form would be "Love is a flower." The act of the imagination conjoins love and flower by means of a direct metaphoric transfer, a copula, and links "idea" and "thing." In a Williams poem such an initial conjunction would be extensively explored through a sequence of related metaphors. Characteristic of Stevens's metaphors is a phrase like "Winter and spring, cold copulars, embrace." The transfers of metaphor tend to occur within an appositional phrase. They give physical form to abstractions but in the process move back again into abstraction, as is the case with the phrase *cold copulars*. The object or concept in question will be defined by a series of such modifying phrases, which parallel one another. For Pound the characteristic metaphor is the compound word. It often occurs in a three-word phrase, such as *nymphs white-gathered*. The metaphoric transfer occurs by means of the hyphen, which yokes two elements of a perception and points to a relation between them.

Although they have important individual differences, all three poets share many of the most basic assumptions in their approaches to metaphor and to poetry. They share the belief that metaphor is not ornament or decoration but is central to poetic vision: it can reveal the truth. The belief in the intrinsic truth of the metaphoric transfer is accompanied, in their critical writings, by a stress upon metaphor as a language form. All of the poets grant to language the power to achieve something that is impossible in either action or thought alone, and to metaphor a particularly vital role in that achievement. This has much to do, it seems to me, with the fact that language has both a figurative and literal dimension. Each of the poets uses metaphor to indicate relations that are at the core of his poetic concerns: for Williams it is the nature of the relation between "idea" and "thing"; for Stevens, that between abstract and concrete; for Pound, that between emotion and action. Each is aware of a gap, in some form, between inner and outer, and his use of language utilizes the existence of the nonliteral as a means of bridging that gap. Finally, perhaps because of the power they grant to language, all three write poems that call attention to themselves as language acts.

Looking for a common basis for their beliefs, one easily turns to that literary movement, or moment, called Imagism, with its accompanying pronouncements, programs, and propaganda. Historically, both Pound and Williams were associated with those poets whom Pound called "imagistes" and published in *Des Imagistes: An Anthology* in 1914. In New York before the war Stevens was connected with Williams and others, notably Kreymbourg and Arensberg, editors of *Others*, which published much of his (and Williams's) early poetry.[1]

Whether or not one wishes to classify that fluid assemblage of poets as a movement or school, Imagism, as Stanley Coffman points out in his *Imagism: A Chapter for the History of Modern Poetry*, has a fuller meaning: "it was the first attempt by contemporary poets to formulate a change of direction that would mark them as contemporary."[2] Williams, Pound, and Stevens all envisioned change, and of necessity in the contemporary manner; the nature of such change is generally in accord with the aesthetics of Imagism.

Imagist theory, as articulated at various moments in the movement's history by Pound, Flint, Hulme, and Amy Lowell, attempts to stress the objective, the particular, the precise, the concrete, the visual. In Flint's essay from *The Egoist* of May 1915, he describes the earliest days (1909) of the new movement, with Hulme as "ringleader": "He insisted too on absolute accurate presentation and no verbiage." In the March 1913 issue

---

1. Robert Buttel, in his *Wallace Stevens: The Making of "Harmonium"* (Princeton, N. J., 1967), writes on p. 126:

Stevens' association with Arensberg, who, according to Kreymbourg, was "passionately fond of Pound and the Imagists" (*Troubadour, An Autobiography* [New York, 1925], p. 221) and with William Carlos Williams, who remained in close touch with Pound, brought him near the vortex of Imagist theory and practice; and the Imagists' poetry generally, reaching its height in the years between 1913 and 1917, no doubt spurred his own experiments in this vein.

2. Norman, Oklahoma, 1951, p. 4.

of *Poetry* there appeared this list of Imagist principles in Flint's article, "Imagisme":

1. Direct treatment of the "thing," whether subjective or objective.
2. To use absolutely no word that does not contribute to the presentation.
3. As regarding rhythm: to compose in the sequence of the musical phrase, not in the sequence of a metronome.[3]

and also, in "A Few Don'ts by an Imagiste," appeared Pound's famous definition of the image:

An "Image" is that which presents an intellectual and emotional complex in an instant of time.[4]

Amy Lowell expanded the original three rules into six in her first Imagist anthology, *Some Imagist Poets* (1915). Among them are the following:

1. To use the language of common speech, but to employ always the *exact* word, not the nearly exact, nor the merely decorative word.
2. To present an image (hence the name: "Imagist"). We are not a school of painters, but we believe that poetry should render particulars exactly and not deal in vague generalities, however magnificent and sonorous. It is for this reason that we oppose the cosmic poet, who seems to us to shirk the real difficulties of his art.
5. To produce poetry that is hard and clear, never blurred nor indefinite.
6. Finally, most of us believe that concentration is of the very essence of poetry.

"Hard and clear" comes, as does so much of what the poets themselves write, from the philosopher associated with the Imagist movement, T. E. Hulme. "It is essential to prove that beauty may be in small, dry things."[5]

---

3. *Poetry* 1, no. 6 (March 1913): 199.
4. Pp. 200–201.
5. "Romanticism and Classicism," *Critiques and Essays in Criticism, 1920–1948,* ed. Robert Stallman (New York, 1949), p. 12.

The Imagist poem presents the image, which is the "thing" itself, but as perceived by the poet; that is, the image has to be impression or "sensation" (Hulme) as much as it is object. "Poetry," said Hulme,

> is not a counter language, but a visual, concrete one. It is a compromise for a language of intuition which would hand over sensations bodily. It always endeavors to arrest you, and to make you continuously *see a physical thing*, to prevent you gliding through an abstract process. . . . Images in verse are not mere decoration, but the very essence of an intuitive language.[6] [Italics mine]

Objective, however, implies the existence, if not the expression, of the subjective; *particular*, of the general; *precise*, of the imprecise; *concrete*, of the abstract; *concise*, of the expanded; *visual*, of the unseen. These are the other side of experience, which is something recognized by the Imagist poets in their poetry, if not in their manifestos. Yet Pound's conception of an image as an "intellectual and emotional complex" surely indicates that the image has a dual function, that of expressing both the inner and the outer components of an experience. So does his redefinition of the image as the vortex: "The image is not an idea. It is a radiant node or cluster; it is what I can, and must perforce, call a VORTEX, from which, and through which, and into which, ideas are constantly rushing,"[7] even as does his description of the one-image poem, "In a Station of the Metro": "In a poem of this sort one is trying to record the precise instant when a thing outward or objective transforms itself, or darts into a thing inward and subjective."[8]

Josephine Miles, describing vocabulary and objects in modern poetry, comes to the heart of the issue: "In all these versions of the natural world, things mean or be not in themselves but as objects which are under pressure from meanings beyond them."[9]

---

6. P. 13.
7. *Gaudier-Brzeska* (London, 1916), p. 106.
8. P. 103.
9. *Pathetic Fallacy in the Nineteenth Century* (New York, 1965), p. viii.

The problem faced by the Imagist poet (and by those poets who are his heirs) is to state and stress one aspect, or pole, of the complex that is the total experience, yet in such a way that it will imply or evoke the other. If one looks at early Imagist poetry, such as the poems by Flint, Aldington, H.D., Amy Lowell, Williams, Pound, Joyce, and others in the very first Imagist anthology, *Des Imagistes,* the struggle with this problem and the always tentative solutions are readily apparent.

The following are all "images" by Imagistes—words or phrases that represent sense experience.

1) Here the mist moves
   Over the fragile leaves and rushes,
   Colourless waters and brown fading hills (Aldington)

2) The light is a wound to me.
   The soft notes
   Feed upon the wound. (Aldington)

3) Each leaf of the aspen
   is caressed by the wind,
   and each is crying. (Flint)

4) Let a strong mesh of roots
   feed the crimson of roses
   upon my heart;
   and then fold over the hollow
   where all the pain was. (Flint)

5) Apples on the small trees
   Are hard,
   Too small,
   Too late ripened
   By a desperate sun
   That struggles through the sea-mist. (H.D.)

6) The light of her face falls from its flower,
   As a hyacinth,
   Hidden in a far valley,
   Perishes upon burnt grass. (H.D.)

7) Damp smell the ferns in tunnels of stone,
   Where trickle and plash the fountains,
   Marble fountains, yellowed with much water. (Amy
   Lowell)

8) I hear an army charging upon the land,
   And the thunder of horses plunging; foam about their
   knees:
   Arrogant, in black armour, behind them stand,
   Disdaining the reigns, with fluttering whips, the
   charioteers. (Joyce)

9) Your hair is my Carthage
   And my arms the bow
   And our words arrows
   To shoot the stars,
   Who from that misty sea
   Swarm to destroy us. (Williams)

10. The petals fall in the fountain,
    the orange coloured rose-leaves,
    Their ochre clings to the stone. (Pound)

Even these brief stanzas, which have been lifted out of the
context of their poems, indicate the difficulty, if not futility of
coming anywhere near to handing over sensations bodily: of being
"objective." They also indicate the several linguistic possibilities
available to a poet with which to create an image. Rarely are these
images rendered in literal language. The description of objects
and actions is complicated by the comparisons of simile and, more
often, by the subtle identifications of metaphor, which move from
simple personification ("each [leaf] is crying"; "the desperate
sun") to more complex personifications ("I hear an army charging upon the land") to the intricate configuration of objects, states
of being, and events ("The light is a wound to me"; ". . . .
roots/feed the crimson roses/upon my heart"; "The light of her
face falls from its flower"; "Their ochre clings to the stone";
"Your hair is my Carthage/ . . . our words arrows/To shoot the
stars") .
   Yet it must also be emphasized that these images come from

poems in which there also exist stanzas and statements that create no images whatsoever:

> White grave goddess,
> Pity my sadness,
> O silence of Paros. (Aldington)
>   or
> Where wert thou born
> O thou woe
> That consumest my life?
> Whither comest thou?

> Let all whom the sea loveth,
> Come to its altar front,
> And I
> Who can offer no other sacrifice to thee
> Bring this. (H.D.)

As an aesthetic movement, Imagism is clearer in theory than in practice. To present an intellectual and emotional complex in an instant of time is not a simple matter. One senses in Imagist poetry the poet's technical struggles to create such images. Often the Imagists alternate between concreteness and abstractness, subjectivity and objectivity, and do not seem to know how to link them.

Each of the following poems, however, moves purposefully beyond the objective, the particular, the concrete. Here the method of approach to that beyond (perhaps even the rationale behind the move) has been suggested to the poet by the "foreign" tradition that has influenced him, be it that of French symbolism, the classical Greek lyric, or the Chinese ideogram.

The Swan

> Under the lily shadow
> and the gold
> and the blue and the mauve
> that the whin and the lilac
> pour down on the water,
> the fishes quiver.

Over the green cold leaves
and the rippled silver
and the tarnished copper
of its neck and beak,
toward the deep black water
beneath the arches,
the swan floats slowly.

Into the dark of the arch the swan floats
and into the black depth of my sorrow
it bears a white rose of flame.
F. S. Flint

Oread (published in the *Egoist,* 1914)

Whirl up, sea—
whirl your pointed pines,
splash your great pines
on our rocks,
hurl your green over us,
cover us with your pools of fir.
H.D.

Liu Ch'e

The rustling of the silk is discontinued,
Dust drifts over the courtyard,
There is no sound of footfall, and the leaves
Scurry into heaps and lie still,
And she the rejoicer of the heart is beneath them:

A wet leaf that clings to the threshold.
Ezra Pound

Flint's "The Swan" is unhesitatingly imagistic. The first two
stanzas articulate briefly, with precision, the concrete, visual components of a perception, the objects that he sees. He sees flowers,
water, fishes, arches, and a swan. He describes them primarily
by their colors and at times lack of color (shadow, black water).
The phrases in these opening stanzas are only faintly figurative:
"silver" and "tarnished copper" are commonly used as color-
words, although literally they refer to metals and not to water

or swan beaks; the color of the flowers does not literally "pour" down on the water, the water pours, but since what Flint is trying to describe is the reflection of the flower colors in the water, the metaphorical merging of flowers and waters is a logical one.

The last stanza with its metaphors "the black depth of my sorrow" and "a white rose of flame" is what gives to the poet's perception its subjective dimensions. By this point the dark, the water, the arch, and the swan have all been described; now we see the swan, quite literally, floating into the dark of the arch. But at the same time "it" (the swan) is also floating into an analagous blackness, the depth of his sorrow, so that the "deep black water beneath the arches" ("the dark of the arch") and the black depth of his sorrow become identified: reflections of one another, perhaps, in keeping with the series of reflections already presented in the poem. Outer is inner and vice versa. The flowers of stanza one also reappear, as the swan that is disappearing into the black depth of sorrow carries a white rose of flame, obviously a symbolic image for something (anguish, pain). The poem itself does not establish the exact nature and meaning of that flower-flame, because it concentrates on flowers (beauty?) to the exclusion of flames (pain?). Nevertheless, the contrast between dark and light, initially established between sunlit colors and shadowed waters, is carried into a subjective dimension as the white flame rose illuminates the black depths of sorrow.

In "Oread," perhaps H.D.'s most famous poem and foremost among those poems consistently offered as examples of Imagism, the image, that of the splashings of the sea, is also a developed metaphor. "Pointed pines," "great pines," "pools of fir" do not literally belong to the sea but to the land. The rationale for the transfer is found in the phrase "your green," which links together the green of the ocean and the green of the forest. Someone is addressing the sea, asking the sea to splash on "our rocks," to hurl its green "Over us," to "cover us" with pools of fir. The title supplies the identity of the speaker, an oread, a Greek forest nymph. The identity of the speaker, in turn, supplies a rationale for (and a theory of) subjective experience. A creature of the forest, as in this instance, cannot help but see everything in terms of forest: the act of perception cannot be objective.

"Liu Ch'e" is one example of Pound's brilliance in creating imagistic poetry in the Chinese and Japanese style. The first five lines of the poem offer a series of careful, physical details, primarily noteworthy for their negative element: there is *no* rustling of silk, *no* sound of footfall. Used in this fashion, the negative both gives and takes away (which is precisely Pound's point). The reader images the rustling, then has to stifle the sound because the words tell him it is "discontinued." The details are to convey this same sense of absence, of the cessation of something. The leaves are shown in an activity that brings them to stasis; "she," most passive of all, "is beneath" them. Only dust, barely moving, drifts over the courtyard, its motion a symbol of the end of things.

Following the colon that concludes the first stanza, the poem blossoms into metaphor. What is the "wet leaf that clings to the threshold"? It is "she, the rejoicer of the heart." It is also all that has been said in the poem to this point, summed up with that phrase. This inclusive metaphor is not the poem's first metaphor, however. Previously the leaves have been personified as they "scurry into heaps and lie still." Personification strengthens the link between lady and leaves, a link established by the similarity of their actions (she once rustled silk and walked in the courtyard but now is still; the leaves scurry into heaps and then lie still) and by their present contiguity (she lies beneath them). This connection is further underlined and perhaps explained by the description of the specific leaf that "clings to the threshold," even as, it seems, she is still the "rejoicer of the heart." Only syntax and punctuation create this metaphor, but the rationale for its existence and its ultimate meaning come from the whole, overtly, "objective" poem.

Although each of these poets uses metaphor to express the totality of his perception, metaphor is not the only possible

solution for the Imagist's problems, which result from his desire
for an objective poetry (a poetry of images) that will at the
same time be able to reveal the whole of the experience, its subjective elements as well.

The lines that follow, Robert Frost's poem, "The Road Not
Taken," and a passage from T. S. Eliot's *The Wasteland,* are
examples of other ways in which modern poetry attempts to
render the complexity of experience. Both can be identified as
operating within the symbolic mode.

The Road Not Taken

Two roads diverged in a yellow wood,
And sorry I could not travel both
And be one traveler, I stood
And looked down one as far as I could
To where it bent in the undergrowth;

Then took the other, as just as fair,
And having perhaps the better claim,
Because it was grassy and wanted wear;
Though as for that the passing there
Had worn them really about the same,

And both that morning equally lay
In leaves no step had trodden black.
Oh, I kept the first for another day!
Yet knowing how way leads on to way,
I doubted if I should ever come back.

I shall be telling this with a sigh
Somewhere ages and ages hence:
Two roads diverged in a wood, and I—
I took the one less traveled by,
And that has made all the difference.
                    (*The Complete Poems of Robert Frost*
                    [New York, 1949], p. 131)

. . . The nymphs are departed.
Sweet Thames, run softly till I end my song.
The river bears no empty bottles, sandwich papers,
Silk handkerchiefs, cardboard boxes, cigarette ends

Or other testimony of summer nights. The nymphs are departed.
And their friends, the loitering heirs of city directors:
Departed, have left no addresses.
> (T. S. Eliot, *The Complete Poems and Plays, 1909–1950*
> [New York, 1962], p. 42)

In the Frost poem the poet has given the reader the physical
details of an experience. There is no metaphor here. We discover that a traveler has chosen between two roads; he chooses
one that is grassy, wanting wear, although on that particular
morning both were worn about the same, being covered with
leaves that had not yet been stepped upon that day. Although
both seem appealing, he knows that he will probably never get
the chance to return to the crossroads and try the other one. He
has chosen "the one less travelled by"; it has made all the difference.

The wood and the roads are symbols; the situation is symbolic.
The successive details of the poem and its total form point to a
symbolic interpretation. Particular clues are the ambiguous reference of the word "way," the great weight that the final phrase,
"And that has made all the difference," attaches to the action,
and the very conventionality of the symbolism involved (that of
life as a journey). The roads are "paths of life" and stand for
choices to be made with reference to the "course" of the traveler's
life; the woods are life itself, and so on. Read this way, each
description or comment in the poem refers both to the physical
event and to the concepts that it is meant to symbolize.

I define a literary symbol as the depiction through language
of an object or set of objects that stands for a concept, an emotion, or a complex of emotion and thought. The symbol provides
tangible form for something that is conceptual and/or emotional
and, therefore, intangible. The use of symbols in Frost's poem is
so simplistic that one might categorize it further as parable.
Symbolism is a complex mode, existing in many varieties and
forms. A symbol may be specific and specified, such as a fish
standing for Christ in early Christianity, or the two roads in
Frost's poem. Sometimes a symbol is a complex of associated

meanings, such as Yeats's use of the rose or swan. Sometimes its reference is deliberately vague, "implying emotions often unstated or attitudes so complex as to be unstatable."[10] Symbols of this sort are especially common in modern poetry; for example, in the poems of T. S. Eliot.

In the passage from *The Wasteland* past is juxtaposed against present to ironically display the inadequacies of the modern condition (inadequate largely because the resonances of the past have been ignored). The use of a line from Spenser's "Prothalamion," "Sweet Thames, run softly till I end my song," initiates the particular comparison made in these lines between modes of love and art. It is the same river for both Eliot and Spenser, but the times, and the scene, have changed. The nymphs that frolicked through Spenser's poem, as Eliot tells us, "are gone." For Spenser these waters were decorated with nymphs, swans, elegant birds, and other accessories to pure, nuptial love. Eliot sees nothing on the water, not even the empty boxes, sandwich papers, silk handkerchiefs, cardboard boxes, cigarette ends, and other "testimonies" of the sordid love of modern-day "nymphs" and their "friends." The notion of love itself has changed, and so, accordingly, has the poetry of love, which now must offer "Departed, have left no addresses," in place of traditional beauties such as "That shone as heaven's light."[11] Here the bottles, papers, handkerchiefs, boxes, and cigarette ends are all isolated objects—concrete particulars, fragments of experience—that stand for or symbolize the "idea" of modern love.

Eliot's famous definition of the objective correlative helps to describe this kind of symbol, which dominates his poetry. To express emotion in the form of art, says Eliot, one has to find "a set of objects, a situation, a chain of events which shall be the formula of that *particular* emotion; such that when the external facts, which must terminate in sensory experience, are given, the emotion is immediately evoked."[12] Eliot's symbol,

---

10. P. ix.
11. *Spenser's Minor Poems*, ed. Ernest de Selincourt (Oxford, 1960), p. 475.
12. "Hamlet and His Problems," *Selected Essays* (New York, 1950), p. 125.

the objective correlative, represents parts that stand for their wholes, external facts that are used to evoke and express complexes of emotion and thought. In his definition Eliot mentions the emotion but leaves out the thought, yet the thought is really the end-product of the process. This fact is illustrated by the passage under discussion, as well as by critical remarks of his own, such as the following statement from his essay "The Metaphysical Poets."

> When a poet's mind is perfectly equipped for his work he is constantly amalgamating disparate experience; the ordinary man's experience is chaotic, irregular, fragmentary. The latter falls in love or reads Spinoza, and these two have nothing to do with each other, or with the noise of the typewriter or with the smell of cooking; in the mind of the poet these experiences are always forming new wholes. (*Selected Essays*, p. 247)

The Sweet Thames passage is not about cigarette ends; it is about modern love. Experience as presented in an Eliot poem imitates the ordinary man's experience in that it, too, is chaotic, irregular, and fragmentary; the difference is that it has been selected and shaped by the poetic mind. The poet is presenting fragments from wholes that he has already formed, wholes that are composed of amalgamated experiences plus his own interpretation of their meaning. The details are *characteristic* details. They are, as Eliot says, a "formula." The fragments are isolated (and thereby emphasized) in the hope that they will evoke their correspondent emotions (they are the tangible aspects of experience that will imply the intangible) and the two together will then reveal the meaning itself, the concept of which they are symbolic. These fragments may be objects (as in the Sweet Thames passage), actions ("Do I dare to eat a peach?"[13]), or events (". . . the moment in the rose-garden,/The moment in the arbour where the rain beat,/The moment in the draughty church at smokefall"[14]). Always these symbols imply complex

---

13. *Complete Poems and Plays, 1909–1950*, p. 7.
14. Pp. 119–20.

emotions and attitudes, unstated and perhaps unstatable. The fragments are symbols because they are means to an end. They stand for his ideas, even as the wasteland itself stands for something like the modern condition, which is what the poem is *about*.

Symbol, image, and metaphor are terms that are frequently associated, often confused, that have much in common and important differences. An image is the representation—in language if it is a poetic image—of sense experience. It may be created with literal language (the high, green tree), figurative language (the smiling tree), or symbolic language (the high, green tree—by which the poet *means* the life force) : with metaphors, symbols, or neither. Once formed, the image itself may be a symbol, but it does not have to be one. This depends upon the purposes of the poet. An image made up of symbols will most probably be itself a symbol (or symbolic complex). An image made from metaphors may be used as a symbol, or it may not. An image made with literal language may or may not be used as a symbol. One source of the confusion between these terms is the fact that while metaphor is, at least generically, a language act (a figure of speech), both symbols and images exist in forms other than language. The cross upon which Christ was crucified may be a symbol, or a symbol may be the representation of that cross in gold, worn about a person's neck, or in paint, or in words (or even in sound and movement). We can say that the word "cross," each time that it is mentioned in a poem, is a symbol; or we can say that the accumulation or combination of references to crosses, nails, blood, and thorns throughout the poem creates a symbol. In the same way, "image" describes sense experience: that which the eye sees, the ear hears, and so on. An image can exist in nature or in any art form. As with symbols, it is difficult to pin down a poetic image. In the first of my Imagist passages, Aldington's "Here the mist moves/Over the fragile leaves and rushes,/Colourless waters and brown fading hills," the image may be the entire phrase (because it depicts a relatively self-contained event), or one may say that each one of the following phrases is an image: "the mist moves," "the fragile leaves and rushes," "colourless waters," "brown fading hills."

In other words, when we talk about poetic symbols or images we can refer to various levels of language. When I compare metaphor to symbol I usually am talking about particular words or phrases that can combine to make an image. In this way I am distinguishing between phrases or sets of words that function as metaphors, those which function as symbols, and those which have neither one of these functions. But whereas the image itself can be used as a symbol, it cannot be used as a metaphor. For the difference between metaphor and symbol as modes of discourse, as language forms, is fundamental. A symbol has to be symbolic, pointing beyond itself and not meaningful for its own sake alone. In metaphor, on the other hand, meaning is created by, and contained within, the relation established between two terms, each of which must therefore be significant in its own right for a meaning to be established. Metaphor depends for its meaning on the perception of relation between its components. A symbol says that $A=B$, while a metaphor says that $A+B=C$. C is the meaning, or the total experience, while A and B are the components, often the inner plus the outer, the objective plus the subjective, the concrete plus the abstract, and so on. This is why metaphor, creating either the single image or combining images, is especially suited to express the complex goals of the Imagist poet. Although symbolism concerns itself with similar goals, its procedure is different.

Where do Williams, Stevens, and Pound fit in to this discussion of metaphors, symbols, and images; of objectivity and subjectivity; of experience and poems? We have already seen something of Pound, for he is closest of the three to Imagism as a movement and essential to any discussion of it. We have seen both the basis of his poetics in his definition of image and vortex and the basis, in the Liu Ch'e poem, of his use of metaphor. For Pound, as this brief exposure indicates, the relation, both theoretically and technically, between image and metaphor is a very close one.

Both Williams and Stevens, each in the terms of his own theoretical vocabulary, reveal their recognition of poetry's need to express the total experience.

In *Kora in Hell* (Boston, 1920) Williams writes:

> A poet witnessing the chicory flower and realizing its virtues of form and color so construes his praise of it as to borrow no particle from right or left. He gives his praise over to the flower and its plant themselves, that they may benefit by those cooling winds of the imagination which thus returned upon them will refresh them at their task of saving the world. (p. 106)

Here is Stevens in "The Noble Rider and the Sound of Words":

> The subject matter of poetry is not that "collection of solid, static objects extended in space" but the life that is lived in the scene that it composes; and so reality is not that external scene but the life that is lived in it. . . . It is not that the imagination adheres to reality, but, also, that reality adheres to the imagination and that the interdependence is essential.[15]

Williams, "borrowing no particle from right or left," is advocating direct treatment of the thing and all that it implies, but in describing the function of poetry he also talks about the cooling winds of the imagination that will benefit the flower and its plant. Likewise Stevens, in his phrase "the life that is lived in the scene," challenges the equating of external and real: what is "essential" is the interdependence of reality and the imagination. Throughout their critical writings—in Williams's insistence upon the power and ultimate reality of the imagination, in Stevens's unceasing attempt to link the mind and the world—both poets express the belief that poetry does, must, reveal the total experience.

A difference between their early poetry (much of which is often labeled Imagistic) and most of the minor poetry in the Imagist anthologies is that both Williams and Stevens more consistently make the attempt to write "pure" Imagist poems: that is, to be completely objective, which should mean non-

---

15. *The Necessary Angel* (New York, 1965), pp. 25, 33.

figurative. As I point out in more detail about Williams later, there is a full range in his early poetry from the nonfigurative to the totally figurative. Yet look at the following two poems, both of which, although perhaps for different reasons, seem to want to be "objective."

The Red Wheelbarrow

So much depends
upon

a red wheel
barrow

glazed with rain
water

beside the white
chickens.
William Carlos Williams (XXI of *Spring and All*)

Study of Two Pears

I

Opusculum paedagogum.
The pears are not viols,
Nudes or bottles.
They resemble nothing else.

II

They are yellow forms
Composed of curves
Bulging toward the base.
They are touched red.

III

They are not flat surfaces
Having curved outlines.
They are round
Tapering toward the top.

IV

In the way they are modelled
there are bits of blue.
A hard dry leaf hangs
From the stem.

V

The yellow glistens.
It glistens with various yellows,
Citrons, oranges and greens
Flowering over the skin.

VI

The shadows of the pears
Are blobs on the green cloth.
The pears are not seen
As the observer wills.

                              Wallace Stevens

In Williams's almost infamous "The Red Wheelbarrow," objects and their components are formally as independent of one another (and of the poet), as clear, as intense, as perfect in themselves as the poet can make them. Yet they are linked by the pressure of the imagination upon them, revealed by the phrase "so much depends/upon" and also by the one hint of metaphor that the poem contains, "*glazed* with rain/water." For the acknowledgment that so much depends upon the perceived scene admits the one perceiving into its fabric, even as the word "glazed" connects other realms of experience to the identity of a red wheelbarrow.

Stevens's "Study of Two Pears" is representative of a recurring mode in his poetry, poems that dispute the right of metaphor in poetry. In my study of Stevens later on, I discuss this kind of poem, what happens in it, and the reasons for its existence, in some detail. At present I want to point out the existence in the poem of what seems a constant in poems of this type: metaphor. The poem begins by resolutely announcing the fact that pears are pears (not possible metaphors for pears, objects that they "resemble," such as viols, nudes, bottles). It concludes by stressing the important extension of that idea: that the mind does not create the world ("seen/As the observer wills"), but the objects exist in the world, independent of the mind's egocentricity. Yet as Stevens attempts to describe what is actually there, curves and flat surfaces, he moves, with the word "modelled" of IV and the developed color imagery of V, into metaphor.

"Modelled," the pears, it is at least hinted, appear as sculptures created by an artist, grouped in a classical still-life arrangement. The "various yellows" with which the pears glisten are not pears at all, but citrons and oranges, even greens which "flower" over the skin, so that the specific pears under observation become the essence, in the associative complexity of their yellowness, of growing, blooming things. They are essence and pattern, as "modelled" emphasizes: the pears are the subject matter of art, which truly creates and reveals them. Unwittingly (perhaps) the observer cannot help but admit the subjective into the objective domain.

Critically, Williams and Stevens have frequently been associated under the banner of Imagism, if not always for reasons that coincide with my own.

Coffman lists them, along with Marianne Moore and Hart Crane, as poets "less closely associated with it [Imagism]," to whom it offered "a discipline in conciseness of expression" (p. 221). Coffman writes about Williams:

> One quality that has always dominated his work is its objectivity: he has tried to bring the word as close as possible to the object, cutting away any conventional, sentimental, too human associations it might have. He is interested in objects, using language to reproduce their appearance as concisely, exactly, scientifically, as possible. He *presents* his materials in a way that Pound approved. . . . Yet there is often in his choice of objects a comment which is stronger for its being unstated. (p. 222)

Again, here is Coffman on Stevens:

Certain of his poems may be called Imagistic; "Study of Two Pears," for example, is a still life which expresses shape, color, the reality of things that is so important a part of his aesthetic. His attention to metaphor, his use of color, his fastidiousness in selecting the materials of poetry also recall the Imagist; but Stevens' poetry is perhaps less Imagistic . . . [in that] this interest [in the world of actuality and in the extent to which the imagination can transform this world] has led him to poetic speculations on broad questions of religion and aesthetics. (p. 223)

William Pratt includes Williams and Pound in his anthology, *The Imagist Poem* (New York, 1963), and discusses them in his "Introduction."

Because their first distinctive work was written during the Imagist period, it is best understood in the context of other Imagist poems, not apart from them.

It is true that both Williams and Stevens recognized the limits of Imagism, and went considerably beyond it in their later poetry. . . . For these poets . . . Imagism might have failed as a movement, but as theory it succeeded, and in the later poems of both Williams and Stevens there is convincing proof that the Imagist discipline continued to work on them to the end of their lives. (p. 37)

In agreeing with Pratt, I would suggest that it is through their use of metaphor especially, through their growing awareness of its necessity and its function, as revealed in both their critical remarks and their poetry itself, that all three poets deal with Imagism and make use of it. Metaphor is one important way by which the poet can render fully the complexity that is perception, the basic unit of experience.

Metaphor is also important to these poets for another reason. Each of them attempts to write a great long poem (a modern "epic," perhaps), but these long poems are very different from those which have gone before, from either an *Iliad* or a *Prelude*. One of the most common charges raised against the Imagist poem was that it was too small, and it was static; its proportions were far from epic. Yet in a note at the end of his "Vorticism" essay Pound wrote:

> I am often asked whether there can be a long imagiste or vorticist poem. The Japanese, who evolved the hokku, evolved also the Noh plays. In the best "Noh" the whole play may consist of one image. . . . Its unity consists in one image, enforced by movement and music. I see nothing against a long vorticist poem.[16]

William Pratt also discusses the relation of the image, the Imagist poem, and the modern long poem.

> Indeed, after all, what are the longer poems of Williams, Pound, or Eliot but aggregate Imagist poems, set in a sort of mosaic pattern around a dominant image—a super image, like *The Waste Land,* for example, or arranged in successive "ideograms," as in the *Cantos?* (p. 38)

Pound speaks of "movement and music"; Pratt of "mosaic pattern" and succession. The image has to do with a moment of perception, but long poems require many moments. Images must, and can, be bound together or organized in some way to make a long poem. Metaphor can provide this organization. Williams, Pound, and Stevens all create long poems that are composed of parts toward a whole; I believe that these poems are structured by the patterns of metaphor that they contain.

Patterns of metaphor, as I shall show in the subsequent chapters of this book, structure these long poems by creating a significant relation between their own form and the overt content of the poem. The progression of metaphors is a formal realization of thematic materials in the poem. It is a controlling force behind the poem's moment-to-moment progression and has a definite, substantiating role to play in creating the meaning of the poem as a whole.

In the following chapter I shall concentrate more closely upon definitions and examples of metaphor and of pattern, before I

---

16. *Gaudier-Brzeska*, p. 109.

apply these terms to close studies of the three poets. In these chapters I shall often be emphasizing the individuality of each of the poets: his particular aesthetic position; his particular, characteristic linguistic techniques, especially as they concern his use of metaphor. I link Williams, Pound, and Stevens together in this volume because each does make use of metaphor as an integral ingredient of his poetry, so that an understanding of this use of metaphor can lead to a fuller understanding of his poetry as a "whole." Yet these poets do not arbitrarily and independently stress metaphor. Metaphor answers needs and solves problems that are similar for all three poets and that have their roots in Imagism.

2
Definition as Example

Metaphor in Short Poems by William Carlos Williams

However people disagree about the nature of metaphor, it is generally agreed that it is a figure of speech in which a word or phrase is applied to an object or concept that it does not literally denote. One good way to talk about what is and what is not metaphor in poetic language is to look at poems. When poetic metaphors are viewed in their indigenous contexts—namely, poems—the process of identifying them proves very different from that which is implied by theoretical definitions and disembodied examples of metaphor.

The early short poems of William Carlos Williams display a range from no metaphor, through some metaphor, to much metaphor indeed.

There is no metaphor in "Proletarian Portrait."

> A big young bareheaded woman
> in an apron
>
> Her hair slicked back standing
> on the street
>
> One stockinged foot toeing
> the sidewalk

> Her shoe in her hand. Looking
> intently into it
>
> She pulls out the paper insole
> to find the nail
>
> That has been hurting her[1]

Here the poet is exploring, carefully and with precision, the details of a perception. While he is depicting them, the present moment is prolonged by the sustained use of present participles. Only after the young woman's action is finally rendered ("She pulls out the paper insole") does the moment begin to slip away—presumably into another act, which would be another poem. In nonfigurative poems like this Williams tries to present what he calls the "perfection" of a perceived object or event without the aid of metaphor.

Poems of this type, for which Williams is so well known, are actually rare in his work. More often, poems that begin in a determinedly nonfigurative fashion do not continue that way to the end, and the movement into metaphor usually provides the thrust of the poem. The following small poems exemplify this tendency.

> To a Poor Old Woman
>
> munching a plum on
> the street a paper bag
> of them in her hand
>
> They taste good to her
> They taste good
> to her. They taste
> good to her
>
> You can see it by
> the way she gives herself

---

1. *The Collected Earlier Poems of William Carlos Williams* (New York, 1951), p. 101. Hereafter the two volumes of Williams's collected poems will be referred to as *CEP* and *CLP*.

to the one half
sucked out in her hand

Comforted
a solace of ripe plums
seeming to fill the air
They taste good to her (*CEP,* p. 99)

The Girl

The wall, as I watched, came neck-high
to her walking difficulty
seaward of it over sand and stones. She

made the effort, mounted it while I
had my head turned, I merely
saw her on top at the finish rolling

over. She stood up dusted off her skirt
then lifted her feet
unencumbered to skip dancing away (*CEP,* p. 462)

In "To a Poor Old Woman" the poem concludes with one out-right metaphor and the phrase that has been repeating throughout the poem, "they taste good to her." The metaphor is "a solace of ripe plums," which seems to fill the air. The phrase is a metaphor for at least two reasons. The first is that plums do not literally have, or feel, or offer solace: plums have been given human qualities. The second is that solace, an abstraction, in seeming to fill the air, begins to achieve a physical form, which it literally does not have.

The poem describes an old woman to whom plums are tasting good. It is about what the tasting good looks like and is. However, there is a difference between *looks like* and *is*: *is* includes more than surface qualities and characteristics. That is why and when the transmuting and transferring power of metaphor is necessary. Williams is using metaphor to "objectify" something that is literally not visible and not objective: the solace that the good taste has given her. What a solace of ripe plums that seems to fill the air looks like is hard to say, but Williams has been able to write about the woman's emotions by somehow making them external to her. Also, another phrase in the brief poem—"the way she gives herself/to the one half/sucked out in her hand"—offers sexual connotations, which provide additional and very real dimensions to the old lady's tasting pleasure.

Again, "The Girl" ends with "to skip dancing away" (without a punctuation mark), which is a metaphor, albeit a slight one, because the girl's movements are not literally a dance. In this poem expression imitates its subject matter. While the girl moves slowly and with difficulty, so the language is awkward, almost laborious. When she is "unencumbered," so the language itself is, so that the function of the dancing metaphor is to heighten the sense of exuberance and beauty of motion that propels her out of the scene and the poem.

At the other extreme are those early poems of Williams which are filled with metaphors. These tend to deal with two subjects, love and nature, subjects much less common to the poems with no or little metaphor. For Williams nature, women, and love have a special relation to one another, and talking about any one of them usually entails the introduction of the others. The process of understanding both women and things of nature, like flowers, is a physical act; it is an act of loving. Women and flowers have much in common because both are beautiful; the true apprehension of beauty, the love of it, is a physical act.

Arrival

And yet one arrives somehow,
finds himself loosening the hooks of
her dress
in a strange bedroom—
feels the autumn
dropping its silk and linen leaves
about her ankles.
The tawdry veined body emerges
twisted upon itself
like a winter wind . . . ! (*CEP*, p. 215)

Blizzard

Snow:
years of anger following
hours that float idly down—
the blizzard
drifts its weight
deeper and deeper for three days
or sixty years, eh? Then
the sun! A clutter of
yellow and blue flakes—

Hairy looking trees stand out
in long alleys
over a wild solitude.
The man turns and there—
his solitary tracks stretched out
upon the world. (*CEP*, p. 198)

Winter Quiet

Limb to limb, mouth to mouth
with the bleached grass
silver mist lies upon the back yards
among the outhouses.
                    The dwarf trees
pirouette awkwardly to it—
whirling round on one toe;
the big tree smiles and glances
                            upward!
Tense with suppressed excitement
the fences watch where the ground
has humped an aching shoulder for
                    the ecstasy. (*CEP*, p. 141)

Song

The black-winged gull
of love is flying—
hurl of the waters'
futile might!

Tirelessly
his deft strokes plying

> he skims free in the licking
> waves' despite—
>
> There is no lying
> to his shrill mockery
> of their torment
> day or night. (*CEP*, p. 460)

In each of these four short poems the experiences being rendered are composed of both human act and human perception
of nature. The action of transfer that metaphor initiates is the
poet's means for expressing the fullness of such experiences. For
example, in "Arrival" the depiction of the prostitute is as much
a comment upon the nature of autumn as the seasonal details
are a description of the woman, and it is the centrally located
metaphor—"feels the autumn/dropping its silk and linen leaves/
about her ankles"—that controls this structure. Even the metaphor itself is balanced: its first line is of nature; its last line is
of the woman; its middle line shares both with leaves that are
silk and linen, or with silks and linens that are leaves. Again,
in "Blizzard" the initial colon creates a complex statement: snow
might be read as a metaphor for the "drift" of a man's life, or
it might be the other way around; both, however, are correct.
Metaphor is used to establish a fundamental relation between
the two. The first seven lines continue to develop this situation.
Then the sun comes out, yet the sun is "a clutter of/yellow and
blue flakes." Storms do not end, they merely change: this sun
is not the storm's opposite, but rather its complement, both being
composed of flakes, differing in that the sun brings color, while
the storm did not. The natural scene begins to be developed
now with descriptions of sun and trees, yet the words of metaphor bespeak the human world: "clutter" and "alleys." (Simile
assists, too: "hairy looking.") The trees "stand out" "over a wide
solitude." The latter phrase again establishes a metaphoric
balance of components: a solitude is a mental phenomenon,
while wild refers to an aspect of nature. The landscape of the
poem is both mental and physical, so that "the world" on which
the man's "tracks" are stretched is most certainly an inner as

well as an outer one. In "Winter Quiet" metaphor (especially personification) creates a vision of all of nature engaged in human copulation. Literally, mist and grass have neither the limbs nor mouths that would allow them to engage in an embrace. Nor is mist literally "silver." It is as if the moon had taken from one of the partners (bleached the grass) to strengthen and give new beauty to the other. In such a way the metaphor "silver" relates to the almost-metaphoric "bleached" by adding yet another sexual dimension to the scene. Trees dance awkwardly; another tree smiles and glances; fences can be tense with excitement. In the final metaphor the entire earth assumes a sexual posture and emotion; the words "humped," "aching," "shoulder," and "ecstasy" all contribute to the achieved metaphor.

In "Song" an introductory metaphor—"the black-winged gull/ of love"—makes of a description of nature a description of the nature of love. This is because the relation established by the preposition "of" is a compound one: at once possession (love's black-winged gull) and equation (love is a black-winged gull; or vice versa: a black-winged gull is love). Although love is never mentioned again in this short poem, subsidiary metaphors, primarily of personification, maintain the existence of this dimension as the poem continues. The waters possess "futile might"; they lick; the bird acts in their "despite"; they "torment." The scene described is that of a bird flying over the waves and perpetually escaping contact with them—a contact that would, presumably, drown him. Yet the relation between bird and waves is more complex than that of simple attack and successful flight. This is indicated both by the endless perpetuation of the encounter (created through the persistent present tense of the poem, as well as by a phrase like "day or night") and also by a metaphor like "his deft strokes plying." In depicting his flying act as one of swimming, it thus immerses him (metaphorically) in the very waves from whose attack he is shown in the next stanza to be skimming free.

This series of poems indicates how complex Williams finds a moment of perception to be. Metaphor is one means for rendering in his poetry certain aspects of that complexity, such as the relation between observer and observed, the relation between physical and nonphysical components, and even the relation between denotations and connotations.

As my discussion to this point has shown, I am using the word *metaphor* as loosely as has been traditional in the long history of its definition. By *metaphor* I mean that kind of linguistic transfer (in whatever syntactic form it occurs, such as verbal, adjectival, or nominal) which implicitly moves a literal into a nonliteral statement. I am focusing on metaphor as "figurative" in order to discuss distinctions between figurative and literal language. For example, the following are nominal, adjectival, and verbal metaphors (in that order) : "love is a spring day"; "sunny love"; "love dawns." In other words, a metaphoric word or phrase is applied to or substituted for a word it does not literally denote, as "love is a kind of emotion" might do. For the purposes of this study I have largely ignored the fine distinctions of rhetoric between kinds of tropes and between tropes and kinds of figures. Rather, I have concentrated upon metaphor's position as the most extreme of figures, in that it states the figurative as literal truth, and establishes a relation between figurative and literal within a simple statement.

Williams, Pound, and Stevens, among other modern poets, have found a special use for the powers of metaphor: the creation of a pattern of relations among metaphors has become an aspect of the organization of modern long poems.

Such patterns are created through consistency in both the function and form of a poet's metaphors. "Mary, a lovely rose" and "rain, the angels' tears" are consistent in form; in each case the metaphor is formed by a noun phrase in apposition to another noun. These two metaphors are not consistent in function but would be if the first were changed to "the rose, a blushing girl." Then each would function to personify an aspect of nature. Their function could remain consistent if their form were different—for example, if the first were altered once again to become "the blushing rose."

Patterns of metaphor organize the works in which they occur

because they create a significant relation between their own form and the overt content of the poem. The progression of metaphors is a formal realization of thematic materials in the poem. Thematic progression is literal, while metaphoric progression is figurative. From the relation created between the two develops the complex meaning of a poem. In a poem in which the thematic progression shows how love must inevitably lead to death, metaphors might display a pattern that would include "hearts are plants which blossom in the sun"; their clasped hands were entangled roots exposed by autumn winds"; and "Dead and at peace, the lovers lay: birds whose song was silenced by the fall of night." The metaphors are consistent in form. All are constructed by direct equivalence: a copula or, in the last example, an appositional phrase. They are also consistent in function, for in each the human is viewed as a natural object. All express stages of the thematic progression by figurative extension. In the first there is no mention of death, yet it is an accepted and understood fact that plants that blossom in the sun will very soon wither and die. In the second the advent of death has been introduced: not, however, in reference to the humans, but to the natural cycle with which the human has been linked. In the last the lovers are dead. Their peace is explained by the metaphoric transfer, which relates their state to an inevitable and ordinary natural event. In this way patterns of metaphor act as a controlling force behind the moment-to-moment progression of a poem. If, however, the function of the metaphors of this hypothetical poem remained consistent but the form of the metaphors became too disparate (as might happen if the original sequence were changed to read "hearts are plants which blossom in the sun"; "rooted, entangled hands, bared by autumn winds"; and "Dead and at peace, the lovers no longer warbled in the sunlight, for night had come"), pattern would not be established. On the other hand, if the same poet had used metaphors such as "hearts are ruby pendants" or "their clasped hands were silent testaments to love," a descriptive and ornamental function for metaphor in the poem would seem to be indicated, rather than a structural one.

Patterns of metaphor will show characteristic differences from poet to poet. For each poet his particular pattern of metaphor has a definite, substantiating role to play in creating the meaning of the poem as a whole. Especially in poems that are composed of parts toward a whole, a form common to Williams, Pound, and Stevens, the pattern of metaphors develops through all the parts as a unifying force.

Patterns of Metaphor in Williams's "Asphodel, That Greeny Flower"

William Carlos Williams's "Asphodel, That Greeny Flower" aptly demonstrates how patterns of metaphor may have a structural function in the organization of long poems. The need to speak in terms of "metaphor," "pattern," "function," and "organization" is especially clear in the study of this thirty-page poem, which moves forward upon a single metaphor. There are few modern long poems in which complexities stem from so simple a structural pattern, which is why this poem makes an excellent subject for examination.

"Asphodel" is the poem of an old man speaking to his wife of their love, at last giving love (a personal love; his love for his wife) its place—a dominant one—in the philosophical system of art, reality, and the imagination that Williams has evolved: "love/rules them all."

Throughout his career Williams used the flower as a metaphor for his most important themes—especially, for love, beauty, and fruition. Here it serves as a metaphor for every theme and image developed in the poem: for love, death, beauty; for sea and storm; for the mind, the bomb, the world. The poem achieves its profundity by means of the metaphoric transfers it enacts among its themes, joining one to another in a dazzling array of combinations. Nowhere in Williams's poetry does metaphor more clearly reveal its function as the linguistic embodiment of the imagination, causing "all things and ages" to "meet in fellowship"; causing them, "peculiar and perfect," to find their release."[2] The lines of relation that metaphor establishes between the poem's concepts are essential to the creation of its meaning.

As well as serving as a metaphor for all of the poem's major themes, the flower has many other forms in the poem. Asphodel is a flower in hell, a flower from Greek myth; it is a pressed flower that Williams kept as a boy; it represents flowers or gardens in general; it is a memory of the many flowers that the poet and his wife have known in their life together, flowers that bloomed both in fields and in poems. All these exist concurrently in the space of the poem, which is the space of memory and art (the realm of the imagination), defying time and death.

J. Hillis Miller writes of "Asphodel":

> The poem prolongs indefinitely the moment just before death. It is speech in the shadow of death and dwells in the light of a perpetual present, between the lightning and the thunderclap, between the sight of the exploding bomb and the coming annihilating heat. . . . [T]he poem maintains forever in living poise the moment between birth and death.[3]

Yet the poem is not static; it progresses and develops and so establishes the manner in which the lines that end the poem—

<pre>
Asphodel
            has no odor
                        save to the imagination
    but it too
                celebrates the light.
                        It is late
    but an odor
                as from our wedding
                        has revived for me
    and begun again to penetrate
                into all the crevices
                        of my world.
</pre>

are a restatement of its beginning—

---

2. "Prologue" to *Kora in Hell, Selected Essays of William Carlos Williams* (New York, 1954), p. 16.
3. *Poets of Reality* (New York, 1969), p. 358.

> Of asphodel, that greeny flower,
>> like a buttercup
>>> upon its branching stem—
> Save that it's green and wooden—
>> I come, my sweet,
>>> to sing to you.

Metaphor is the agent by which this is accomplished. The introduction of a figurative ("wooden") flower within the description of a literal asphodel ("greeny"; "like a buttercup/upon its branching stem—/save that it's green . . .") is the initial extension of meaning necessary for much more complex transfers. Upon these depends the existence, in the concluding lines, of a figurative odor within literal odorlessness.

The poem includes three books and a coda. In Book I the many references to the flower occur separately, scattered through its nine pages, serving to link as in a web the assorted themes that are beginning to develop. In the following two books and coda a different pattern emerges. The metaphors cluster together in metaphoric sequences, so that individual metaphors are difficult to extricate from their contexts. In Book II there are long passages of literal language in addition to the sequences of metaphor. Later, in Book III and the Coda, literal and figurative interpenetrate in a manner prepared for by the poem's formal and thematic development. (Appendix A includes all of the metaphors in "Asphodel," showing the complete sequence with which the poem's pattern of metaphors is developed.)

In Book I the flower is referred to twenty-two times. Almost all of these references are metaphors. That is, the flower is not in a literal sense or scene but continually exists and functions in a variety of figurative meanings and dimensions. The first six references follow one another rapidly on the opening page of the poem. The poet begins by announcing the subject of his poem. It is the asphodel; he comes to sing of it to his beloved.

> 1) Of Asphodel, that greeny flower,
>> like a buttercup
>>> upon its branching stem—
> save that it's green and wooden—   (p. 153)

In capsule form numbers two, three, four, and five establish most of the contexts in which flowers are to occur: the flowers they knew together; the flower that awaits one after life; the flowers of memory; the specific asphodel that is the occasion for the poem.

2)   a life filled,
                    if you will,
       with flowers.   (p. 153)

3) that there were flowers also
              in hell.   (p. 153)

4) I'm filled with the fading memories of those flowers
                                                             (p. 153)
5)   even to this poor
       colorless thing—   (p. 153)

In number six the asphodel is personified: it becomes the poet himself, speaking as he does (although in hell).

6)   Of love, abiding love
         it will be telling
              though too weak a wash of crimson
                    colors it
       to make it wholly credible.   (p. 154)

On the next page the poet announces matter-of-factly the purpose of his poem. There is "something, something urgent" that he has to say to her. He asks her to listen while he talks on "against time." "It will not be/for long." A shape appears before him, paralleling the vision of the asphodel that appears to the dead, described on the preceding page:

       but the dead see,
                    asking themselves:
       What do I remember
              that was shaped
                    as this thing is shaped?   (p. 153)

The shape, when identified, will also tell of love, abiding love.

> I have forgot
>> and yet I see clearly enough
>>> something
>> central to the sky
>>> which ranges round it.   (p. 154)

Suddenly "An odor springs from it!" The odor brings to mind honeysuckle, the buzzing of a bee, "and a whole flood/of sister memories!"

> Only give me time,
>> time to recall them
>>> before I shall speak out.   (p. 154)

The poem is the speaking out of these memories, occasioned by the perception of an asphodel. This is one reason why each of the themes that memory provides is expressed in terms of the flower.

Number seven is the poet's first memory, that of his boyhood collection of pressed flowers, which included the asphodel.

> 7) I had a good collection,
>> The asphodel,
>>> forbodingly,
> among them.   (p. 155)

It is immediately followed by number eight, which is a restatement, in terms of the flower, of what the movement of the poem will be: an offering to his wife of reawakened memories of flowers.

> 8)   I bring you,
>> reawakened,
> a memory of those flowers.   (p. 155)

In the next sequence (numbers nine through twelve) the nature of his love for Flossie is described with flower-metaphors.

He approaches her by means of the reawakened odor of his pressed flower—"a moral odor."

9) It is a curious odor,
        a moral odor,
                that brings me
    near to you.
        The color
                was the first to go.   (p. 155)

Ten is a series of sexual allusions, and to anyone familiar with Williams the profounder implications of the sexual metaphor are immediately apparent.

10) There had come to me
        a challenge,
                your dear self,
    mortal as I was,
        the lily's throat
                to the hummingbird!
    Endless wealth,
        I thought,
                held out its arms to me.
    A thousand topics
        in an apple blossom.   (p. 155)

As a flower Flossie represents for him the principle of earth, of fecundation. Love of her gave him access to the world.

11)   The whole world
                became my garden!

Yet "the sea . . . is also a garden" (twelve).

12) But the sea
        which no one tends
                is also a garden
    when the sun strikes it
        and the waves
                are wakened.
    I have seen it
        and so have you
                when it puts all flowers
    to shame.   (p. 156)

In "Asphodel" metaphor is most often achieved in the most direct manner, by means of the copula. The description of the sea that follows shows it may be likened to a flower ("the starfish/stiffened by the sun/and other sea wrack/and weeds"), yet the fact that sea and flower have been conjoined is what is most important.[4]

Number thirteen follows the poet's first reference to death. It is not the end of love, he says, for a hierarchy can be attained in love's service. Naturally its sign, or guerdon, is a flower.

13)   Its [love's] guerdon
              is a fairy flower;
  a cat of twenty lives.
      If no one came to try it
          the world
would be the loser.   (p. 157)

The storm, which is to have a major role in the poem, is first introduced as a simile for the "spectacle of our lives," which the poet and his wife have watched "from year to year" "with joined hands." "Yet as the storm unfolds, it is called (in number fourteen) a flower, too."

14) The storm unfolds . . .
      It is a flower
          that will soon reach
  the apex of its bloom.   (p. 157)

The sexual orchid of fifteen and sixteen is a figure for the love

---

4. Williams's early poem, "Flowers by the Sea," may serve as a gloss to the nature of the metaphoric transfer enacted here:

> When over the flowery, sharp pasture's
> edge, unseen, the salt ocean
>
> lifts its form—chickory and daisies
> tied, released, seem hardly flowers alone
>
> but color and the movement—or the shape
> perhaps—of restlessness, whereas
>
> the sea is circled and sways
> peacefully upon its plantlike stem (*CEP*, p. 87)

of Helen and Paris, for the poet is now remembering the *Iliad* (as one of the books they have read together), and his comments point out the importance of the poem to him. Through the use of a figure (through literature) the love of Helen and Paris found expression and has endured.

15)   those crimson petals
     spilled among the stones,   (p. 158)

16) The sexual orchid that bloomed then   (p. 158)

Number seventeen is "and the will becomes again/a garden . . ." (p. 159). It occurs at the heart of an important passage in Book I, which extends the allusion to the *Iliad* as a poem to the very moralistic function of poetry—and especially of figure—that Williams envisioned.

                              It is the mind
              the mind
                     that must be cured
                              short of death's
              intervention,
                     and the will becomes again
                              a garden. The poem
              is complex and the place made
                     in our lives
                              for the poem.
              Silence can be complex too,
                     but you do not get far
                              with silence.
              Begin again,
                     It is like Homer's
                              catalogue of ships:
              it fills up the time.
                     I speak in figures,
                              well enough, the dresses
              you wear are figures also,
                     we could not meet
                              otherwise . . .   (p. 159)

Dresses also are figures because they are, in the sense that poetry is, imaginative recreations or interpretations of the body, as poetry is of the world. "We could not meet/otherwise." That is—"through metaphor to reconcile the people and the stones," as Williams wrote in his poem "A Sort of Song." For the will to become a garden implies a perfect conjoining of the intellectual and the physical; subjective and objective; male and female— all that Williams hopes for poetry to accomplish.

In number eighteen the poet returns with increased insight to the speaking of his poem.

```
18)                    . . . When I speak
        of flowers
              it is to recall
                    that at one time
        we were young.                    (p. 159)
```

It is followed by "All women are not Helen,/I know that,/but have Helen in their hearts./My sweet,/you have it also . . . ," an idea that unites literary and physical with new and closer ties. In nineteen and twenty flowers, women, love, gardens, and the sea all conjoin to describe "the love of love/the love that swallows up all else/. . . a love engendering gentleness and goodness":

```
19)                    Imagine you saw
        a field made up of women
              all silver-white.               (p. 160)
```

```
20)          Love is something else,
                    or so I thought it,
        a garden which expands,
              though I knew you as a woman
                    and never thought otherwise,
        until the whole sea
              has been taken up
                    and all its gardens.       (p. 160)
```

Yet love also contains pain.

```
21) I should have known
              though I did not,
                    that the lily-of-the-valley
        is a flower makes many ill
              who whiff it.                    (p. 160)
```

With these next lines the poet once again brings the poem into its present tense: the confrontation of his wife.

> You understand
>> I had to meet you
>>> after the event
> and have still to meet you.   (p. 161)

In number twenty-two love is directly presented as a flower.

> 22)   Love
>>>> to which you too shall bow
>> along with me—
>>> a flower
>>>> a weakest flower
> shall be our trust   (p. 161)

The reason for this is offered in the lines that follow the metaphor:

>   and not because
>> we are too feeble
> to do otherwise
>> but because
>>> at the height of my power
> I risked what I had to do,
>> therefore to prove
>>> that we love each other
> while my very bones sweated
>> that I could not cry to you
>>> in the act.   (p. 161)

Then once again the poet proclaims his opening lines ("Of asphodel, that greeny flower,/I come, my sweet,/to sing to you"); now we have some understanding of what singing of an asphodel has to do with his desire, expressed in the lines that follow, to bring her news of something that concerns her and many men.

>   It is difficult
>> to get the news from poems
>>> yet men die miserable every day
>>>> for lack

of what is found there.
Hear me out
for I too am concerned
and every man
who wants to die at peace in his bed
besides.   (pp. 161–62)

The poem can provide salvation, and this particular poem is meant, as is only too clear, to provide personal salvation for an old man who is close to death, Williams himself.

Book II concentrates upon death: death as the bomb, seen as avarice, hatred through fear, waste—all that silences. What the bomb silences (and thus obstructs) are voyages of discovery (i.e., love). These voyages, also described in Book II, make up the other half of a duality being explored. Metaphor is used to conjoin the elements of the duality, here in an especially powerful way, since the same metaphor is used for both halves of the duality: both love and the bomb are a flower.

Early in Book II the poet announces his intentions for that book:

So to know, what I have to know
about my own death,
if it be real,
I have to take it apart.   (p. 162)

Taking it apart entails the investigation of memory after memory of voyages, of peaks and pinnacles achieved by Williams and by others, too. These are described first in literal language, then in metaphoric language. Thus number one occurs after Williams has described three of his own experiences of "pinnacles": one with a young artist who admired his poem about the parts of a broken bottle, another about his sight of the Jungfrau, a third about the Alhambra. His experiences of death have been occasioned by "the world's niggardliness." "I was lost/failing the poem."

This is the first metaphoric sequence:

1)   But if I have come from the sea

```
                    it is not to be
        wholly
                fascinated by the glint of waves.
                    The free interchange
        of light over their surface
                which I have compared
                        to a garden
        should not deceive us
                or prove
                        too difficult a figure.
        The poem
                if it reflects the sea
                        reflects only
        its dance
                upon that profound depth
                        where
        it seems to triumph.
                The bomb puts an end
                        to all that.
        I am reminded
                that the bomb
                        also
        is a flower
                dedicated
                        howbeit
        to our destruction.
```
                                                    (pp. 164–65)

Here Williams speaks once again of figure, acknowledging
again that poetry is figure. The poem, in "reflecting" the sea,
reflects only its dance ("the glint of waves"; "the free inter-
change/of light over their surface") upon the profound depths.
This is a statement of Williams's theory of poetry, which views
the poem as the movement of the imagination over objects. Thus
the garden, to which the surface motion of the sea has been
"compared"—the flower—is also a sign for the poem. Yet the
bomb is also a flower: initially because it *looks* like one when
it explodes, but ultimately because it represents a perversion of
the power of love (release of "light" for the purposes of destruction rather than creation). As such it is at once similar to and

different from both love and flowers. Metaphor requires us to see these relations and distinctions.

The second sequence beautifully epitomizes Williams's metaphoric technique in "Asphodel."

<pre>
2) Meanwhile
            we are sick to death
                        of the bomb
      and its childlike
            insistence.
                        Death is no answer,
      no answer—
            to a blind old man
                        whose bones
      have the movement
            of the sea,
                        a sexless old man
      for whom it is a sea
            of which his verses
                        are made up.
      There is no power
            so great as love
                        which is a sea,
      which is a garden—
            as enduring
                        as the verses
      of that blind old man
            destined
                        to live forever.
      Few men believe that
            nor in the games of children.
                        They believe rather
      in the bomb
            and shall die by
                        the bomb.   (p. 166)
</pre>

The connecting lines of metaphor establish relations between sea, verses, love, and garden in a dense interpenetration of the thematic subjects of the poem.

bones	have movement of	the sea	
verses	are made up of	the sea	
love		is	a sea
love		is	a garden

a syntactical ambiguity: either/or, or both

sea		is	a garden
no power	as great as	love	
no power	as enduring as	verses	
verses	destined to live	forever	
blind old man destined to live	forever		

syntactical ambiguity

In this discussion of Homer (the arch-poet), metaphoric transfer, which is contained in the middle column of phrases, is like an electric charge of meaning between the left and right columns.

The second sequence follows a comparison of Darwin's voyage of the *Beagle*, "a voyage of discovery if there ever was one," to the death "incommunicado" of the Rosenbergs.

> It is the mark of the times
> that though we condemn
> what they stood for
> we admire their fortitude.   (p. 167)

Number two thus rephrases the literal lines in the metaphoric vocabulary of gardens and vision.

Similarly, the third and fourth sequences follow the mention of

> . . . that other voyage
> which promised so much
> but due to the world's avarice
> breeding hatred
> through fear
> ended so disastrously . . .   (p. 167)

that of the *Nina, Pinta,* and *Santa Maria.*

> 3)   But Darwin
>   opened our eyes

> to the gardens of the world (p. 167)

4)   How the world opened its eyes!
                    It was a flower
    upon which April
            had descended from the skies!
                    How bitter
    a disappointment! (p. 167)

Finally, the poem's dance, the opening of eyes, is connected to the concept of measure, rephrasing succinctly much of the content of *Paterson*:

> In all,
>   this led mainly
> to the deaths I have suffered.
>   For there had been kindled
>   more minds
> than that of the discoverers
>   and set dancing
>   to a new measure,
> a new measure!
>   Soon lost.
>   The measure itself
> has been lost
>   and we suffer for it.
>   We come to our deaths
> in silence.
>   The bomb speaks. (pp. 167–68)

The list of metaphors for Book III, as the Appendix indicates, is even more dense than was that for Book II: it includes a large percentage of the book. The book opens with these lines:

> What power has love for forgiveness?
>   in other words
>   by its intervention
> What has been done
>   can be undone.
>   What good is it otherwise? (p. 169)

They immediately precede the first metaphoric sequence.

1) Because of this
        I have invoked the flower
            in that
    frail as it is
        after winter's harshness
            it comes again
  to delect us.
        Asphodel, the ancients believed,
            in hell's despite
  was such a flower.
        With daisies pied
            and violets blue,
  we say, the spring of the year
        comes in!
            So may it be
  with the spring of love's year
        also
            if we can but find
  the secret word
        to transform it.   (pp. 169–70)

The "great power" of love, discussed in Book II, is here identified as that of forgiveness. The act of forgiveness, which is to become the central action in the poem, is related to two kinds of movement, both of which can undo the done. They are linear ascension and cyclical recurrence. The voyages and pinnacles of Book II lead into "the steps/if it may be/by which you shall mount/again to think well/of me" (p. 171); and the flower, frail as it is, comes again after winter's harshness.

The flowers of number one have the universal-particular, general-specific kind of relation that is characteristic of Williams's technique. Here the asphodel, identified as the flower of ancient myth, presents again the idea of undoing the done with its reference to the myth of Persephone in the line "in hell's despite." Then Williams quotes Shakespeare's song from *Love's Labour's Lost* to present once again the notion of spring and rebirth. This line is especially interesting, since it seems at first to be a direct contradiction of Williams's expressed hatred of Eliot's "literary" technique which, as Williams says in his *Auto-*

biography, "set me back twenty years."[5] But later in the book, the Shakespearean line reappears: "But in their pride/there comes to my mind/the daisy. . . ." "Pride" evokes daisy in the speaker's mind, because it sounds like "pied." This time the poet comments upon his use of the quotation. "Not the shy flower of England," he writes, but those flowers which "we knew as children." Not the literary generality but the specific, experienced flower. When he wishes to recall "many other flowers" for her pleasure, it is, of course, the violet that is singled out and, like the daisy, made particular as the violets he once saw that grew in marshy places.

Thinking to have lost his wife's love, the poet comes to her proudly, "in the name of love," "as an equal/to be forgiven." He then offers to her the steps by which she shall mount again to think well of him.

The long series of memories that are the "steps" are a portrait of the male (of Williams himself) who combines both "crude force" (the naked sword of the rider of Colleoni's horse; the horse rampant in "Venus and Adonis"; a fast freight) and imaginative sensitivity. Two of the images of crude force exist in (are realized by) works of art, and the long description of "another man . . . in the subway," which ends in a revelation of the dirty Negro man as a type for Williams's own father, as a type for the male principle itself, presents a perfect example of poetry realizing (in both of the word's connotations) the nature of the man being observed by capturing his integral "measure" or rhythm in verse form.

The flowers of number two—conjoined to the experience of the man in the subway station—are, significantly, flowers rendered through art, both linguistic and pictorial.

> 2) Fanciful or not
>   it seemed to me
>   a flower
>   whose savor had been lost.
>   It was a flower

5. (New York, 1951), p. 174.

```
                    some exotic orchid
        that Herman Melville had admired
            in the
                    Hawaiian jungle.
        Or the lilacs
            of men who left their marks,
                    by torchlight,
        rituals of the hunt,
            on the walls
                    of prehistoric
        caves in the Pyrenees—
            what draftsmen they were—
                    bison and deer.
        Their women
            had big buttocks.
                    But what
        draftsmen they were!
            By my father's beard,
                    what draftsmen.
        And so, by chance,
            how should it be otherwise?
                    from what came to me
        in a subway train
            I build a picture
                    of all men.                    (p. 174)
```

The exclamation *By my father's beard* is meant quite literally here, for it is precisely by means of his "father's beard" that he has built this "picture/of all men."

```
                    Then I remembered:
        When my father was a young man—
            it came to me
                    from an old photograph—
        he wore such a beard.
            This man
                    reminds me of my father.
        I am looking
            into my father's
                    face! . . .                    (p. 173)
```

Number three introduces and number four concludes the

section that is the heart of the poem: the poet's vision of his wife pouring reviving water at the roots of her plants.

                I say to myself
                        Kindness moves her
                                shall she not be kind
                also to me? At this
                        courage possessed me finally
                                to go on.   (p. 175)
        3) It is winter
                        and there
                                waiting for you to care for them
                are your plants.
                        Poor things! you say
                                as you compassionately
                pour at their roots
                        the reviving water.   (p. 175)

        4)   These heads
                        that stick up all around me
                are, I take it,
                        also proud.
                                But the flowers
                know at least this much,
                        that it is not spring
                                and will be proud only
                in the proper season.   (p. 176)

The pouring of reviving water is the act of forgiveness and is the power of love in action. It has been prepared for by and is related to both major and minor metaphors in each book. I refer to the sea-garden metaphors, but also to the many examples of language that initially seems to be but barely metaphoric:

        a life filled with flowers (p. 153)

        I'm filled with the fading memory of these flowers (p. 153)

        while our eyes fill with tears (p. 153)

        while I drink in

the joy of your approach (p. 154)

But the sea
        which no one tends
                is also a garden
    when the sun strikes it
            and the waves
                    are wakened. (p. 156)

    How the world opened its eyes!
            It was a flower
    upon which April
            had descended from the skies! (p. 167)

gasp dying
        for want of love. (p. 170)

In a complex statement the poet confesses the explicit nature of his failing—women—and yet explains why his failing is necessary.

                    . . . After that manner
    I call on you
            as I do on myself the same
                    to forgive all women
    who have offended you.
            It is the artist's failing
                    to seek and to yield
    such forgiveness.
            It will cure us both.   (p. 175)

In his play *A Dream of Love,* the poet-doctor, Doc, and his wife, Myra, confront one another upon the same issue, and in their speeches the relation of sex to poetry, as it affected Williams—not only in his aesthetic theory, but personally—is made especially clear.

MYRA:
What could you tell me that I do not know? Tell me, tell me, dear. We have so little time.

DOC:
Well, I'll tell you. A man must protect his price, his integrity

as a man, as best as he is able, by whatever invention he can cook up out of his brains or his belly, as the case may be. He must create a woman of some sort out of his imagination to prove himself. Oh, it doesn't have to be a woman, but she's the generic type. It's a woman—even if it's a mathematical formula for relativity. Even more so in that case—but a woman. A woman out of his imagination to match the best. All right, a poem. I mean a woman . . . bringing her up to the light, building her up and not merely of stone or colors or silly words—unless he's supremely able—but in the flesh, warm, agreeable, made of pure consents. That means they're not married, of course—unless he unmarries them by hard work for a moment now and then. Something—to that time unconceived by him or anyone in the world. Do you follow me?

MYRA:
Is that all?

DOC:
When a man, of his own powers, small as they are, once possesses his imagination, concretely, grabs it with both hands —he is made! Or lost, I've forgotten which . . . And just as woman must produce out of her female belly to complete herself—a son—so a man must produce a woman, in full beauty out of the shell of his imagination and possess her, to complete himself also . . .

MYRA:
The rape of the imagination.

DOC:
Good. It *is* a kind of rape. You often surprise me by your felicitous phrasing.

The true purpose, Doc says later, because he "will not lie," for what she terms "perverted and disgusting" is "to renew our love, burn the old nest and emerge transcendent, aflame—for you? Do you know any other way?" (p. 207)

It is necessary to include the entire conclusion of Book III in number five, for it is a composite of all the forms of flowers that have been contributing to the poem's development.

5)   I say to you
                    privately
     that the heads of most men I see
            at meetings
                    or when I come up against them
     elsewhere
            are full of cupidity.
                    Let us breed
     from those others.
            They are the flowers of the race.
                    The asphodel
     poor as it is
            is among them.
                    But in their pride
     there comes to my mind
            the daisy,
                    not the shy flower
     of England but the brilliance
            that mantled
                    with white
     the fields
            which we knew
                    as children.
     Do you remember
            their spicy-sweet
                    odor? What abundance!
     There are many other flowers
            I could recall
                    for your pleasure:
     the small yellow sweet-scented violet
            that grew
                    in marshy places!
     You were like those
            though I quickly
                    correct myself
     for you were a woman
            and no flower
                    and had to face
     the problems which confront a woman.
            But you were for all that
                    flowerlike
     and I say this to you now
            and it is the thing

which compounded
my torment
        that I never
                forgot it.
You have forgiven me
        making me new again.
                So that here
in the place
        dedicated in the imagination
                to memory
of the dead
        I bring you
                a last flower. Don't think
that because I say this
        in a poem
                it can be treated lightly
or that the facts will not uphold it.
        Are facts not flowers
                and flowers facts
or poems flowers
        or all works of the imagination,
                interchangeable?
Which proves
        that love
                rules them all, for then
you will be my queen,
        my queen of love
                forever more.   (pp. 176–78)

Again the poet comments on his wife's act: "You have forgiven me/making me new again." Again he uses a phrase that,
revivifying a "dead" metaphor, is at once literal and figurative.
Such phrases can occur "here/in the place/dedicated in the
imagination/to memory/of the dead." It is in such a place that
he can bring her such a flower. In the final lines of number
five the burden of Williams's *Paterson V*—that art is reality—
is introduced in a very short space. Williams begins by setting
up poems and facts in opposition. But this position is raised
merely to be annihilated, once and for all, in the most concise
expression in all of Williams's writing of his final aesthetic
position: "Are facts not flowers/and flowers facts/or poems

flowers/or all works of the imagination/interchangeable?" *Interchangeable* refers not to identify but to function. Poems, flowers, and facts can be "interchangeable" because all find their reality by means of an act of the imagination—that is, within a work of art. Love rules them all, because love is the finest, the ultimate creation of the imagination.

The Coda returns to the image of the storm to define "the huge gap/between the flash/and the thunderstroke," when "spring has come in/or a deep snow fallen." The flower is mentioned only briefly in the Coda. Through metaphor the poem has arrived at the tremulous point where metaphor is in a sense unnecessary. The gap between flash and thunder stroke is the realm of the imagination itself, whereas metaphor embodies in language the action of the imagination upon something outside of itself in order to contain that thing. The gap is also "that interval . . . when love will blossom," which is, as we have seen, that moment when the poet's wife compassionately pours at the roots of her plants the reviving water. This equation can be made because "love and the imagination/are of a piece/swift as the light/to avoid destruction" (p. 179), or again, "Light, the imagination/and love . . ./maintain/all of a piece/their dominance" (p. 180). Therefore, when the poet says "Only the imagination is real!/I have declared it time without end," the phrase "time without end," another revived dead metaphor, is at once literal and figurative. It means both "I have said it over and over" and "I have said the following: there can be such a thing as time without end." Phrases like this become extremely important in the latter part of "Asphodel." They represent the power of the imagination to conjoin the literal and the figurative to reveal, through art, the true reality, which is both literal and figurative.

If the imagination could assert its ascendancy, that alone would "geld the bomb" ("permitting/the mind contain it"). Then

> The light
> for all time shall outspeed
> the thunder crack. (p. 181)

The ultimate celebration of the light is "All the pomp and ceremony of wedding." Perhaps as a lesson to Eliot, to show him the proper use of literary quotations, Williams, too, quotes from Spenser's "Prothalamion." But it is for the purpose of moving, as he had done with Shakespeare's flowers, from the literary back to the personal and particular: in this case, to his own wedding:

> For our wedding, too,
>   the light was wakened
>   and shone. The light!
> the light stood before us
>   waiting!
>   I thought the world
> stood still.
>   At the altar
>   so intent was I
> before my vows,
>   so moved by your presence
>   a girl so pale
> and ready to faint
>   that I pitied
>   and wanted to protect you.
> As I think of it now,
>   after a lifetime,
>   it is as if
> a sweet-scented flower
>   were poised
>   and for me did open.
> Asphodel
>   has no odor
>   save to the imagination
> but it too
>   celebrates the light.
>   It is late
> but an odor
>   as from our wedding
>   has revived for me
> and begun again to penetrate
>   into all the crevices
>   of my world.   (pp. 181–82)

"I thought the world stood still" is yet another revived metaphor. Although the flower is almost entirely absent from the Coda, it reappears again in the final lines, which return, in their own way, to the poem's beginning. Here a simile is followed by a statement that is neither figurative nor literal, but simply a truth. Asphodel as a pressed flower has no odor (hence the simile). Yet the "save" is a powerful litotes, in that the imagination is actually the defining agent of reality. Therefore, the move can be made, by means of the many metaphoric resonances that the flower evokes (especially its conjunction with love itself) to the statement that an odor has revived (the verb can have transitive as well as intransitive force). Its penetration of the crevices of the poet's world is again the act of forgiveness—the act of love, with all of its implications. Even as the asphodel, in the opening lines of the poem, was a "poor/colorless thing," so now it "celebrates the light"—by virtue of the transformations and transcendence that metaphor, as the agent of the imagination, has effected upon it.

The structuring function of metaphor in "Asphodel, That Greeny Flower," a poem about the power of the imagination, is not arbitrary. By building a long poem around one figure only, the figure of the flower, Williams forces form and theme to be absolutely interdependent. Metaphor, since it is for Williams the linguistic embodiment of the imagination, is the only language structure that could create the proper form in which to speak of love and the imagination. Since all of the poem's metaphors evolve from one center, the flower, the pattern they create from their pronounced consistency in function and form, moving and developing through the three books and coda, is almost solely responsible for the structure of the total poem. In this way Williams's poem exemplifies how a pattern of metaphor may be used to organize a long poem.

---

6. *Many Loves and Other Plays* (Norfolk, Conn., 1961), pp. 200–201.

3
Metaphor in **The Cantos** of Ezra Pound

Earlier I spoke of modern long poems that were "parts toward a whole." *The Cantos* is the most extreme case in point in modern poetry. Its "parts" have been published independently and in groups over a span of fifty years. That they are nevertheless "towards a whole" is something about which Pound expended a great deal of rhetoric. This is why in my study of *The Cantos* I have concentrated upon an examination of its parts. A detailed analysis of the complete working out of the pattern through all of the cantos would be, if not impossible, certainly monotonous and ultimately redundant. I have chosen rather to demonstrate, through selected examples, the principle of metaphoric patterning that is at work throughout the poem. A canto is usually in its own right a long poem, often a difficult long poem to read. The same principle that governs the organization of individual cantos also governs their relation to one another. In addition, in a work as long as this, special emphasis must fall upon the functioning of the parts if only because the whole is so extensive and, for that matter, was not completed. A canto needs to be understood somehow as it is being read, not in some distant future.

The manner in which a reader reads many of the cantos is (or should be) directed by its use of metaphor. A theory of metaphor and image (which, as I shall show, Pound associates together) is at the heart of Pound's ideas about the role and effect of poetry in society. He calls for a new kind of reading process, a process based on a moment-to-moment physical, rather than intellectual, response to poetry. His use of metaphor especially is directed toward that end, in that metaphor, because of its association in Pound's view with image and rhythm, demands that kind of mental process in order to be understood. In developing his theory of poetry Pound has created his own vocabulary: to understand Pound's meaning and use of metaphor I shall need to employ, and therefore to investigate, terms like *vortex, ideogram, phanopoeia, logopoeia,* and *melopoeia,* as well as Pound's own interpretation of words like *image, idea, equation,* and *god.*

In addition, metaphors are Pound's most effective means for depicting the true relations that exist in the world. He denies to metaphor any decorative function: figure is important because it can present true relations in a way that no other language structure can achieve. This second characteristic of metaphor is an aspect of the first. Poetry, at its best, is a depiction of actions and results in action. Poetry should express ideas by means of things and actions, for, as Pound reiterates again and again, "Ideas are true as they go into action."[1]

My assumption that metaphor can structure the reading of a canto makes the cantos accessible to readers in a way that most critics of *The Cantos* would deny. The prevailing critical approaches to the poem seem to propose two alternate positions. The first is that *The Cantos* cannot stand as a poem in their own right but must exist in some kind of relation to other specialized bodies of knowledge. The second is that any given canto cannot work as a poem in its own right but exists only as it relates to the total structure of one-hundred-plus cantos; that is, one canto cannot be understood unless all have been

---

1. *Culture* (New York, 1938), p. 188.

read. The underlying theses of these points of view seem to me to be inadequate and inappropriate to Pound's poem. He has purposely created the individual cantos so that they can communicate, although perhaps not in the way that his critics would want them to.

In this study I have been primarily concerned with the first thirty cantos, and with the opening cantos in particular. This study is therefore an introduction to *The Cantos* by means of its own introductory cantos. From these poems I have moved both backwards and forwards in time in order to investigate the source and development of a particular kind of image that clearly exemplifies Pound's use of metaphor in *The Cantos*. It is the image of gods. Through an examination of instances of this image as it moves from the earlier versions of the first thirty cantos to the final version, one can observe the development of Pound's metaphoric technique in *The Cantos*. This technique can best be characterized by Pound's own phrase from an early letter concerning *The Cantos:* "condensation to maximum attainability."[2] The notion of maximum attainability is as important as that of condensation (a key term in any description of Pound's form), for it points to Pound's unceasing effort to alter violently his reader's mental process—to the whole question of what constitutes "attainability." The image of gods persists into the later cantos; its function and form there remains consistent with the first thirty cantos. In this essay I compare the final form of the opening cantos to their earlier versions, which are the original publication of three cantos in *Poetry* of June, July, and August, 1917 (Vol. X, Nos. III, IV, and V, 113–21, 180–89, and 248–54), a second version, *Three Cantos of a Poem of Some Length* (published in *Lustra of Ezra Pound,* New York, 1917, pp. 181–202), and *A Draft of XVI Cantos of Ezra Pound for the Beginning of a Poem of Some Length* (Paris, 1925). I also discuss briefly Cantos 95 and 91 of *Section: Rock-Drill: 85–95 de los cantares* (New York, 1956).

In publication after publication Pound harangued about

---

2. D. D. Paige, ed., *The Letters of Ezra Pound* (New York, 1950), p. 322.

his ideas concerning literature and language, sculpture and music, economics and politics, history and culture. The intense and diverse learning that can be both the delight and the bane of readers of *The Cantos* (for it contributes both to the profundities and to the confusions of the work) is on display in his critical writings. Consequently, critics have devoted much effort to them—describing them, assessing their values, and, what seems to have been most important, relating them to Pound's poetry. This kind of work often leads to the first of the two critical stances that I have mentioned. It has produced innumerable articles with titles like the following: "The Italian Background to *The Cantos*,"[3] "Some Considerations Arising from Ezra Pound's Conception of the Bank,"[4] and "Ezra Pound and Music."[5] It is epitomized, however, by John Edwards and Williams Vasse's *Annotated Index to the Cantos of Ezra Pound* (Berkeley and Los Angeles, 1959). Implicit in this index is the point of view that *The Cantos*, to be appreciated, must be understood, and that understanding means getting the references. Each of the critics who take this approach has found his own formula for cracking the Poundian code, while Edwards and Vasse have in effect written their own *Cantos*. The question that is involved here is whether or not the poem requires of its readers that they be as knowledgeable as its poet—and as knowledgeable about the same things. Both Pound and the poem have answered this question. Pound's letter to Hubert Creekmore, which I have already mentioned, contains the following:

> I believe that when finished, *all* foreign words in the Cantos, Gk, etc., will be underlinings, not necessary to the sense, in one way. I mean a complete sense will exist without them; it will be there in the American text, but the Greek, ideograms, etc., will indicate a *duration* from whence or since

---

3. John Drummond in Peter Russel, ed. *An Examination of Ezra Pound* (London, 1950), pp. 100–118.
4. Max Wykes-Joyce in Russel, pp. 218–28.
5. Murray Shafer in Walter Sutton, ed., *Ezra Pound: A Collection of Critical Essays* (Englewood Cliffs, N. J., 1963), pp. 129–42.

whence. If you can find any *briefer* means of getting this repeat or resonance, tell papa, and I will try to employ it.

Narrative not the same as lyric; different techniques for song and story. "Would, could," etcetera: Abbreviations save *eye* effort. Also show speed in mind of original character supposed to be uttering or various colourings and degrees of importance or emphasis attributed by the protagonist of the moment.

All typographic disposition, placing of words *on* the page, is intended to facilitate the reader's intonation, whether he be reading silently to self or aloud to friends. Given time and technique I might even put down the musical notation of passages or "breaks into song."

There is *no intentional* obscurity. There is condensation to maximum attainable. It is impossible to make the deep as quickly comprehensible as the shallow.

The order of words and sounds *ought* to induce the proper reading; proper tone of voice, etc., but can *not* redeem fools from idiocy, etc. If the goddam violin string is not tense, no amount of bowing will help the player. And *so* forth.

As to the *form* of *The Cantos:* All I can say or pray is: *wait* till it's there. I mean wait till I get 'em written and then if it don't show, I will start exegesis. I haven't an Aquinas-map; Aquinas *not* valid now.————(pp. 322–23)

In the middle of Canto 96 (in *Thrones 96–109 de los cantares,* New York, 1959, p. 11) we find:

If we never write anything save what is already understood the field of understanding will never be extended. One demands the right, now and again, to write for a few people with special interests and whose curiosity reaches into greater detail.

These two statements are complementary when viewed in the light of the poem itself. *The Cantos* do try to create understanding where there was no understanding before; they do this by means of their peculiar form. Naturally, whatever knowledge a reader possesses when approaching any poem becomes part of his equipment for dealing with that poem. That is why the *Annotated Index* approach has a limited usefulness. However, the poem and its readers need not be dependent upon it.

In his comparison of *The Cantos* to "what covers much of the same ground, culture-history," I think that Harold Watts accurately defines the poem's purpose.

> Orderly narrative, study of causal relationships, precise state-ments of the basis for comparisons made—all this is an invi-tation to comprehend or (the same thing) to escape the ur-gency of real experience which puts (or should put, Pound feels) the will in chancery; for the mind is encouraged to catalogue and file for delayed reference the very "ideas in action" that ought to be seminal. But another method of presentation—naturally, the method of *The Cantos*—will com-pel the reader to an act of direct experiencing, confused (why not?) and intense. And only from this latter sort of reading— the argument must run—do conviction and action come.[6]

Watts calls the poem a "calculated assault on indurated modern sensibility: sensibility that an orderly attack (cultural histories, analyses of Western thought) leaves unaltered" (p. 43).

Watts's justification and source for these statements lies in Pound's theoretical and critical writings. Perhaps the most im-portant fact about this great body of prose is that it does go over much the same ground as do *The Cantos*. Not only do the theories about money, culture, history, and literature reappear in the poem, but the poetic theory, too, appears, in the poem's structure. Therefore, before I proceed to the second critical position, which attempts to deal with this structure, I think it important to present some of Pound's remarks about language and poetry. Pound's theories concerning imagism, vorticism, and so on have been described in much detail by individual essayists and in book-length studies such as Hugh Kenner's *The Poetry of Ezra Pound* (New York, 1951). What I wish to emphasize here is the similarity and consistency in all of these remarks. For example, Pound's 1912 principles of imagism reappear in many other guises in his later writings. They are:

1. Direct treatment of the "thing" whether subjective or ob-jective.

---

6. Harold H. Watts, *Ezra Pound and the Cantos* (London, 1952), p. 41.

2. To use absolutely no word that does not contribute to the presentation.

3. As regarding rhythm: to compose in the sequence of the musical phrase, not in sequence of a metronome.[7]

One might compare this list with another one, from "How To Read," in which Pound, after "looking at what actually happens," defines the manners in which language is charged or energized: melopoeia, phanopoeia, and logopoeia. We might relate principle number three to melopoeia, one to phanopoeia, and two to logopoeia.

MELOPEIA, wherein the words are charged, over and above their plain meaning, with some musical property, which directs the bearing or trend of that meaning.

PHANOPOEIA, which is a casting of images upon the visual imagination.

LOGOPOEIA, "the dance of the intellect among words," that is to say, it employs the words not only for their direct meaning, but it takes count in a special way of habits of usage, of the context we *expect* to find with the word, its usual concomitants, of its known acceptances, and of ironical play. It holds the aesthetic content which is peculiarly the domain of verbal manifestation, and cannot possibly be contained in plastic or in music. It is the latest come, and perhaps most tricky and undependable mode.[8]

In the *ABC of Reading* Pound redefines these terms, calling melopoeia "inducing emotional correlations by the sound and rhythm of the speech," phanopoeia "throwing the object (fixed or moving) onto the visual imagination," and logopoeia "inducing both of the effects by stimulating the associations (in-

---

7. From "A Retrospect," in T. S. Eliot, ed., *Literary Essays of Ezra Pound* (London, 1954), p. 3.
8. *Literary Essays,* p. 25.

tellectual or emotional) that have remained in the receiver's consciousness in relation to the actual words or word groups employed."[9]

The second type of criticism to which I have referred wants to stress, not the translating of Pound's words, but their structure. The key term is *juxtaposition*. I quote from Hugh Kenner: ". . . the *peripeteia* . . .juxtaposes two worlds of perception to strike light from their interaction,"[10] and again from Harold Watts: ". . . juxtaposition (the association from canto to canto or within a single canto of opposed or apparently unrelated elements or blocks of ideograms) is perhaps the fundamental method of procedure in the poem."[11] Thinking about *The Cantos* along lines such as these stems from Pound's definitions of image, vortex, and ideogram.

1) An "Image" is that which presents an intellectual and emotional complex in an instant of time.[12]

2) The image is not an idea. It is a radiant node or cluster; it is what I can, and must perforce, call a VORTEX, from which, and through which, and into which, ideas are constantly rushing. In decency one can only call it a VORTEX.[13]

3) By contrast to the method of abstraction, or defining things in more and still more general terms, Fenollosa emphasizes the method of science, "which is the method of poetry," as distinct from that of "philosophic discussion," and that is the way the Chinese go about it in their ideograph or abbreviated picture writing . . .

But when the Chinaman wanted to make a picture of something more complicated, or of a general idea, how did he go about it?

---

9. (New York, 1960) , p. 63.
10. P. 63.
11. P. 87.
12. "A Retrospect," *Literary Essays*, p. 4.
13. *Gaudier-Brzeska* (London and New York, 1916) , p. 106.

He is to define red. How can he do it in a picture that isn't painted in red paint?

He puts (or his ancestor put) together the abbreviated pictures of

ROSE	CHERRY
IRON RUST	FLAMINGO . . .

The Chinese word or ideogram for red is based on something everyone KNOWS.[14]

I agree that the 117 canto structure is one of juxtaposed images, or ideograms, which are, to use Pound's phrase from *Culture*, "ideas in action." ("Ideas are true as they go into action." P. 188) And if it is also true, as Watts convincingly argues, that *The Cantos* are meant by Pound to perform that function which Pound thinks art and the artist ought to perform—to shape or reshape culture, then a reader's ability to perceive the total shape of the smaller and larger blocks of juxtaposed images is one step toward Pound's goal. Yet the very fact that the first thirty cantos were consistently written and published canto by canto, and then in small groups (first three, then sixteen, then another fourteen, and finally thirty), is historical proof of the status that Pound has allotted to the parts of his long poem. If they did—and, as I maintain, do—have this status, then how, given an awareness of both the extensive factual information behind the work and its overarching formal structure, can a single canto communicate some kind of meaning to a reader?

It is my belief that Pound's use of metaphor is directly involved in the establishment and communication of meaning in a canto. If we return for a moment to Pound's definitions of the image, vortex, and ideogram, it may be seen that, although they make sense, especially in the light of what does happen in Pound's poetry, they are not very specific. Thus an image might be "Seal sports," or

---

14. *ABC of Reading,* pp. 21, 22.

> Seal sports in the spray-whited circles of cliff-wash,
> Sleek head, daughter of Lir,
>   eyes of Picasso,
> Under the black fur-hood, lithe daughter of Ocean . . .

or it could be all of the Tyro episode in Canto II. An ideogram could be synonymous with an image, but it could also be a cluster of images. It is therefore perhaps clearer to begin by looking at the words—and the language—with which these images are composed.

Pound's poetic language is highly metaphorical, particularly when he is at his most lyrical and most colloquial. Thus in the opening cantos we find:

> Sun to his slumber, shadows o'er all the ocean,
> Came we then to the bounds of deepest water,
> To the Kimmerian lands, and peopled cities
> Covered with close-webbed mist, unpierced ever
> With glitter of sun-rays
> Nor with stars stretched, nor looking back from heaven
> Swartest night stretched over wretched men there.
>   (Canto I)

But also:

> And Dos Santos fattened, a great landlord of Portugal
> Now gathered to his fathers . . .
> Go to hell Apovitch, Chicago ain't the whole punkin.
>   (Canto XII)

or again:

> So that in the end that pot-scraping little runt Andreas
>   Benzi, da Siena
> Got up to spout out the bunkum
> That that monstrous swollen, swelling s. o. b.
>   Papa Pio Secundo
>   Aeneas Silvius Piccolomini
>   da Siena
> Had told him to spout, in their best bear's-greased latinity
>   (X)

Pound, like Williams, is forever reviving dead metaphors. In this way they charge the language anew by adding sudden and new images to the context. ("Great Literature is simply language charged with meaning to the utmost possible degree." *ABC of Reading*, p. 28.) In addition, these few examples indicate the extent to which Pound's metaphors (as we might expect in view of his theory) are characterized by a commitment to the concrete, rather than the abstract—"direct treatment of the thing," the object, in lieu of the concept. (His rejection of abstraction in literary form is, as Watts has shown, directly related to Pound's politics and economics—his hatred of usury, for example. Usury represents an act of abstraction, giving to paper money a value that is not inherent in the paper as paper. Creating money out of nothing, buying and selling it, without a true correspondence to the existing wealth of concrete objects, of natural resources, is in Pound's view the greatest of all evils and a sign of the state of moral and artistic decay of a culture.)

Just as there is a noticeable difference between the style of the pre-*Canto* poems and *The Cantos*, so there is a difference in the form of the metaphors that are used. Watts argues that the method of *The Cantos* is different from that of Pound's early, "imagistic" poetry (including the Chinese translations) because the program of imagism was not wrong but incomplete.

> It led to the production of static poetry, poetry devoted only to objects and what could be their precipitate when introduced into the minds of readers [i.e., "a totality of apprehension that takes in far more than what, in the poem, is stated," p. 38]. Imagism was incapable of presenting, of "rendering" things which were dynamic rather than static. (p. 39)

Watts goes on to say that the presenting of "ideas in action" is necessary in *The Cantos*, a poem that purports to alter that cluster of customs by which we live by directing our attention to that which is always changing, culture itself. But beyond pointing at "ideas in action," Watts never defines how this great change from imagistic to *Canto*-esque form was to be accomplished.

However, it seems to me that Pound's concept of the image, as clarified by his term *vortex,* does involve movement. And the definition of vortex is really but another way of saying "ideas in action." The ideogram is not static: when Pound defines the term in his *ABC of Reading,* his stress is on its lack of abstraction, its relationship to things, but one has only to compare Fenollosa in *The Chinese Written Character as a Medium for Poetry* (Pound's source for his notions about ideogram) on the ideogram with Pound on vortex to see the connection.[15]

> A true noun, an isolated thing, does not exist in nature. Things are only the terminal points, or rather the meeting points, of actions, cross-sections cut through actions, snapshots. Neither can a pure verb, an abstract motion, be possible in nature. The eye sees noun and verb as one: things in motion, motion in things, and so the Chinese conception tends to represent them.[16]

Fenollosa goes on to point out that the ideogram is in truth metaphor: the use of material images to suggest immaterial relations, for Chinese characters are more than vivid shorthand pictures of actions and processes in nature. They describe the unseen as well as the seen. Metaphors are possible only because they follow objective lines of relationship in nature herself.

> Relations are more real and more important than the things which they relate. The forces which produce the branch-angles of an oak lay potent in the acorn. Similar lines of resistance, half-curbing the out-pressing vitalities, govern the branching of rivers and of nations. Thus a nerve, a wire, a roadway, and a clearing-house are only varying channels which communicate forces for itself. This is more than analogy, it is identity of structure. Nature furnishes her own clues. Had the world not been full of homologies, sympathies, and identities, thought

---

15. The Fenollosa essay is extremely important to Pound's poetics, for it contains the bases of his ideas about both healthy and degenerate language and society and the relationship between them. As Pound himself wrote in a February 1939 letter to Hubert Creekmore: "For Ars Poetica, gorrdamit, get my last edn. of Fenollosa's 'Chinese Written Character' vide my introduction." (*Letters,* p. 322)
16. (San Francisco, 1936), p. 10.

would have been starved and language chained to the obvious. There would have been no bridge whereby to cross from the minor truth of the seen to the major truth of the unseen.[17]

This is exactly the kind of truth that Pound is after in his use of metaphor. In his essay "Vorticism," he talks about the process of creating his early "one image poem," "In a Station of the Metro" ("The apparition of these faces in the crowd:/Petals, on a wet black bough"). He describes its structure as a "form of super-position, that is to say, it is one idea set on top of another. . . . In a poem of this sort one is trying to record the precise instant when a thing outward and objective transforms itself, or darts into a thing inward and subjective."[18] The poem is a metaphor; the colon (or semi-colon, as in the version printed in *The Selected Poems,* New York, 1957) reinforces the analogy created by juxtaposition. The apparition of faces in a crowd is the minor truth of the seen; the petals are the major truth of the unseen. Most important of all is the fact that the two are related to one another, so that their juxtaposition (the assertation of metaphor) is a way of trying to record the "precise instant" of transformation (the lines of relation). Characteristically of Pound, although he talks in his comment of subjective and objective, inward and outward, his actual recording of the experience speaks in terms of two objective, outward manifestations; only the word *apparition* hints at the emotional, inner experience of which the whole poem is an expression.

The theory behind this kind of metaphor (which results from the combination of Fenollosa's and Pound's own ideas on image, vortex, and ideogram) does not change as Pound begins to write *The Cantos.* What does happen is that Pound begins to achieve forms that seem better able to transmit both the truth and the force inherent in metaphor. The altered form of *The Cantos,* including the form of its metaphors, has resulted from a two-fold process. Its first element is ellipsis, what Pound called "condensation to maximum attainability." Pound's procedure has

17. P. 22.
18. *Gaudier-Brzeska,* p. 103.

been to condense (or omit) statement of any kind, the logical or explicit links between images. Yet there is a second element to the process: Pound has not simply removed certain kinds of linking devices; he has replaced them with other devices. For by deliberately removing most traces of what I have called "statement," Pound has made his strongest bid for the replacement of this kind of reading process (logical, intellectual) in his audience with a different process. In the *ABC of Reading* he calls it starting

> the reader or hearer from what he actually sees or hears, instead of distracting his mind from that actuality to something which can only be approximately deduced or conjectured FROM the actuality, and for which the *evidence* can be nothing save the particular and limited extent of the actuality. (p. 31)

Pound is asking for a more direct, more emotional and physical reading process. To achieve this he has replaced logopoeia (the dance of the intellect among words) as chief aid to phanopoeia (the throwing of the object onto the visual imagination) with melopoeia (wherein the words are charged, over and above their plain meaning, with some musical property that directs the bearing or trend of that meaning, thereby inducing emotional correlations by the sound and rhythm of the speech).

Although melopoeia has always been a primary element in Pound's poetics, it has received little attention from the critics (which in itself may be a verification of Pound's criticism of the Western sensibility). Pound has extended his basic idea of melopoeia in several essays about music. The following excerpts are from *Antheil* (Chicago, 1927).

> A SOUND OF ANY PITCH, OR ANY COMBINATION OF SUCH SOUNDS, MAY BE FOLLOWED BY A SOUND OF ANY OTHER PITCH, OR ANY COMBINATION OF SUCH SOUNDS, providing the time interval between them is properly gauged; and this is true for ANY SERIES OF SOUNDS, CHORDS, OR ARPEGGIOS. The limits for practical purposes of music depend solely on our capacity to produce a sound that will last long enough, i.e. remain audible long

enough, for the succeeding sound or sounds to catch up, traverse, intersect it. (pp. 3–4)

In a poem the images persist for traversal or intersection in the reader's apprehension, in modalities governed by adroit rhythmic recall or imagistic analogy. For the poet and/or the reader of poetry, it means that the secret of major form consists in the precise adjustment of the intervals between disparate or recurrent themes or items or rhythms. And anything at all may be put into a poem, provided its mode and degree of definition, and its relation with the other things in the poem, be suitably managed. (p. 6)

. . . the lateral motion, the horizontal motion, and the time interval between succeeding sounds MUST affect the human ear, and not only the ear but the absolute physics of the matter. The question of where one wave-mode meets another, or where it banks against the course of another wave to strengthen or weaken its action, must be considered. (p. 17)

Hugh Kenner devotes a brief chapter to this theory of "Great Bass" (as Pound calls it in *Culture*), but the conclusion that he draws from all this is just a reinforcement of the juxtaposition idea.

Pound, quite consciously, never thinks of using two motifs, two blocks of rendering, except as parts, integral parts, of a larger rhythm of juxtaposition and recurrence. This balancing and recurrence of motifs is what holds together single cantos. It also holds together the entire work. . . . (p. 280)

Kenner is correct as far as he goes, but he cannot see beyond (or into) image patterns and motifs—although Pound specifically couples imagistic analogy with rhythmic recall. The problem with total reliance upon blocks of rendering or motifs as the smallest units of perception is that, as I have said earlier, often it is very difficult to establish any logical connection between them. On the other hand, Pound's notion of proper time interval between sounds, or of where and how one "wave node" meets another, can be shown to clarify many such transitions.

In a note at the end of his "Vorticism" essay Pound wrote:

I am often asked whether there can be a long imagiste or vorticist poem. The Japanese, who evolved the hokku, evolved also the Noh plays. In the best "Noh" the whole play may consist of one image. I mean it is gathered about one image. Its unity consists in one image, enforced by movement and music. I see nothing against a long vorticist poem.[19]

Both versions of the original *Three Cantos* seem to have been constructed according to this principle. Both versions, the cantos as published in *Poetry* and in *Lustra,* still contain an extensive use of statement and a more traditional usage of metaphor; they are organized around the recurrence of one "image." This image is a vision of spirits or ghosts or gods. While the image continues into the final versions, Pound's method of presentation alters greatly.

Much of the original material in the earliest versions of *The Cantos* has been omitted (for the purpose of "condensation to maximum attainability"), yet this particular kind of image persists and is, if anything, strengthened. There is a special reason for this, which has to do with metaphor. Tied to his discussions of image, vortex, and ideogram is another series of statements about metaphor and poetry, and they are concerned with Pound's notion of "equation" in poetry and with the presence of the gods. They reveal much more explicitly his interest in the truth of metaphor.

Hugh Wittemeyer, in his study of Pound's early poetry, *The Poetry of Ezra Pound: Forms and Renewals, 1908–1920,* discusses the high value that Pound places upon states of consciousness themselves as the ultimate knowable truths. "For Pound," he writes, "only the states of mind themselves are 'vivid and undeniable,' and the gods are metaphors or 'explications of mood.' "[20] Again, "The poem is a verbal equation which seeks to adumbrate the epiphany in images of sunlight and flowers, and expressions of gratitude and triumph" (p. 27). His notion that "the gods are metaphors" is based upon a series of remarks

---

19. *Ibid.,* P. 109.
20. (Berkeley and Los Angeles, 1969) , p. 27.

by Pound in his earliest prose, which are important not only for the early poems of *Personae*, and also for the earliest *Cantos*, but for the total development of *The Cantos* into their most recent installments.

1) I believe that every emotion and every phase of emotion has some toneless phrase, some rhythm-phrase to express it. (*Gaudier-Brzeska*, p. 97)

2) By the "image" I mean such an equation; not an equation of mathematics, not something about *a, b,* and *c,* having something to do with form, but about *sea, cliffs, night,* having something to do with mood. (*Gaudier-Brzeska*, p. 106)

3) Poetry is a sort of inspired mathematics, which gives us equations, not for abstract figures, triangles, spheres, and the like, but equations for human emotions. If one have a mind which inclines to magic rather than to science, one will prefer to speak of these equations as spells or incantations; it sounds more arcane, mysterious, recondite. (*The Spirit of Romance* [London, 1910], p. 14)

4) The first myths arose when a man walked sheer into "nonsense," that is to say, when some very vivid and undeniable adventure befell him, and he told someone else who called him a liar. Thereupon, after bitter experience, perceiving that no one could understand what he meant when he said that he "turned into a tree" he made a myth—a work of art that is—an impersonal or objective story woven out of his own emotion, as the nearest equation that he was capable of putting into words. That story, perhaps, then gave rise to a weaker copy of his emotion in others, until there arose a cult, a company of people who could understand each other's nonsense about the gods. ("Arnold Dolmetsch," in T. S. Eliot, ed., *Literary Essays of Ezra Pound,* p. 431.)

5) The perception of the intellect is given in the word, that of the emotions in the cadence. It is only then, in perfect rhythm joined to the perfect word that the two-fold vision can be recorded. . . .

It is only when the emotions illumine the perceptive powers that we see the reality. It is in the light born of this double current that we look upon the face of the mystery unveiled. (Introduction to *Cavalcanti—Sonnets and Ballate* [Cambridge, Mass., 1912], xxi, xxiii)

Finally, Hugh Kenner (in "The Broken Mirrors and the Mirrors of Memory") quotes Pound (he does not give the source) as saying quite succinctly that "A god is an eternal state of mind"; he is manifest "when the states of mind take form."[21]

It is from this interesting blend of mysticism and poetics that Pound's use of the gods in his poetry springs. The gods themselves are incarnate metaphor, yet—and this is of more importance to our present concerns—descriptions of the appearance of gods most regularly involve the use of metaphoric language. They do so because the vision of gods is for Pound the perfect moment for rendering the true relations between inner and outer, for recording "the precise instant when a thing outward and objective transforms itself, or darts into a thing inward and suggestive." Again, this does not represent a change in tactics for Pound, but rather a greater clarification of function as well as an omission of other kinds of material—and metaphor—which does not contribute to that function. Metaphors are used in *The Cantos* to reveal the nature of the gods and the importance of those moments of vision in which they are observed. The lists that follow show my attempts to trace several occurrences of this image of the gods as it appears in the various versions. (The 1925 *XVI Cantos* is rarely included, because it usually does not show significant textual change. Its most interesting feature is that, although it is almost identical to the

---

21. Lewis Leary, ed., *Motive and Method in The Cantos of Ezra Pound* (New York, 1969), pp. 14–15.

1934 text, with the exception of one canto (VI) and a few miscellaneous passages, it still "explains" much more than does the final version. This is owing to its device of marginal annotation and also to the woodcut illustrations for each canto, which certainly help to indicate what that canto is "about.")

Example 1 is not that image per se but shows the progress of the original opening to *The Cantos,* when they were directly indebted to Browning for their existence. These lines begin the running, one-sided dialogue with "Bob Browning" that characterizes the early versions. The two early texts change very little— only punctuation is altered. But with the changing of this "invocation" of Browning to Canto II in an extremely shortened version one can see how the direct connection lines to Browning have been edited out of the final work. Browning's Sordello becomes just one more incarnation or aspect of a composite figure that also contains the historical Sordello, the poet Sordello, Dante's Sordello, and Pound's Sordello. It also is a brief example of how Pound's condensation process can work. Lengthy lines of chat have evolved into "But Sordello, and my Sordello?", followed by the first phrases of the most "historical" account of Sordello in a manuscript in the Ambrosian library at Milan. In the proverbial nutshell we now have the ideas about Sordello that the speaker of the 1917 Canto I was trying to express. (How these lines function more specifically in Canto II will be discussed in the analysis of that poem, which follows shortly.)

1

from *Poetry:*

Hang it all, there can be but one Sordello!
But say I want to, say I take your whole bag of tricks,
Let in your quirks and tweeks, and say the thing's an art-
    form,
Your Sordello, and that the modern world
Needs such a rag-bag to stuff all its thoughts in;
Say that I dump my catch, shiny and silvery
As fresh sardines flapping and slipping on the marginal
    cobbles?

(I stand before the booth, the speech; but the truth
Is inside this discourse—this booth is full of the marrow of
   wisdom.)

from *Lustra:*

Hang it all, there can be but the one "Sordello,"
But say I want to, say I take your whole bag of tricks,
Let in your quirks and tweeks, and say the thing's an art-
   form,
Your "Sordello," and that the "modern world"
Needs such a rag-bag to stuff all its thoughts in;
Say that I dump my catch, shiny and silvery
As fresh sardines flapping and slipping on the marginal
   cobbles?
I stand before the booth (the speech), but the truth
Is inside this discourse: this booth is full of the marrow of
   wisdom.

from Canto II

Hang it all, Robert Browning,
There can be but the one "Sordello."
But Sordello, and my Sordello?
Lo Sordels si fo di Mantovana.

The complete omission of the extended metaphor of Browning's rag bag and Pound's "catch" is important. One reason for
its demise could well have been that it is simply not the kind
of metaphor that Pound ultimately used in *The Cantos:* it is
much too decorative. Pound seems to be trying to resurrect the
dead metaphor *bag of tricks,* but it does not work. That it does
not work (that it does not help or interest the reader to see
Browning's poems as a rag-bag) is shown by the fanciful nature
of the thoughts: fish metaphor. True, "shiny," "silvery," "flapping," and "slipping" catch a quality of his thought, but they
are not what Pound calls the "proper and perfect symbol."
(These remarks about symbol are equally applicable to Pound's
notion of metaphor.)

I believe that the proper and perfect symbol is the natural object, that if a man uses "symbols" he must so use them that their symbolic function does not obtrude; so that *a sense*, and the poetic quality of the passage, is not lost to those who do not understand the symbol as such, to whom, for instance, a hawk is a hawk.[22]

In example 2 the changes from the *Poetry* to *Lustra* versions of this detailed presentation of the vision of gods are few but significant. "North-most rocks" to "square-shaled rocks"; "not dark and shadowy ghosts" to "not dark and shadow-wet ghosts"; references to Arnaut and Catullus omitted as well as some of the discussion with Browning. "Square-shaled" and "shadow-wet" are the first examples we have met of what becomes in *The Cantos* a basic unit of metaphor, of image, and of melopoeia.

2

from *Poetry:*

As well begin here. Began our Catullus:
"Home to sweet rest, and to the waves' deep laughter,"
The laugh they wake amid the border rushes.
This is our home, the trees are full of laughter,
And the storms laugh loud, breaking the riven waves
on "north-most rocks"; and here the sunlight
Glints on the shaken waters, and the rain
Comes forth with delicate tread, walking from Isola Garda—
                Lo soleils plovil,
As Arnaut had it in th' inextricable song.
The very sun rains and a spatter of fire
Darts from the "Lydian" ripples; *"locus undae,"* as Catullus,
        "Lydiae,"
And the place is full of spirits.
Not *lemures,* not dark and shadowy ghosts,
But the ancient living, wood-white,
Smooth as the inner bark, and firm of aspect,
And all agleam with colors—no, not agleam,
But colored like the lake and like the olive leaves,

---

22. "A Retrospect," *Literary Essays,* p. 9.

Glaukopos, clothed like the poppies, wearing golden greaves,
Light on the air.
Are they Etruscan gods?
The air is solid sunlight, *apricus,*
Sun-fed we dwell there (we in England now) ;
It's your way of talk, we can be where we will be,
Sirmio serves my will better than your Asolo
Which I have never seen.

from *Lustra:*

As well begin here, here began Catullus:
"Home to sweet rest, and to the waves deep laughter,"
The laugh they wake amid the border rushes.
This is our home, the trees are full of laughter,
And the storm laughs loud, breaking the riven waves
On square-shaled rocks, and here the sunlight
Glints on the shaken waters and the rain
Comes forth with delicate tread, walking from Isola Garda,
                    Lo Soleils plovil.
It is the sun rains, and a spatter of fire
Darts from the "Lydian" ripples, *lacus undae,*
And the place is full of spirits, not *lemures,*
Not dark and shadow-wet ghosts, but ancient living,
Wood-white, smooth as the inner-bark, and firm of aspect
And all a-gleam with colour?
Not a-gleam
But coloured like the lake and olive leaves,
GLAUKOPOS, clothed like the poppies, wearing golden greaves,
Light on the air. Are they Etruscan gods?
The air is solid sunlight, *apricus.*
Sun-fed we dwell there (we in England now)
For Sirmio serves my whim, better than Asolo,
Yours and unseen.

from Canto IV:

            Actaeon . . .
            and a valley,
The valley is thick with leaves, with leaves, the trees,
The sunlight glitters, glitters a-top,
Like a fish-scale roof,
            Like the church roof in Poictiers

If it were gold.
           Beneath it, beneath it
Not a ray, not a slivver, not a spare disc of sunlight
Flaking the black, soft water;
Bathing the body of nymphs, of nymphs, and Diana,
Nymphs, white-gathered about her, and the air, air,
Shaking, air alight with the goddess,
          fanning their hair in the dark,
Lifting, lifting and waffing:
Ivory dipping in silver,
        shadow'd, o'ershadow'd
Ivory dipping in silver,
Not a splotch, not a lost shatter of sunlight.
Then Actaeon: Vidal,
Vidal. It is old Vidal speaking,
        stumbling along in the wood,
Not a patch, not a lost shimmer of sunlight,
        the pale hair of the goddess . . .

Thus the light rains, thus pours, *e lo soleils plovil*
The liquid and rushing crystal
        beneath the knees of the gods.
Ply over ply, thin glitter of water;
Brook film bearing white petals.

In example 4 we shall also encounter "ship-work," "bird-cry," "green-gray," "gate-cliffs," "glare-purple," "sea-worn," and "gull-cry." This list can serve to display some of the variations that Pound's use of the compound word can take, and also a common identity and function that they all share. In my discussion of Canto II I will show how the structure (and its extended forms) operates in a complete poem. At this point I would like simply to explain this figure and its function as I understand it.

    These compound words are often a form of kenning, a periphrastic expression used instead of the simple name of a thing, such as "oar-steed" for "ship." Kenning is characteristic of both Greek (wine-dark sea) and Old English poetry (cf. Pound's *Seafarer* translation), so that one reason for using them in the opening cantos is to evoke the "feel" of the cultures from which this style of verse sprang. But even more important to Pound, I think, is the fact that these compound words seem to be the realization of his ideas of image, vortex, and ideogram. They are also the ultimate form of the condensation of metaphor that I have said characterizes the style of *The Cantos*. With this form Pound is isolating concrete elements from a given perception or experience and presenting them, juxtaposed against one another, to form a new and third entity—an image. He is omitting any linguistic rendering of their relation—that is, verb or preposition. As Fenollosa argues, things imply actions, and so do these "things" imply the lines that connect them and thus the entire perception (an intellectual and emotional complex in an instant of time). The hyphen points to and emphasizes the fact that a relationship is being established. These hyphenated words are ideograms in exactly Fenollosa's (and Pound's) sense of the term. They are a shorthand way of presenting the intellectual and emotional complex, a radiant node or cluster, if only because of the effect that such a device must have on the reader. The hyphen is like an arrow pointing to a relation. The reader is asked to fill it in. He might do it by thinking—stop reading and remark to himself: square-shaled rocks means rocks that are square and shaled or perhaps square because they are shaled; shadow-wet ghosts means ghosts that are shadows, or dark like shadows, and wet as things often are that are in the shadows, or seem wet because they are dark and shadowy; odor of ship-work means the odor connected with the work that is done to make a ship move; bird-cry means cry of birds; cliff green-gray means a cliff that is a color at once green and grey; gate-cliffs mean cliffs that act as gates to something; and so on. But a simpler way to supply the links, given the fact that the reader is presented with concrete things, is to image, for these ideograms are powerful creators of phanopoeia—throwing a visual image into the mind. An image, by its very nature—because it is an active re-creation—is a more motoric, more physical and more emotional act on the part of the reader than is thinking.[23] Yet even if, for some reason, the reader does not image

---

23. Theodore R. Sarbin and Joseph B. Juhasz, "Toward a Theory of the Imagination," *Journal of Personality* 38, no. 1 (March 1970) : 52–76.

but only supplies intellectually the implied relationships, he has still been induced into action of some kind. This is a step toward the fulfillment of Pound's purpose in writing the poem, as I have understood it. Elsewhere in the work Pound employs the same kind of structure with similar effects without actually using a hyphen, for example: "sea churning shingle" or "cave salt white." Usually he uses these compound words as a foundation unit for the building of extended metaphoric statements.

Not all compound words, or images, or ideograms are metaphors in my own sense of the term. "Shadow-wet ghosts" is a metaphor, while "bird-cry" is not, primarily because the former is a figurative expression while the latter is literal. The hyphenated form in "bird-cry" is a substitute for something like "cry of birds." The hyphenated form strengthens the words' imagistic impact by pointing to the relation between "bird" and "cry," which might otherwise be ignored, since the phrase is such a common one. In addition, the choice of compound words, whether or not they are metaphors, reinforces the visual and auditory pattern that Pound has been carefully creating. "Shadow-wet ghosts," on the other hand, is figurative, in that nothing, not even a ghost, can be literally "shadow-wet." But the metaphoric nature of such an expression is more complicated than this, and points toward Pound's own definitions of metaphor, which are not at all conventional. "Shadow-wet ghosts" is also a metaphor because none of the explanations offered on the preceding page for the phrase could actually translate or duplicate its meaning: the creation of "shadow-wet" from "shadow" and "wet," while readily understood, cannot be explained by literal language. Nor is the phrase "understood" by logical reasoning, but rather by imaging. In this way "metaphor" and "image," which are usually not at all interchangeable, come very close together, as they do in all of Pound's theoretical writing. For Pound all images are metaphor, because an image is a verbal equation for an emotional and intellectual complex in an instant of time. He is nowhere careful to distinguish between meanings of "image," "vortex," "ideogram," and even "symbol" and "metaphor," for he sees them all as instances of the proper use of poetry—that is, creating the verbal equation for an action in such a way that it requires action, rather than idea, on the part of the reader to comprehend it.

Yet if one cares to distinguish between metaphor and other varieties of image, one can say that Pound's metaphors, and especially his compound-word metaphors, are perhaps the fullest realization of these ideas about poetry simply because they, unlike "bird-cry," cannot be understood by any other process save the "active" one of direct experience. This is more clearly exemplified by phrases that are less obviously metaphoric than "shadow-wet," such as "gate-cliff" or "sea-surge." A "gate-cliff" is neither a gate nor a cliff, but an entity that is a composite of the two in a way that "cliffs that act as gates" cannot approximate, even as "sea-surge" is something other than "the surge of the sea": it is a "thing" (in Pound's view a crucial achievement) that can be directly treated.

The passage I have chosen from Canto IV is not a direct rendering of the lines from *Poetry* and *Lustra*. It depicts Diana and her nymphs bathing, as Pound, via Golding, tells Ovid's story of Actaeon. But all share sun, water, rain, white spirits— now goddesses—and Daniel's phrase "lo soleils plovil." If not identical, the spirit is surely similar. In the passages from *Poetry* and *Lustra* personifying and more conventional metaphors establish the sense of a fluid relationship among the elements: "the trees are full of laughter"; "the storms laugh loud"; "the rain/Comes forth with delicate tread"; "the very sun rains" (translated in *Lustra* as "It is the sun rains"), and so on. The spirits, however, remain uninvolved in this movement. In the Actaeon passage, precisely because the underlying theme is that of metamorphosis, the elements again merge, but only, as its metaphors reveal, through and by means of the goddess: "Not a slivver, not a spare disc of sunlight/flaking the black, soft water"; "air alight with the goddess"; or "ivory dipping in silver/Not a splotch, not a lost shatter of sunlight." It is "thus" that (the Daniel line again) "the light rains, thus pours . . ./The liquid and rushing crystal/beneath the knees of the gods." The goddess is providing light in the dark place, embodying in herself various light-making or bright elements in nature: sunlight, ivory, silver, crystal. Even the water, a reflector of light, becomes an extension of herself. The statement, "the pale hair of the goddess," occasions a subsequent metaphor: "ply over ply, thin glitter of water." Pound has created the metaphors that carry the meaning of the passage by underlining the truth of his earlier personifications, and even more directly, that of a metaphor of Golding's (changing only the color) :

> Such colour as appeares in Heaven by *Phebus* broken rayes
> Directly shining on the Cloudes, or such as is alwayes
> The colour of the Morning Cloudes before the Sunne doth show,
> Such sanguine colour in the face of Phoebe gan to glowe
> There standing naked in his sight.[24]

There is just one compound word in this passage: "nymphs white-gathered around her." The image is, in miniature, that of the entire passage, and the quality that is indicated by the yoking of *white* and *gathered* is precisely that which I have been trying to describe: the sense of the presence of the goddess (here all of the goddesses, or spirits) : of their radiance and power, its relationship to and effect upon nature. In this way an extended metaphor is organized about one compound word.

Finally, the effect of melopoeia as a device that "directs the bearing or trend" of the "plain meaning" of the words must be mentioned. (We cannot see it linking disparate images in this excerpt.) Assonance, internal rhyme, alliteration, and sheer repetition create the spirit or mood of the image.

Example 3 does not change significantly in its progression toward Canto III. The most interesting section of the passage is its conclusion, in which the speaker wants to move from Tuscany to Egypt and China. Pound's continual whittling away at the passage results, finally, in the inclusion of only the key image

---

24. W. H. D. Rouse, ed., *Shakespeare's Ovid, Being Arthur Golding's Translation of the Metamorphoses* (New York, 1966) , p. 67.

for each culture. (In the 1925 version he was still changing: the second to the last line read "Scarabs, green veins in the turquoise.") By the final version there is nothing in the context that says Egypt or China. The transition is made by means of assonance (glazes>green>grey; upturned>turquoise) and imagistic analogy (swimmers moving through the air; veins moving through the turquoise; steps moving through the cedars). I have also included another "gods floating in the air" sequence, from Canto XX, to demonstrate how melopoeia aids the presentation of the image. One has only to read the passage aloud to note how both visual and auditory elements combine to create the sense of slow floating: the stress upon nouns and adjectives formed from nouns, examined in careful detail, the enjambed consonants, the repetition, alliteration, and assonance.

3

from *Poetry:*

                        And set out your matter
As I do, in straight simple phrases:
        Gods float in the azure air,
Bright gods, and Tuscan, back before dew was shed,
It is a world like Puvis'?
                     Never so pale, my friend,
'Tis the first light—not half light—Panisks
And oak-girls and the Maenads
Have all the wood. Our olive Sirmio
Lies in its burnished mirror, and the Mounts Balde and Riva
Are alive with song, and all the leaves are full of voices.
"Non e fuggito."
               "It is not gone." Metastasio
Is right—we have that world about us.
And the clouds bow above the lake, and there are folk upon
    them
Going their windy ways, moving by Riva,
By the western shore, far as Lonato,
And the water is full of silvery almond-white swimmers,
The silvery water glazes the up-turned nipple.
How shall we start hence, how begin the progress?
Pace naif Ficinus, say when Hotep-Hotep

Was a king in Egypt—
> *When Atlas sat down with his astrolabe*
> *He, brother to Prometheus, physicist—*
> Say it was Moses' birth-year?
Exult with Shang in squatness? The sea-monster
Bulges the squarish bronzes.
(Confucius later taught the world good manners.
Started with himself, built out perfection.)
> With Egypt!
Daub out in blue of scarabs, and with that greeny turquoise?
Or with China, *O Virgilio mio,* and gray gradual steps
Lead up beneath flat sprays of heavy cedars . .

from *Lustra:*

> Gods float in the azure air,
Bright gods and Tuscan, back before dew was shed;
It is a world like Puvis.?
> Never so pale, my friend,
'Tis the first light—not half-light—Panisks
And oak-girls and the Maelids have all the wood;
> Our olive Sirmio
Lies in its burnished mirror, and the Mounts Balde and Riva
Are alive with song, and all the leaves are full of voices.
"Non e fuggi."
> "It is not gone." Metastasio
Is right, we have that world about us.
And the clouds bowe above the lake, and there are folk
> upon them
Going their windy ways, moving by Riva,
By the western shore, far as Lonato,
And the water is full of silvery almond-white swimmers,
The silvery water glazes the upturned nipple.
> *"When Atlas sat down with his astrolabe,*
> *He brother to Prometheus, physicist."*
We let Ficino
Start us our progress, say it was Moses' birth year?
Exult with Shang in squatness? The sea-monster
Bulges the squarish bronzes.
Daub out, with blue of scarabs, Egypt,
Green veins in the turquoise?
> Or grey gradual steps
Lead up beneath flat sprays of heavy cedars:

from Canto III:

Gods float in the azure air,
Bright gods and Tuscan, back before dew was shed.
Light: and the first light, before ever dew was fallen.
Panisks, and from the oak, dryads,
And from the apple, maelid,
Through all the wood, and the leaves are full of voices,
A-whisper, and the clouds bowe over the lake,
And there are gods upon them,
And in the water, the almond-white swimmers,
The silvery water glazed the upturned nipple,
        As Poggio has remarked.
Green veins in the turquoise,
Or, the grey steps lead up under the cedars.

from Canto XX:

And then the faceted air:
Floating. Below, sea churning shingle.
Floating, each on invisible fluid,
Borne over the plain, recumbent,
The right arm cast back,
        the right wrist for a pillow,
The left hand like a calyx,
Thumb held against finger, the third,
The first fingers petal'd up, the hand as a lamp,
A calyx.

Example 4 is a yet more vivid example of the process that
we have been observing.

4

from *Poetry:*

(Canto I)

I have but smelt this life, a whiff of it—
The box of scented wood
Recalls cathedrals. And shall I claim;
Confuse my own phantastikon,
Or say the filmy shell that circumscribes me
Contains the actual sun;
        confuse the thing I see

With actual gods behind me?
        Are they gods behind me?
How many worlds we have! If Botticelli
Bring her ashore on that great cockle-shell—
His Venus (Simonetta?)
And Spring and Aufidus fill all the air
With their clear-outlined blossoms?
World enough. Behold, I say, she comes
"Apparalled like the spring, Graces her subjects,"
(That's from *Pericles*) .
Oh, we have worlds enough, and brave *décors,*
And from these like we guess a soul for man
And build him full of aery populations.

        (Canto III)

And a certain Cretan's
                Hymni Deorum:
(The thin clear Tuscan stuff
    Gives way before the florid mellow phrase.)
Take we the Goddess, Venus:
                Venerandam,
Aurean coronam habentem, pulchram
Cypri munimenta sortita est, maritime,
Light on the foam, breathed on by zephyrs,
And air-tending hours. Mirthful, *orichalci,* with golden
Girdles and breast bands.
                Thou with dark eye-lids,
Bearing the golden bough of Argicida.

from *Lustra:*

(both passages are almost exactly the same as above.)

from Canto XVII:

                Between them,
Cave of Nerea,
        she like a great shell curved,
And the boat drawn without sound,
Without odor of ship-work,
Nor bird-cry, nor any noise of wave moving,
Nor splash of porpoise, nor any noise of wave moving,

Within her cave, Nerea,
                    she like a great shell curved
In the suavity of the rock,
                    cliff green-gray in the far,
In the near, the gate-cliffs of amber,
And the wave
                    green clear, and blue clear,
And the cave salt white, and glare-purple,
        cool, porphyry smooth,
        the rock sea-worn.
No gull-cry, no sound of porpoise,
Sand as of malachite, and no cold there
        the light not of the sun.

from Canto I:

        Venerandam,
In the Cretan's phrase, with the golden crown, Aphrodite,
Cypri munimenta sortita est, mirthful, oricalchi, with golden
Girdles and breast bands, thou with dark eyelids
Bearing the golden bough of Argicida. So that:

In the selection from *Poetry's* Canto I (all of the preceding examples have been drawn from that canto, which works and reworks the central image and the ideas it embodies) the speaker relates another vision of a goddess. This time it is of Venus.

In a passage from the original *Poetry* version, Pound, talking to Browning, sets forth a concept of history.

. . . Ghosts move about me
Patched with histories. You had your business:
To set out so much thought, so much emotion;
To paint, more real than any dead Sordello,
The half or third of your intensest life
And call that third Sordello;
And you'll say, "No, not your life,
He never showed himself."
Is't worth the evasion, what were the use
Of setting figures up and breathing life upon them,
Were't not *our* life, your life, my life, extended?
I walk Verona. (I am here in England.)
I can see Can Grande. (Can see whom you will.)
                    You had one whole man?

And I have many fragments, less worth? Less worth?
Ah, had you quite my age, quite such a beastly and can-
    tankerous age?
You had some basis, had some set belief.
Am I let preach? Has it a place in music?

Here he talks, even as he had done in reference to Sordello, about the convergence of worlds (and time) upon a single figure. He juxtaposes the Venus of Botticelli and Shakespeare and at the end of the third canto (which later became Canto I) the Venus of a Latin translation of a Homeric hymn to Venus. These lines continue, only slightly condensed, into the final version. The point, once again, is that the thing we call Venus contains all of these visions of her—that she is, in a sense, created by them.

There is no longer any "talking about" in the passage from Canto XVII. (Although Edwards and Vasse identify Nerea as a possible reference to the Nereids, I am considering the passage to be about Venus because of the cockle-shell motif—here "she like a great shell curved"—and also the final line, "and light not of the sun," which has been used previously to evoke the concept *goddess*, albeit not Venus in particular. In the earlier Venus-passage Pound talks about ideas. He says that his concept of Venus is the result of a series of other concepts or visions of her. Here the concern seems to have been to re-create that vision, employing each of the early principles of imagism: direct treatment of the "thing," whether subjective or objective; using absolutely no word that does not contribute to the presentation; composing in the sequence of the musical phrase. The cluster of compound words represents condensation within an extended image at its most extreme and also, because the two are related, an expression of the greatest lyrical intensity. The sheer number of such words seems to me to force the reader to image as hard as he can, and his act is in direct accord with the meaning of the passage—glorification of the goddess. Once again the compound words are at once agents of phanopoeia and melopoeia. In the first section of the passage, which tries to create a sense of the absence of sound, there is no metaphor and only two compound words, *ship-work* and *bird-cry*. The lines convey silence as a positive, rather than a negative quality, by presenting that which is absent: "nor bird-cry, nor any noise of wave moving," and so on. The reader is asked to call these noises into being for a moment—i.e., to image them—but the images are meager in comparison to those in the second section. Here the concern is with presenting what is there—rocks, water, and sand —and then relating these to what is missing ("no gull cry, no sound of porpoise . . . no cold there"). The cluster of compound words is therefore to be found here, as well as an accelerated assonance:

cliff > cliff > clear > clear > cave > cool > smooth > cry > malachite > cold
green > grey > gate > green > clear > glare > purple > gull-cry
gray > far > amber > wave > cave > glare > sand > malachite

Of the several compound words in the passage, some are metaphor while some are not. This distinction is often difficult to make, because the function of all of the compound words is so similar. Metaphors like "gate-cliffs," "green clear," "blue clear," and "glare-purple" are distinctive primarily because, since they are metaphors, they most successfully fulfill the common function. That is, it is difficult to explain "glare-purple" but not difficult to understand it. Again, in a phrase like "the rock sea-worn," by its structure, seems more than simply another form of "worn by the sea." The yoking of "sea" and "worn" into the new entity "sea-worn" has created an image, "a radiant node or cluster," for a diffuse condition.

All of this imaging activity leads into the final line of the passage. Bearing in mind the source of light in the Actaeon sequence, one can see why the light in the cave is not of the sun. It is of the Morning Star, Venus. It is a manifestation of her power. In this way all of the vivid color that the reader has been asked to image, because of the structure of the words on the page, owes its existence to the goddess and is there to reflect or enhance her presence.

Canto II is an especially clear example of a canto with a structure that is based upon compound words and in which phanopoeia and melopoeia carry the "meaning" of the poem. To repeat Pound's words from *Antheil:* "the secret of major form consists in the precise adjustment of the intervals between disparate or recurrent *themes* or *items* or rhythms"; the reader's apprehension is governed by "rhythmic recall" and "imagistic analogy." I have already tried to show how melopoeia can control a given image. Therefore, the following chart represents my attempt to demonstrate how tonal qualities—patterns of assonance, alliteration, repetition, and the like—can provide the links between extended images or episodes.

Canto II: Melopoeia as linking device

1. Hang it all, Robert Browning,
   there can be but the one "Sordello."
   But Sordello, and my Sordello?
   Lo Sordels si fo di Mantovana.

2. So-shu churned in the sea.

3. Seal-sports in the spray-whited circles of cliff-wash,
   Sleek head, daughter of Lir,
             eyes of Picasso
   Under black fur-hood, lithe daughter of Ocean;

4. And the wave runs in the beach-groove:

5. "Eleanor, ἐλέναυς and ἑλέπτολις!"
             And poor old Homer blind, blind, as a bat,

6. Ear, ear for the sea-surge, murmur of old men's voices: . . .

---

1. to 2. to 3.: Lo Sordels si fo>so-shu
             si>sea>seal>sleek

4. And the wave runs in the beach groove—thematic meaning.
5. Sordello>Lo Sordels>seal>sleek>Eleanor

6. So-shu churned in the sea>ear, ear for the sea-surge

7. And by the beach-run, Tyro,
           Twisted arms of the sea-god,
Lithe sinews of water, gripping her, cross-hold,
And the blue-grey glass of the wave tents them,
Glare azure of water, cold-welter, close cover.
Quiet sun-tawny sand-stretch,
The gulls broad out their wings,
           nipping between the slay feathers;
Snipe come for their bath,
           bend out their wing-joints,
Spread wet wings to the sun-film,
And by Scios,
           to left of the Naxos passage,
Naviform rock overgrown,
           algae cling to its edge,
There is a wine-red glow in the shallows,
           a tin flash in the sun-dazzle.

8. The ship landed in Scios,
           men wanting spring-water,
And by the rock-pool a young boy loggy with vine-must,
           "To Naxos? Yes, we'll take you to Naxos,
cum' along lad.". . .

---

7. And the wave runs in the beach-groove>And by the beach-run

8. lithe>snipe>Scios>ship>Scios>spring-water
wing-joints>wet wings>wine-red>wanting spring-water
sun-film>tin flash in sun-dazzle>spring water
Naviform rock + shallows>rock-pool
wine-red>vine-must

---

9. And of a later year,
           pale in the wine-red algae,
If you will lean over the rock,
           the coral face under wave-tinge,
Rose-paleness under water-shift,
           Ileuthyeria, fair Dafne of sea-bords,
The swimmer's arms turned to branches,
Who will say in what year,
           fleeing what band of tritons,

The smooth brows, seen, and half seen,
      now ivory stillness.

10. And So-shu churned in the sea, So-shu also,
      using the long moon for a churn-stick . . .

11. Lithe turning of water,
      sinews of Poseidon,
  Black azure and hyaline,
      glass wave over Tyro,
  Close cover, unstillness,
      bright welter of wave-cords,
  Then quiet water,
      quiet in the buff sands,
  Sea-fowl stretching wing-joints,
      splashing in rock-hollows and sand-hollows
  In the wave-runs by the half-dune;
  Glass-glint of wave in the tide-rips against sunlight,
      pallor of Hesperus,
  Grey peak of the wave,
      wave, colour of grape's pulp,

12. Olive grey in the near,
      far, smoke grey of the rock-slide,
  Salmon-pink wings of the fish-hawk
      cast grey shadows in water,
  The tower like a one-eyed great goose
      cranes up out of the olive-grove,

  And we have heard the fauns chiding Proteus
      in the smell of hay under the olive-tree,
  And the frogs singing against the fauns
      in the half-light.
  And . . .

---

9. Algae cling to its edge, wine-red glow in the shallow
carried along through whole metamorphosis section by
vine-must, vine-trunk, grape-leaves, heavy vine, grape-cluster,
vines grow>wine-red algae
pale in the wine-red algae>coral face under wave-tinge>
    rose-paleness
under water-shift

10. smooth>seen>seen>stillness>So-shu churned in the sea

11. churn-stick>turning
    moon>sinews

12. accumulation of all of the sound patterns so that it becomes harder to chart, for example:

    glass-glint of wave in the tide-rips>pallor of Hesperus
    grey peak of wave>wave>colour of grape's pulp>grey
    smoke grey of rock-slide, etc.

There are other kinds of connections, of course, any of which the reader may know; but he does not have to know them. The most obvious is the setting or background: almost every action occurs in or by the sea. Most of them have to do with Greece (although not Sordello and not So-shu). The earliest published version of this poem (originally Canto VIII in *Dial*, May 1922) makes the thematic function of the sea much more explicit. That poem begins with a Dido passage, most of which can now be found in Canto VII, and then continues:

> And the weeping Muse, weeping, widowed and willing
> The weeping Muse
>   Mourns Homer,
> Mourns the days of long song,
> Mourns for the breath of the singers,
> Winds stretching out, seas pulling to eastward,
> Heaving breath of the oarsmen,
>   triremes under Cyprus,
> The long course of the seas,
> The words woven in wind-wrack,
>   salt spray over voices.

These lines clearly establish the thematic relationship of sea, song, and singers of the sea (Homer, Virgil, and Ovid). In their light one can see how two lines that have remained in the text—"And the wave runs in the beach-groove:" and "Ear, ear for the sea-surge;"—relate, also, to the establishment of theme. These lines are all that remain, but by their sense and also their punctuation they seem a good example of "condensation to maximum attainable." (Punctuation is a factor that must be mentioned. It does serve to separate image blocks—colons, series of dots, paragraphing—so that it is a more cognitive linking device than most of the others.) The elements of the poem are also united by the theme of sea-change, or metamorphosis.

The transition in which the functioning of melopoeia is most noticeable is in the beginning of the canto, because thematic or even imagistic links between cantos seem very tenuous. (See first section of melopoeia chart.) Critics have explained this passage intellectually in various ways. For example, Hugh Kenner has written:

> The theme of Canto 2 is the artist's struggle to bring form (Browning's *Sordello*, Pound's *Cantos*) out of flux (the Sordello documents, the sea) . So-shu, who also churned in the sea, was an Emperor who built roads (form out of flux again, at the political level; you churn the fluid to get a solid). The metamorphosed impious seamen were solidified in punishment by Bacchus, and in epiphanization by Ovid.   (p. 318)

This may very well be the abstract meaning of So-shu in this canto, but it cannot be the immediate effect of the lines upon a reader. If on the other hand the reader can (paradoxically enough) make an effort to relax and to hear the words one at a time without searching, at the same time, for some logical meaning, he will sense the movement from Sordello to So-shu to the sleek-headed daughter of Lir.

The second chart is simply a listing of all of the hyphenated words in the canto. My point in presenting this list is to illustrate Pound's second phrase, imagistic analogy, operating at its simplest level. These ideograms alone present by means of their images a condensed version of the movement of the poem.

Canto II: Compound words

So-shu (churned in the sea)
spray-whited (circles)

cliff-wash
fur-hood
beach-groove
sea-surge
beach-run
sea-god
cross-hold
blue-grey (glass of the wave)
cold-welter
close cover
sun-tawny
sand-stretch
wing-joints
sun-film
wine-red (glow in the shallows)
tin flash
sun-dazzle
spring-water
rock-pool
vine-must
god-sleight

(ship)   stock fast
             sea-swirl
(grapes with   sea-foam
no seed but)

scupper-hole
sea-break
gun whale
vine-trunk
grape-leaves
row locks
oar shafts
lynx-purr
tar smell
pad-foot
eye-glitter

                    pad-foot
                    knee-skin
                    ship-yard
                    grape-cluster
                    pin-rack
                    grape shoots
                    scupper-hole
                    fore-hatch
        (sea)   blue-deep
                    green-ruddy
                    back-swell
                    rudder-chains
                    fish-scales
                    fore-stays
                    fish-scales
                    groin muscles
                    lynx-purr (amid sea)
(pale in the)   wine-red (algae)
                    wave-tinge
                    rose-paleness
                    water-shift
                    sea-birds
        (and)   So-shu (churned in the sea)
                    long moon
                    churn-stick
                    sea-fowl
                    wing-joints
                    rock-hollows
                    sand-hollows
                    wave-runs
                    half-dune
                    glass-glint (of wave)
                    tide-rips
                    olive-grey
                    smoke grey
                    rock-slide

> salmon-pink (wings)
> fish-hawk
> one-eyed (great goose)
> olive-grove
> olive-trees
> half light

Another example of the kind of imagistic analogy that unifies the poem may be seen from the following brief list. The reader's apprehension of the sea as a unifying element is reinforced by specific references to it that occur throughout the poem in each of the episodes and that pick up and play upon the same words and sounds.

> wine-red glow in the shallows
> sea . . . green-ruddy in shadows
> wave colour of grape's pulp
> grey shadows in water

Finally, I think it important to return once again to Pound's notion of poetry, and especially metaphor, as "equation" in order to relate this to the theme of metamorphosis in the opening cantos, which in turn is connected to Pound's concept of history and to the form of his metaphors. Canto II contains this description of Tyro and Poseidon:

> And by the beach-run, Tyro,
>   twisted arms of the sea-god,
> Lithe sinews of water, gripping her, cross-hold . . .

Here a phrase like "lithe sinews of water" exemplifies how Pound's beliefs about myth and poetry find a form in language. The lithe sinews of water describe the appearance of the water, yet the figure is in no sense decorative. The description, although figurative, is true, since Poseidon *is* the water. All poetry is of necessity an "equation" for human emotions; myths, especially, indicate the relation between an emotional experience and the "impersonal and objective story" woven from it. Of all kinds of myth, metamorphoses, in particular, are relevant, since they describe the very moment of transition. The early cantos are filled with metamorphoses, for this if for no other reason.

Here we can also recall Fenollosa's remarks about metaphor and its function of bridging the gap between the seen and the unseen: a relationship that is also a true one. In these cantos of Ovidian metamorphoses things never become dissolved into other things. The verse very carefully maintains a sense of the concurrence of both of their identities. In the Acoetes episode phrases like "fish-scales over groin muscles,/lynx-purr amid sea" indicate a changed state but do not dissolve its components, thereby establishing a complex identity for the seamen. The same kind of effect is achieved earlier in that section, when the wild cats appear, as a result of "god-sleight," out of the air. Each line that presents the change is carefully balanced: "out of nothing, a breathing"; "eye-glitter out of black air." These figures from Ovid are thus very like Pound's presentation of Sordello or of Venus as I have described it. (This may even be the rationale for beginning the canto with "Hang it all, Robert Browning.") For the Sordello who can and does exist in the present day is simultaneously each of his "incarnations." What I have been describing is, finally, characteristic of the structure of ideogram (or image or vortex) as it occurs in *The Cantos*—the compound word, too, represents a metamorphosis: sea and surge into sea-surge. But here again the form, rather than dissolving its components into itself, establishes at once their identities and the implicit relation between them. This construction is particularly suited to the purposes of *The Cantos*, since, because of its form, it directly assaults the reader and forces him to participate, to act—if only to be able to understand.

> Properly, we shd. read for power. Man reading shd. be man intensly alive. The book shd. be a ball of light in one's hand. (*Culture,* p. 55)

A close reading of the introductory cantos will show that while most of them follow the pattern of transitions as I have described it, some do not. (IV and V are two more good examples of those that do, while III is one that does not. It is my opinion that in III, which remains closest of all the cantos to the original version, Pound has not performed the second half of the process well. He has omitted almost all of the intellectual links, but, in lifting the episodes almost verbatim from the earlier versions, he has not rewritten into them connectives of a melopoeiac nature.)

In a Note to his essay on Vorticism in *Gaudier-Brzeska,* Pound wrote that "no artist can possibly get a vortex into every poem or picture he does. . . . Certain things seem to demand metrical expression, or expression in a rhythm more agitated than the rhythms acceptable to prose, and these subjects, though they do not contain a vortex, may have some interest, an interest as 'criticism of life' or of art" (p. 109). This comment provides a helpful insight into the varieties of style that Pound uses. Just as his early long poem, *Hugh Selwyn Mauberley,* contains very few metaphors, so some of the earlier Cantos—and great blocks of the later cantos—are likewise without metaphors. Some subjects demand a vortex—they demand metaphor, image, ideogram, phanopoeia, and melopoeia—while others do not, yet remain necessary to Pound's verse as kinds of criticism of life and art. The first thirty cantos contain both types of subjects, what Kenner is talking about with his divisions of *passion* ("myths, metamorphoses, modes of love and violence") and *action* (Sigismundo Malatesta). In later sequences of cantos the subjects are more separate (for example, the Adams and Jefferson cantos are "criticism of life"). The bulk of the middle cantos, in which Pound is setting out his "facts," belong to this style. But in the latest cantos, the Pisan sequence, *Section: Rock-Drill* and *Thrones,* the gods—and metaphor—begin to reappear.

The Cantos have often been compared, implicitly and explicitly, to Dante's *Divine Comedy.* In her comparison of *The Cantos* to Langland's *Piers Plowman,* Christine Brooke-Rose writes:

He has himself described them [in "An Introduction to the Economic Nature of the United States" (*Money Pamphlets* by £ No. 1, London, 1950)] as "an epic poem which begins 'In the Dark Forest,' crosses the Purgatory of human error, and ends in the light." It is certainly possible to think of Cantos I–XXX as Hell; of Cantos XXXI–XLVI (Jefferson-Nuevo Mundo), the 5th Decad (Sienna-Leopoldine Reforms) and LII–LXXI (the Chinese dynasties and back to Adams in action) as Purgatory, with the synthesis of the *Pisan Cantos* (LXXIV–LXXXI) as a personal Purgatory; *Rock-Drill* (LXXXV–XCV) and *Thrones* (XCVI–CIX), which are flooded with light, as Paradise.

But Hell, Purgatory, and Paradise are constantly super-imposed on one another throughout.[25]

Certainly this model has something to do with resurgence, as the poem seeks for paradise, of concern for the gods and for the reappearance of light after a great deal of darkness.

Even in these later cantos the frequency of metaphor varies. There are cantos like 95, in which metaphors occur only occasionally, interspersed with much nonmetaphoric material, and there are cantos such as 91, which is primarily a series of metaphors that develop and extend a single theme. Yet in each case the basic function of metaphor, as I have described it, is similar.

For example, the following is a list of the compound words of Canto 95, plus an additional few metaphors that did not contain this structure. Without knowing anything more about this canto, one can still see a pattern emerging from the phanopoeia and melopoeia displayed in this brief list. One might note, for example, pairs of images that are separated from one another by long sections of text. (I have tried to indicate them with connecting lines.) Pound seems to be relying on these words having the capacity to produce sounds lasting long enough "for the succeeding sound or sounds to catch up, traverse, and intersect it." Since my chart follows the lyrical as opposed to the more narrative mode of the poem, it seems

---

25. Noel Stock, ed., *Ezra Pound Perspectives* (Chicago, 1965), pp. 168–69.

fcasible that these "notes" would carry and form a counterpoint to the other tonal pattern.

from Canto 95

LOVE, gone as lightning
Mist weighs down the wild thyme plants
oak-wood
Queen of Heaven bringing her repose . . .
    bringing light
white-foam
sea-gull
That the crystal wave mount to flood surge
The light there almost solid
boar-hunt
mooring-ropes
lone rock
sea-gull
oak-leaf
vine-leaf
yard-arm
thistle down
sea-god

Canto 91 is a "god" canto; since it is about goddesses, light, and the mystical process of metaphor itself, it is naturally a canto where one expects—and finds—much metaphor. This canto has been a favorite of critics of *The Cantos,* so that several interpretations of its general meaning and specific references exist. However, I would like to begin by looking first at metaphor, phanopoeia, and melopoeia, to see what they alone indicate about the poem.

The following is a list of metaphors in Canto 91. Also included is a phrase (indicated by a numeral in parenthesis) that is not a metaphor but that contains compound words that act in the pattern being established.

1. that the body of light come forth
    from the body of fire

2. And that your eyes come to the surface
   from the deep wherein they were sunken,
Reina

3. That your eyes come forth from their caves
      a light then
                        as the holly-leaf
            qui laborat, orat

4. and the stone eyes again looking seaward

5. in the green deep of an eye:
      Crystal waves weaving together toward the gt/healing
   Light *compenetrans* of the spirits

6. She has entered the protection of crystal

7. Light & the flowing crystal

8. Gods moving in crystal

9. Love moving the stars παρὰ βώμιον

10. They set lights now in the sea
       and the sea's claws gathers them outward.

11. That the sun's silk
       hsien　　顯　　tensile

12. Ra-Set over crystal
                  ⚊ moving
    in the Queen's eye the reflection
    & sea-wrack—
                  green deep of the sea cave

(13) . . . nor had fear of the wood-queen, Artemis
     that is Diana

14. Lord, thast scop the dayes lihte,
    all that she knew was a spirit bright,
  a movement that moved in cloth of gold
    into her chamber.

15. the light flowing, whelming the stars.
    In the barge of Ra-Set
On river of crystal

16. & from fire to crystal
    via the body of light,
        the gold wings assemble

17. The water-bug's mittens
      petal the rock beneath,
The natrix glides sapphire into the rock-pool.

18. "Ghosts dip in the crystal,
    adorned"

Although the compound word is no longer so insistently prevalent as it was in the earlier cantos, the method by which metaphors are formed creates a similar effect. The vocabulary is a very limited one, so that the same words move through all of the phrases. Metaphors are created from the continually changing combinations they afford. For example, the fact that number five's "in the green deep of an eye" results from a succession of other phrases in which occur the words "light," "eyes," "deep," and "cave" makes it unparaphrasable. Understanding of its meaning results from direct experience of the words, or imaging. The word *crystal,* especially, moves through the canto, forming new combinations, images, and usually metaphors as it appears in one phrase after another: "crystal waves," "the protection of crystal," "flowing crystal," "moving in crystal," "Ra-Set over crystal," "river of crystal," "from fire to crystal," "ghosts dip in the crystal." Melopoeia is active. One can note sequences of progression such as forth $>$ from $>$ fire $>$ surface $>$ from

> sunken > come forth > leaf in 1, 2, and 3; crystal > stars
> sea > sea's claws > sun's silk > hsien > tensile > Ra-Set
> crystal > queen's > sea-wrack > sea-surge in 8 through 12;
queen > green > deep > sea > wood-queen in 12 and 13. A
very limited set of sound patterns is used throughout the canto's
metaphors, concentrating on the sounds produced by combinations of *s, ʃ, c,* and *g.*

The nature of the metaphoric transfer involved in these images
is also very similar. Almost every one of the metaphors depicts
spirit or light achieving a body (the body of light coming forth
from the body of fire), such as "That your eyes come forth from
their caves"; "Gods moving in crystal"; "She has entered the
protection of crystal"; "the light flowing, whelming the stars."

The best, and one of the earliest, glosses for this version of
"ideas into action" comes from Pound's 1912 essay on Cavalcanti, in which he translates "Vedrai la sua virtu nel ciel salita"
as "Thou shalt see the rays of this emanation going up to
heaven as a slender pillar of light, or, more strictly in accordance
with the stanza preceding: thou shalt see depart from her lips
her subtler body, and from that a still subtler form ascends and
from that a star, the body of pure flame surrounding the source
of the *virtu,* which will declare its nature" (xiv). Later in the
same essay he translates "E la beltate per usa Dea la mostra"
as " 'Beauty displays her for her goddess.' That is to say, as the
spirit of God became incarnate in the Christ, so is the spirit
of eternal beauty made flesh dwelling amongst us in her" (xv).

Much has been written upon Pound's use of myth, light
imagery, and light philosophy, but surely the gist of it all is in
passages like these, which have a clear conncetion to his other
observations on gods, myth, and metaphor.

Even if the reader does not know these statements, he has,
presumably, read the earlier cantos, where similar language and
similar images have shown him the importance of moments of
vision like these. George Dekker, discussing the image of the
body of light coming forth from the body of fire as an image of
the transfiguring of sensual passion into devotional and creative

energy, points out its frequent occurrence in *The Cantos*,[26] even
as Hugh Kenner notes that "the reader of the *Cantos* has en-
countered Aphrodite's eyes many times ('your eyen two wol
sleye me sodenly,' Canto 81) and been told of their immersion
in the accidental postures of matter—

> all that Sandro knew, and Jacopo
> and that Velasquez never suspected
> lost in the brown meat of Rembrandt
> and the raw meat of Rubens and Jordaens . . . Canto 80."[27]

These lines from **XXXIX** are relevant:

> Unceasing the measure
> Flank by flank on the headland
> with the Goddess' eyes to seaward
> By Circeo, by Terracina, with the stone eyes
> white toward the sea
> With one measure, unceasing:
> "Fac deum!" "Est factus."
> Ver novum!
> Ver novum!
> Thus made the spring,
> Can see but their eyes in the dark
> not the bough that he walked on.
> Beaten from flesh into light
> Hath swallowed the fire-ball
> A traverse le foglie
> His rod hath made god in my belly
> sic loquitur nupta
> Cantat sic nupta
>
> Dark shoulders have stirred the lightning
> A girl's arms have nested the firs,
> Not I but the handmaid kindled
> Cantat sic nupta
> I have eaten the flame.

as is the following sequence from **XLVII**:

---

26. *The Cantos of Ezra Pound* (New York, 1963), p. 103.
27. "Under the Larches of Paradise," *Gnomon* (New York, 1958), p. 283.

The light has entered the cave. Io! Io!
The light has gone down into the cave,
Splendour on splendour!
By prong have I entered these hills:
That the grass grow from my body,
That I hear the roots speaking together,
The air is new on my leaf,
The forked boughs shake with the wind.
Is Zephyrus more light on the bough, Apeliota
more light on the almond branch?
By this door have I entered the hill.
Falleth,
Adonis falleth.
Fruit cometh after. The small lights drift out with the tide,
sea's claw has gathered them outward,
Four banners to every flower
The sea's claw draws the lamps outward.
Think thus of thy plowing
When the seven stars go down to their rest
Forty days for their rest, by seabord
And in valleys that wind down toward the sea

                      Καὶ Μοῖραι' Ἄδονιν
                KAI MOIRAI' ADONIN
When the almond bough puts forth its flame,
When the new shoots are brought to the altar,

                Τυ Διώνα. Καὶ Μοῖραι
                TU DIONA? KAI MOIRAI
Καὶ Μοῖραι' Ἄδονιν
KAI MOIRAI' ADONIN
            that hath the gift of healing,
that hath the power over wild beasts.

But most important, perhaps (for the reader of this essay) is
the by now familiar

    Thus the light rains, thus pours, *e lo soleils plovil*
    The liquid and rushing crystal
            beneath the knees of the gods.
    Ply over ply, thin glitter of water;
    Brook film bearing white petals. (Canto IV)

Here, in the vision of goddesses, which became the most appropriate way of talking about Pound's use of metaphor in *The Cantos,* is the first use of the word *crystal* in a setting that creates the sense of its essential meaning for Pound.

There is much in discussions of Canto 91, like Kenner's, Dekker's, and Donald Davie's (in *Ezra Pound: Poet as Sculptor,* New York, 1964) that is perceptive and accurate. Dekker discusses Pound's goddesses as "his personal development of the radiant visions of Guinicelli, Cavalcanti, and Dante" (p. 86), and stresses Queen Elizabeth's role in the canto and her relation to the other ladies of Canto 91:

> this canto is, indeed, Pound's "Legend of Good Women"—including (though sometimes only by implication) the Virgin Mary, Eleanor of Aquitaine, Ondine, Helen of Tyre, the Empress Theodora, the goddesses Artemis and Aphrodite, Cleopatra and Helen of Troy. (p. 102)

Kenner identifies the prevailing subject of the final cantos as "'the values that endure like the sea,'" and notes that they move toward "a permanence that contains and requires all orderly movement, not an arrest, nor, we are explicitly told, a stasis" (p. 285). Davie stresses the attempt in these cantos to achieve *forma,* quoting Pound from *Guide to Kulchur* (p. 152):

> "I made it out of a mouthful of air," wrote Bill Yeats in his heyday. The *forma,* the immortal *concetto,* the concept, the dynamic form which is like the rose pattern driven into the dead iron-filings by the magnet, not by material contact with the magnet itself, but separate from the magnet. Cut off by the layer of glass, the dust and filings rise and spring into order. Thus the *forma,* the concept rises from death . . .

He then goes on to say:

> And the point to be made is that Pound in the *Cantos* characteristically aims at recreating not the concept, any or all of them, but rather the *forma,* the thing behind them and common to them all. By arranging sensory impressions he aims to state, not ideas, but the form behind and in ideas, the moment before that "fine thing held in the mind" has precipitated out now this idea, now that. (p. 220)

He speaks of the image of immaculate conception in Canto 91 and of its images of glass and water, and he notes, in concurrence with my own ideas, that "the poet is restoring to life the dead metaphor in the cliché 'crystal clear' " (p. 225).

Davie makes several attempts to explain Pound's technique. One way is involved with the notion of *forma:*

> Perhaps by his arrangement of sensory impressions (that is to say, of images) Pound aimed to express, not "ideas," some of which admittedly cannot be expressed in this way, but rather a state of mind in which ideas as it were tremble on the edge of expression. (p. 218)

Again, he shows his awareness, if not absolute approval, of the effects of Pound's versification:

> What needs to be noticed, however, is that, as we lend ourselves to the liturgical sway of the powerful rhythms, we do not ask for glosses because after a while we are letting the rhythm carry us over details half-understood or not understood at all. However little we like the snapped off, jerking rhythms of the cantos that try to comprehend history, we need them to offset these rhythms of the myth that surpasses history; we need the one to validate the other, and, although Pound may have got the proportions between them wrong, some proportion there has to be. (p. 212)

He is combating statements like these by Noel Stock in *Reading the Cantos* (New York, 1966), speaking of *Rock-Drill* and *Thrones.*

> Much of the time Pound has not thought out the connexions he makes, and does not therefore know what he is saying. But all too often, when we do trace through to a definite meaning, it proves not to have been worthwhile. In short, the material has not been assimilated; or, where it has, is seldom interesting, unless we happen to share, or for some reason wish to support, Pound's view of his subjects. (p. 97)

> Now it is not enough to know a little about these matters if we are to understand what Pound is talking about. We have to have read the books, pamphlets and cuttings, and

to have heard the stories. Everything about the passage above, including the tone, depends upon our knowing the facts and having some definite appreciation of the atmosphere in which it was written. Until we actually look into sources, handle the books, place ourselves in Pound's situation and see as nearly as possible through his eyes, we cannot even begin to know how the material is supposed to function. But function is too serious a word. It suggests the working out of a poetic design. Pound is not here composing poetry, he is keeping a kind of mental diary which includes snatches of poetry. And in this sense, and this sense alone, the matter and form are one. (pp. 102–3)

I have mentioned the main points in some discussions of Canto 91: the critics will also tell one, if he wants to know, who Ra-Set is or why Apollonius asked "Is this a bath house? Or a court house?" It is up to each reader to determine how much information he thinks he needs to have. My point has been primarily to show that the immediate, surface level of the poem has its own relevance and justification, and that intense perception of and at this level seems to be closest to what Pound usually has in mind for his reader.

It is necessary to put these ideas about metaphor, image, and melopoeia in their proper perspective. They are not my formula (thus to be ranked by the side of the other critical formulae) for cracking the code. The reader ought not to sit down and count assonance patterns as I have had to do in order to try to prove my point. He should listen, he should react and allow himself to experience directly whatever there is in the verse that can affect him. By his very distortion of usual language patterns Pound seems to be asking his reader not to respond as he would respond to usual language patterns. If the reader tries to do so, he misses a great deal of the "point" (and probably the poem).

Watts has argued in his final assessment of *The Cantos* that the ideogrammatic method ultimately fails.

Let us put the matter at its simplest, ignoring questions about what the psyche common to humanity may be. Mr. Pound and we, his readers, share a language. So long as he and we move within the confines of that language, we must submit to *its* coercion as well as to that of the ideogram. It is simply impossible to stop at the point where Pound would want us to stop, the point beyond which permissible and necessary time-binding degenerates into abstract thinking— even though we are aware of Pound's unclear caveat, 'Thus far and no farther.' We concede that Pound is no enemy of certain sorts of general statements, as many a passage in *Culture* shows. We know that what he really wishes to do is to discredit certain specific abstractions, bad abstractions that bully and stupefy mankind. To whatever degree we sympathize, we cannot keep from noting that what the poet of *The Cantos* really strives for is not to tear out all abstractions (his expressed programme) but to tear out of the mind and the will the evil abstractions and to implant there concepts no less generalized, even though they are approached obliquely by means of the ideogram. (p. 121)

But Watts's argument is contradictory. He says at the same time that the English language cannot contain the ideogram (because it demands abstract thinking) and will not work as Pound would wish it to, and that, anyhow, Pound *wants* to implant concepts in his reader. He just does not refer directly to them. Yet Pound would be the first to admit this. "An abstract or general statement is GOOD if it be ultimately found to correspond with the facts" (*ABC of Reading*, p. 25). What the poem attempts to do is to give its reader the facts (as Pound sees them) —physical facts, which are images for certain abstract concepts. If we can experience them by responding as directly—and as physically—as possible, they will give us a foundation upon which we may then base our abstractions. "A general statement is valuable only in REFERENCE to the known objects or facts" (*ABC of Reading*, p. 26).

Joseph Frank, in his excellent article "Spatial Form in Modern Literature," makes a similar although more consistent criticism of the structure of *The Cantos*.

To be properly understood, these word-groups must be juxtaposed with one another and perceived simultaneously; only when this is done can they be adequately understood; for while they follow one another in time, their meaning does not depend on this temporal relationship. The one difficulty of these poems which no amount of textual exegesis can wholly overcome is the internal conflict between the time-logic of language and the space-logic implicit in the modern conception of the nature of poetry.[28]

It would seem, however, that the pattern of melopoeia is the counteracting agent. Its structure is a linear one, very much dependent upon time, that is to say, timing. Therefore, while the reader is suspending "the process of individual reference temporarily" (Frank, p. 383), a logopoeiac act, he is following through a linear time pattern, but on another level.

In summary, a study of Pound's use of patterns of metaphor as a structuring agent in *The Cantos* indicates an approach to the reading of the poem that is based upon the demand of such a form and structure. I refer to the moment-to-moment response to image and rhythm (phanopoeia and melopoeia), which Pound sees as more fundamental to the process of reading poetry, and which must be preparatory to the more intellectual (and abstracting) processes of logopoeia, such as picking up references or forming overarching correspondences. A concentration upon the individual status of cantos, the parts of the whole that is yet to be finished, makes the necessity of such a reading process particularly apparent.

Pound has devoted a great deal of effort toward provoking this kind of response in his readers. His dependence upon the depiction of things and action in lieu of ideas and concepts, his development of the vortex, ideogram, and image, his reliance upon assonance patterns and other agents of melopoeia, and his use of metaphor all contribute towards this goal. Pound's metaphors in *The Cantos* are especially suited for such a purpose, because, individually, they are the most compressed and direct

---

28. In Mark Schorer, Josephine Miles, and Gordon McKenzie, eds., *Criticism* (New York, 1958), p. 383.

form of image he can create and, in sequence, they form patterns in accordance with the principles of melopoeia.

Pound's program for the creation and the understanding of art results from a deep and highly moralistic involvement in the process and the problems of human culture. (This is why his interests, of necessity, extended themselves to and entangled themselves in other apparently unrelated fields such as history, economics, and politics.) Literature can both call forth action and serve as an effective means of expressing action—especially emotional experience. Metaphor is also the most powerful form with which verbal equations for human emotions can be achieved, for metaphors depict the true lines of relationship that exist between all the forces of existence. Metaphor is therefore a linguistic agent of the truth, and truth, for Pound, is a fundamental requisite of art in a healthy culture.

4
Metaphor in Wallace Stevens's
Notes Towards a Supreme Fiction

Like both Williams and Pound, Wallace Stevens uses patterns of metaphor in his late, long poem, *Notes Towards a Supreme Fiction*. This work both uses metaphor to create a structuring pattern and discusses the concept of metaphor as it is concerned in the central issue of Stevens's philosophy: the right relation of imagination and reality.

Notes Towards a Supreme Fiction is a sustained attempt at defining the supreme fiction. It revolves around an examination of the relation between imagination and reality, the abstract and the concrete. It is built upon a pattern of metaphors placed in apposition to literal, abstract statements. The metaphors function to embody the abstract statements that they modify. They are usually parallel to one another, forming series of metaphors that in their language move back and forth from the concrete to the abstract. The totality of metaphors (or resemblances, to use one of Stevens's terms) defines the concept in question; it also creates the poem. In addition, the poem sometimes achieves extended, or total metaphors, which are what Stevens calls "fictions," and which are the supreme moments of poetry.

As J. Hillis Miller and other critics have pointed out, Stevens's search to reconcile imagination and reality is "the life of his poetry."[1]

> Imagination and reality are like two charged poles which repel one another as they approach and can never touch, though the relation between them creates a vibrant field of forces. Existence is neither imagination alone nor reality alone, but always and everywhere the endlessly frustrated attempt of the two to cross the gap which separates them. (p. 233)

> This way and that vibrates his thought, seeking to absorb imagination by reality, to engulf reality in the imagination, or to marry them in metaphor. (p. 258)

Miller's conclusion is an important one: in Stevens's philosophy "there is no progress, only an alternation between contradictory possibilities" (p. 259).

Thus although Stevens's definitions of metaphor alter little in the various statements that he makes about it, his evaluation of it does change radically. Sometimes he thinks of it as evil, sometimes as salvation. Therefore, when discussing Stevens's opinions about metaphor, it is essential to note the particular stance toward the subject that he is taking at that moment.

Stevens's 1947 essay, "Three Academic Pieces," is perhaps the best place to find the basic tenets of his theory of metaphor. It has two sections: the first is prose, the second is a poem. The following remarks are from Section I.

> The study of the activity of resemblance is an approach to the understanding of poetry. Poetry is a satisfying of the desire for resemblance. As the mere satisfying of a desire, it is pleasurable. But poetry if it did nothing but satisfy a desire would not rise above the level of many lesser things. Its singularity is that in the act of satisfying the desire for resemblance it touches the sense of reality, it enhances the sense of reality, heightens it, intensifies it. If resemblance is described as a partial similarity between two dissimilar things, it complements and reinforces that which the two dissimilar things have

---

1. *Poets of Reality* (New York, 1969), p. 258.

in common. It makes it brilliant. When the similarity is between things of adequate dignity, the resemblance may be said to transfigure or to sublimate them.[2]

In this ambiguity, the intensification of reality by resemblance increases realization and this increased realization is pleasurable. It is as if a man who lived indoors should go outdoors on a day of sympathetic weather. His realization of the weather would exceed that of a man who lives outdoors. It might, in fact, be intense enough to convert the real world about him into an imagined world. In short, a sense of reality keen enough to be in excess of the normal sense of reality creates a reality of its own. Here what matters is that the intensification of the sense of reality creates a resemblance: that reality of its own is a reality. (p. 79)

Part II of "Three Academic Pieces" is the poem "Someone Puts a Pineapple Together." This, like "Notes," is a poem about poetry (here, specifically about metaphor) using poetry, especially metaphor, to make its statement. In part I of this poem Stevens writes:

> It is as if there were three planets: the sun,
> the moon, and the imagination, or, say
> Day, night and man and his endless effigies. (p. 83)

In III, after saying, "Admit the shaft/Of that third planet to the table and then," he presents twelve numbered one-line metaphors for the pineapple on the table. Some of these are

1. The hut stands by itself beneath the palms.
2. Out of their bottle the green genii come.
3. A vine has climbed the other side of the wall. (p. 86)

He continues:

> These casual exfoliations are
> Of the tropic of resemblance, sprigs
> Of Capricorn or as the sign demands,

---

2. *The Necessary Angel* (New York, 1965), p. 77.

Apposites, to the slightest edge, of the whole
Undescribed composition of the sugar-cone,
Shiftings of an inchoate crystal tableau,

The momentary footing of a climb
Up the pineapple, a table Alp and yet
An Alp, a purple Southern mountain bisque

With the molten mixings of related things,
Cat's taste possibly or possibly Danish lore,
The small luxuriations that portend

Universal delusions of universal grandeurs,
The slight incipiencies, of which the form,
At last, is the pineapple on the table or else

An object the sum of its complications, seen
And unseen. This is everybody's world.
Here the total artifice reveals itself

As the total reality. (pp. 86–87)

In this poem can be seen the basis of both Stevens's theory and
practice of metaphor. Terms like "apposites," "an object the sum
of its complications," "The total artifice reveals itself/As the
total reality" describe a method that is everywhere in Stevens's
poetry and aptly illustrated by the twelve listed metaphors in
the pineapple poem itself.

Stevens's *Adagia* is his list of aphorisms, statements of truths
that come in a steady progression, contradicting rather more
than expanding one another as they go.[3] Many of them have
to do with metaphor, such as the following.

Metaphor creates a new reality from which the original appears
to be unreal. (p. 169)

Reality is a cliché from which we escape by metaphor. It is
only *au pays de la métaphore qu'on est poète.* (p. 179)

The degrees of metaphor. The absolute object slightly turned
is a metaphor of the object. (p. 179)

---

3. *Opus Posthumous* (New York, 1957) , pp. 157–80.

Some objects are less susceptible to metaphor than others. The whole world is less susceptible to metaphor than a tea-cup is. (p. 179)

There is no such thing as a metaphor of a metaphor. One does not progress through metaphors. Thus reality is the indispensable element of each metaphor. When I say that man is a god it is very easy to see that if I also say that a god is something else, god has become reality. (p. 179)

The *Adagia* purport to be nothing more than a random list of truths; yet when the form of this "work" is compared with other forms used by Stevens—that of the pineapple poem, for example, or "Thirteen Ways of Looking at a Blackbird," or for that matter, that of *Notes Towards a Supreme Fiction*—a basic similarity of structure reveals itself. "An object the sum of its complications," writes Stevens in the pineapple poem, and "Poetry is the sum of its attributes," he says in the *Adagia*. A poem presents an object by presenting a series of its complications, or points of view toward the object; very often these complications are metaphors. These metaphors often follow the form of the aphorisms of *Adagia*. They are statements built upon the copula (this is that). Usually they stand in apposition to some thematic statement, and apposition may itself be thought of as compressed copula.

"Poetry," said Stevens in "A High-Toned Old Christian Woman" in *Harmonium,* "is the supreme fiction, madame." Much later, in a letter written to Henry Church in 1942, he says about the *Notes:*

I ought to say that I have not defined a supreme fiction. A man as familiar with my things as you are will be justified in thinking that I mean poetry. I don't want to say that I don't mean poetry; I don't know what I mean. The next thing for me to do will be to try to be a little more precise about this enigma. I hold off from even attempting that because, as soon as I start to rationalize, I lose the poetry of the idea. In principle there appear to be certain characteristics

of a supreme fiction *and the NOTES is confined to a statement of a few of those characteristics.*[4]

One can perhaps say that the supreme fiction is poetry *and* all
that poetry signifies for Stevens (this would take in the imaginative act; man's means of relating to reality; and so on, for
all this is involved, for Stevens, in the production of a poem).
At any rate, the *Notes* are an attempt at definition. The notes
fall under three headings: "It Must be Abstract," "It Must
Change," and "It Must Give Pleasure." These three statements
by themselves offer a definition, so that it becomes necessary
to inquire into the function of the ten blank verse sections
or poems that are listed after each of the headings: what part
do they play in a "definition"?

These sections, as I see them, function much as do the twelve
metaphors for pineapple in the pineapple poem: they are poem-
length extensions of something like those twelve statements about
the pineapple. Stevens's explanation of his procedure in "Someone Puts a Pineapple Together" might very well serve as an
explanation of the way in which "Notes" is put together. The
notions of "apposites," of an object as the sum of its complications, of the total artifice as the total reality all relate to the
structure of the thirty-two sections. They also point toward a
description of the use of metaphor throughout the poem.

As series of metaphors for a central "object" (here the concept of "supreme fiction") the structure of the sections seems to
be more spatial than linear. Although I would not deny a
linear movement in the poem—development of theme, for example—a sense of spatial qualities seems to be of great importance. It negates a redundancy that might be found in the poem
if it is seen not as redundancy but as apposition. If the poems
were thought of as spread out on a table, instead of being ar-
ranged in consecutive sequence, they would then more clearly
demonstrate their relation to one another and to the pineapple
of this poem, the concept of supreme fiction.

---

4. Holly Stevens, ed., *The Letters of Wallace Stevens* (New York, 1966),
p. 435.

In ascertaining the particular stance that Stevens is taking toward metaphor, it is not enough to note what he says about it—one must also observe what he is doing with it. For example, "Poem Written at Morning" is a pro-metaphor poem, which praises the approach of the pineapple poem and concludes by using metaphor to establish this position.

> A sunny day's complete Poussiniana
> Divided it from itself. It is this or that
> And it is not.
> By metaphor you paint
> A thing. Thus, the pineapple was a leather fruit,
> A fruit for pewter, thorned and palmed and blue,
> To be served by men of ice.
> The senses paint
> By metaphor. The juice was fragranter
> Than wettest cinnamon. It was cribled pears
> Dripping a morning sap.
> The truth must be
> That you do not see, you experience, you feel,
> That the buxom eye brings merely its element
> To the total thing, a shapeless giant forced
> Upward.
> Green were the curls upon that head.[5]

In discussing the pineapple poem, "Poem Written at Morning" offers examples for statements like "It is this or that/And it is not" or "By metaphor you paint a thing." "Thus, the pineapple was" is followed by a series of metaphors. Yet even the statement that by metaphor one "paints," later reinforced with the phrase "The senses paint/By metaphor," indicates how Stevens, in this poem, is viewing the imaginative process as metaphoric. Again, to show how fragrant was the juice (presumably of the pineapple) he substitutes metaphor ("It was cribled pears/Dripping a morning sap") for comparison ("fragranter/Than wettest cinnamon"). But the peculiar magic of Stevens's flair for metaphor is reserved for the conclusion of the poem. Here Stevens uses his characteristic form for the presentation

---

5. *The Collected Poems of Wallace Stevens* (New York, 1964), p. 219.

of metaphor: an abstract statement paralleled by a metaphoric statement that embodies that idea. "That the buxom eye brings merely its element/To the total thing, a shapeless giant forced/ Upward" means the same thing as "The truth must be/That you do not see, you experience, you feel." The difference between seeing and experiencing and feeling is that the seeing eye would be objectively analytical; it would not be buxom, it would not bring itself ("merely its element") to the object perceived, it would not force the shapeless giant upward. The act of metaphor (here seen to be irrevocably linked with the act of perception) is the embodiment of abstractions, which is why the eye is "buxom," a human entity in itself, and why the perceived object is a "shapeless giant." Yet with the concluding statement Stevens has moved his position one step further, onto the borders of "fiction." The giant, originating as an exemplifying metaphor, has become a being in his own right—in his own story. Here that story is never continued, so that its introduction acts primarily as an indication of the direction in which such a pro-metaphor position would lead.

One must look, too, at a poem like "The Motive for Metaphor":

> You like it under the trees in autumn,
> Because everything is half dead.
> The wind moves like a cripple among the leaves
> And repeats words without meaning.
>
> In the same way, you were happy in spring,
> With the half colors of quarter-things,
> The slightly brighter sky, the melting clouds,
> The single bird, the obscure moon—
>
> The obscure moon lighting an obscure world
> Of things that would never be quite expressed,
> Where you yourself were never quite yourself
> And did not want nor have to be,
>
> Desiring the exhilarations of changes:
> The motive for metaphor, shrinking from

> The weight of primary noon,
> The A B C of being,
>
> The ruddy temper, the hammer
> Of red and blue, the hard sound—
> Steel against intimation—the sharp flash,
> The vital, arrogant, fatal, dominant X. (*CP*, p. 288)

The motive for metaphor is seen here as essentially more negative than positive. One makes metaphors in the "half" seasons, autumn and spring, where one is surrounded by "the half colors of quarter things," because there in such obscurity things "would never be quite expressed," there "where you yourself were never quite yourself/And did not want nor have to be." Thus one motive is desire for "the exhilarations of changes"; but another comes from the fact that one shrinks from "the weight of primary noon"—because one cannot, does not want to have to take direct, unadulterated reality. But this unvarnished reality, the depiction of which concludes the poem, is presented through a series of seven metaphors that follow the pattern of the pineapple metaphors. On the other hand, there is little metaphor in the first three stanzas of the poem, which describe the seasons for which metaphor is appropriate. The total poetic statement being made here is more complex than it may originally seem.

In the same way when reading *Notes Towards a Supreme Fiction* it is helpful, in keeping track of the points of view toward reality and the imagination that are presented, to have an idea of the stance toward metaphor that is being taken. This requires, especially in this poem, an awareness of its use of metaphor.

I say especially, because the more closely one reads the statements—the pronouncements of truths—in the *Notes,* the more one realizes that it is a definition of its central terms rather than the arrival at a set position toward them that the poem finally achieves. The statements are ultimately as contradictory as the statements of the *Adagia* and are very similar to them. These are from *Adagia:*

In poetry at least the imagination must not detach itself from reality. (p. 161)

The final belief is to believe in a fiction, which you know to be a fiction, there being nothing else. The exquisite truth is to know that it is a fiction and that you believe in it willingly. (p. 163)

All of our ideas come from the natural world: trees=umbrellas. (p. 163)

We live in the mind. (p. 164)

The poem is a nature created by the poet. (p. 166)

The ultimate value is reality. (p. 166)

Life is not free from its forms. (p. 170)

Reality is a cliché from which we escape by metaphor. It is only *au pays de la métaphore qu'on est poète.* (p. 179)

The momentum of the mind is all toward abstraction. (p. 179)

These are from *Notes:*

Perhaps there are moments of awakening,
Extreme, fortuitous, personal, in which

We more than awaken, sit on the edge of sleep,
As on an elevation, and behold
The academies like structures in a mist. (*CP,* p. 386)

The major abstraction is the commonal,
The inanimate, difficult visage . . . (p. 388)

. . . The casual is not
Enough. The freshness of transformation is
The freshness of a world. It is our own,
It is ourselves, the freshness of ourselves,
And that necessity and that presentation

Are rubbings of a glass in which we peer. (pp. 397–98)

We reason of these things with later reason
And we make of what we see, what we see clearly
And have seen, a place dependent on ourselves. (p. 401)

. . . But to impose is not
To discover. To discover an order as of
A season, to discover summer and know it,

To discover winter and know it well, to find,
Not to impose, not to have reasoned at all,
Out of nothing to have come on major weather,

It is possible, possible, possible . . . (p. 403–4)

. . . Perhaps,
The man-hero is not the exceptional monster,
But he that of repetition is most master. (p. 406)

That's it: the more than rational distortion,
The fiction that results from feeling. Yes, that.

They will get it straight one day at the Sorbonne,
We shall return at twilight from the lecture
Pleased that the irrational is rational,

Until flicked by feeling, in a gildered street,
I call you by name, my green, my fluent mundo.
You will have stopped revolving except in crystal. (pp. 406–7)

Notes Towards a Supreme Fiction concludes by addressing a
soldier at war, trying to establish what Stevens sees as a true
relation between himself as poet and the soldier. It begins:

Soldier, there is a war between the mind
And sky, between thought and day and night . . .

. . . It is a war that never ends. (p. 407)

Or, to use Miller's terms, imagination and reality are "like
charged poles which repel one another as they approach and
can never touch." Stevens concludes by admitting, not a solution,
but the perpetual existence of the war.

Stevens's title itself expresses the constant ambiguity of his attitude in its juxtaposition of the words *Notes* and *Supreme*. The former indicates tentativeness, while the latter points toward a possible absolute. In "Three Academic Pieces" Stevens cites metaphor as a means toward the achievement of such an absolute.

> In the fewest possible words since, as between resemblances, one is always a little more nearly perfect than another and since, from this, it is easy for perfectionism of a sort to evolve, it is not too extravagant to think of resemblances and of the repetitions of resemblances as a source of the ideal. In short, metaphor has its aspects of the ideal. (pp. 81–82)

Notes Towards a Supreme Fiction presents full definitions of the essential components in the "war" as Stevens understands them—in terms of words like *abstract, idea, giant, major,* and *fiction. Abstract* means something like a return to essence, what Miller describes as "the power to carry the image of the very thing alive and undistorted into the mind" (p. 248). In *Notes Towards a Supreme Fiction* it means that

> the poet should abstract himself from the layers of interpretation which have piled up over the years on objects in the external world. He must throw out, for example, what science, mythology, theology and philosophy tell him about the sun and see the sun as the first man saw it for the first time. . . . Nothing must come between him and the sun when he gives himself to the act of looking at it and seeing it in its being. (p. 248)

Idea means something like direct sense perception. It is the result of the process of abstracting. Stevens wrote to Henry Church:

> If you take the varnish and dirt of generations off a picture, you see it in its first idea. If you think about the world without its varnish and dirt, you are a thinker of the first idea. (October 28, 1942. *Letters*, pp. 426–27)

"But the first idea was not to shape the clouds/In imitation," writes Stevens in Part IV of "It Must be Abstract." "The clouds preceded us" (p. 383). The *giant* is a "A thinker of the first idea" (VII, "It Must be Abstract," p. 386). "The major abstraction is the idea of man/And major man is its exponent" (X, "It Must be Abstract," p. 388).

Yet the poem *fully* defines these terms, as I have said, because it makes a poem from them. It uses ideas about imagination and reality and makes from them a poem. Metaphor, as Stevens often says, is really the opposite kind of endeavor from that which concerns itself with abstraction and first ideas. There is motive for metaphor in a statement such as the following:

> From this the poem springs: that we live in a place
> That is not our own and, much more, not ourselves . . .
> (IV, "It Must be Abstract," p. 383)

Metaphor changes that into this:

> . . . The freshness of transformation is
> The freshness of a world. It is our own,
> It is ourselves, the freshness of ourselves,
> (X, "It Must Change," pp. 397–398)

For metaphor, whether praised or damned, seems to be inevitable—"From this the poem springs." Even when Stevens writes a poem about the desire to achieve reality, to see the sun clearly in the idea of it, he uses metaphor to do it; he builds his poem upon a structure of metaphor. It may be one thing to see the sun clearly in the idea of it but quite another to write a poem about it.

Always Stevens, in his letters and essays, is hesitant, cagy about defining a fiction. Yet it is in a fiction—the supreme achievement of a poem—where the real and the imagined are reconciled—if only in the fiction. The best way to approach an understanding of what a fiction is is to observe metaphor at work in this poem. To do this, I have selected passages from the *Notes* for closer consideration.

Since the abstract, abstraction, and the act of abstracting are primary considerations in this work, it follows that in discussing the poem's metaphors we should be concerned with the range and relation they establish between abstract and concrete language. This continuum is of especial importance in Stevens's use of metaphor, whereas it is of minimal importance to Williams's, for example.

For Williams the world, man, poems, and even the imagination are seen to be concrete. For Stevens, however, the situation is much more complicated. Given the existence of the world, man, the imagination, and poems, he is never sure, as his contradictory statements on the subject indicate, wherein reality lies, what is concrete, and what is abstract. There are on the one hand his definitions of abstraction, which is for him direct sense perception, a return to essence, "the act of looking at [an object] and seeing it in its being." This is the act of the mind, and as a movement away from "layers of interpretation which have piled up over the years on objects in the external world," it is in that sense a movement toward the concrete and toward reality. Metaphor is not mythology, but it is interpretation (it is "to impose" and not "to discover") . Yet Stevens's statements about metaphor make it clear that metaphor is also an approach toward reality and toward the concrete. "An object the sum of its complications, seen/And unseen. This is everybody's world./Here the total artifice reveals itself/As the total reality." Metaphor is "the intensification of reality by resemblance"; "metaphor creates a new reality from which the original appears to be unreal."

Stevens's definition of "abstract" and "abstraction" is different from mine when I speak of abstract language or an abstraction. Here abstract is the direct opposite of concrete. An abstraction is a concept, a generalized idea rather than a specified object. Abstract language uses a vocabulary that consists primarily of abstract words to express concepts and ideas. Stevens uses the terms *abstract* and *abstraction* to speak of mental processes, while I am using them to describe language—in this case, the language of his poetry. The difference between perception and language, and the movement between one and the other, is at the heart of Stevens's problems in constructing a consistent theory. Stevens's own poetic language is especially interesting in the extreme diversity it displays in its use of abstract and concrete words. Sometimes it is predominantly abstract, as in the dedication to the *Notes.*

> And for what, except for you, do I feel love?
> Do I press the extremest book of the wisest man
> Close to me, hidden in me day and night?
> In the uncertain light of single, certain truth,
> Equal in living changingness to the light
> In which I meet you, in which we sit at rest,
> For a moment in the central of our being,
> The vivid transparence that you bring is peace. (p. 380)

Here the key words of the passage are all concepts: *love, truth, changingness, being, transparence, and peace.* In the last five lines there are fourteen nouns, all of them abstractions except for the pronouns *I* and *you.*

On the other hand, Stevens's fictions, some of which I will discuss in detail later on, are characterized by the concreteness of their language. In between are Stevens's metaphors, whose function throughout the poem has to do with effecting relations, in a variety of interesting ways, between abstract and concrete.

Part I of the *Notes* is called "It Must Be Abstract," and in its first section the poem, beginning its definition of the nature of abstraction and of idea, takes a predictably anti-metaphoric stance.

I

> Begin, ephebe, by perceiving the idea
> Of this invention, this invented world,
> The inconceivable idea of the sun.
>
> You must become an ignorant man again
> And see the sun again with an ignorant eye
> And see it clearly in the idea of it.
>
> Never suppose an inventing mind as source

Of this idea nor for that mind compose
A voluminous master folded in his fire.

How clean the sun when seen in its idea,
Washed in the remotest cleanliness of a heaven
That has expelled us and our images . . .

The death of one god is the death of all.
Let purple Phoebus lie in umber harvest,
Let Phoebus slumber and die in autumn umber,

Phoebus is dead, ephebe. But Phoebus was
a name for something that never could be named.
There was a project for the sun and is.

There is a project for the sun. The sun
Must bear no name, gold flourisher, but be
In the difficulty of what it is to be. (pp. 380–81)

To see the sun clearly in the idea of it requires the expelling of images, such as voluminous masters folded in their fires or purple gods lying in umber harvest; the sun must not be named "gold flourisher." Other than to point out forbidden imagery, the language of the section adheres closely to abstraction, as phrases like "The inconceivable idea of the sun," "And see it clearly in the idea of it," or "but be/In the difficulty of what it is to be" indicate. This kind of abstraction is a negative act, a denial of encumbrances, names, and images, which is to result in clarity and cleanliness. Nevertheless, the passage, seemingly unwittingly, contains an occasional metaphor: "ignorant eye" and "washed in the remotest cleanliness of a heaven/That has expelled us and our images."

This kind of position is difficult for Stevens to maintain, however. By the second section of Part I he has begun to make use of a consistent pattern of metaphor, as is indicated by the following selected examples.

The following passage comes from II of "It Must Be Abstract" and contains metaphors for the abstract statements "And not to have is the beginning of desire," paralleled by "To have what is not is its ancient cycle."

> And not to have is the beginning of desire.
> To have what is not is its ancient cycle.
> It is desire at the end of winter, when
>
> It observes the effortless weather turning blue
> And sees the myosotis on its bush.
> Being virile, it hears the calendar hymn.
> It knows that what it has is what is not
>
> And throws it away like a thing of another time,
> As morning throws off stale moonlight and shabby
>   sleep. (p. 382)

The ending of winter is observed by "desire," whose actions
and observations give apprehensible, concrete form to the original
abstractions. As a figure *desire* might be labeled either personification (the abstract term *desire* observes, hears, sees, and
knows) or synechdoche (desire is singled out as a characteristic
emotion and emotion as a characteristic aspect of man) ; in either
case (the two are not mutually exclusive) the use of metaphor
emphasizes the human element in experience. Desire, because
of what it has experienced (the beginning of spring), throws
away what it has (winter) because it is what is not: winter and
its qualities are negative, as opposed by the positive qualities
displayed by the new spring day. Yet those positive qualities
prove to be complex ones. Desire sees and hears three things:
"the effortless weather turning blue"; "The myosotis on its bush";
and "the calendar hymn." Although parallel phrases, one is literal
(the myosotis) , while the others are metaphors. ("The effortless
weather turning blue" describes the sky brightening, while "the
calendar hymn" refers to the birds' song.) Both phrases personify
natural acts (weather is effortless and birds sing hymns) . In
addition, weather, an abstract noun, becomes through its activity
a concrete entity. "Calendar hymn" again calls attention to the
seasonal importance of the moment being described. It also contributes (since calendars are made by men, not birds) to a
function shared by all the metaphors in this passage. As well as
consistently giving concrete form to abstractions, the metaphors,

each in its own way, connect man and nature, the experiencer and the experienced.

As the passage concludes, the human acts of desire are compared to an event in nature, the dawning of a new day. Yet this event is in turn described with a metaphor that personifies morning and turns moonlight and sleep into objects (the one stale, the other shabby) that can be "thrown off."

The association of weather and man becomes a persistent theme throughout the poem. "The poem [*Notes*] is a struggle with the inaccessibility of the abstract," writes Stevens to Henry Church in the long letter from which I have frequently quoted. "First I make the effort; then I turn to the weather because that is not inaccessible and is not abstract. The weather as described is the weather that was about me when I wrote this. There is a constant reference from the abstract to the real, to and fro" (*Letters,* p. 434). Stevens opposes the art of poetry to myth-making and apotheosis. In I of "It Must Be Abstract" he rejoices in the death of Phoebus, who was a name for the sun. Again, in IV he shows that Adam and Eve had it all wrong (and so, by implication, have the people who view the world through mythologies, through egotism).

> From this the poem springs: that we live in a place
> That is not our own, and, much more, not ourselves
> And hard it is in spite of blazoned days.
>
> We are the mimics. Clouds are pedagogues
> The air is not a mirror but bare board,
> Coulisse bright-dark, tragic chiaroscuro
>
> And comic color of the rose, in which
> Abysmal instruments make sounds like pips
> Of the sweeping meanings that we add to them. (pp. 383–84)

"Eve made the air a mirror of herself," but "The air is not a mirror." By means of its figures this passage does exalt art (and artifice) as the proper mediary by which man relates to nature. Once again this idea is expressed by means of metaphors in an appositional relation to an introductory statement. Metaphoric transfers are usually made directly, by means of the copula, and such metaphors often personify.

The metaphoric sequence is an explanation of a literal statement. It finds its roots and impetus, however, in that very statement with the phrase *blazoned days,* which contains several meanings of blazoned: represented by drawings or engravings (as in heraldic bearings) ; exhibited conspicuously; covered as if with blazons. All of these meanings extend into the metaphors that follow.

These indicate that man imitates nature, the teacher (clouds are pedagogues) , and not vice versa; and yet the series of metaphors also emphatically make the familiar point that the world is a stage in which man, we have already been informed, is but a player (for "mimic" connotes actor as well as student) . Nature is not only a stage: the vocabulary of the metaphors, drawn from painting and music as well as theater, involves additional art forms in the definition. Yet it is men who make theaters, paintings, symphonies—and metaphors. Through metaphor man makes nature into art. However, characteristically, Stevens still feels it necessary to add that our "sweeping meanings" are, after all, added on to the world that is already there, even as he began by announcing that the place is "not our own."

The next two passages, both taken from "It Must Be Abstract," continue to demonstrate a similar construction.

> It feels good as it is without the giant,
> A thinker of the first idea. Perhaps
> The truth depends on a walk around a lake,
>
> A composing as the body tires, a stop
> To see hepatica, a stop to watch
> A definition growing certain and
>
> A wait within that certainty, a rest
> In the swags of pine-trees bordering the lake. (p. 386)

The first passage is a series of appositional phrases, all object of "depend upon." The truth depends upon each of the events mentioned, which are parallel statements. A linear time sequence, however, arranges them in patterns of two: two walkings, two stoppings, two restings. The phrases move from the literal into the figurative. Walking around the lake, composing as the body tires, and stopping to see hepatica are all literal, while stopping to watch "a definition growing certain" is the first metaphor. Yet it is significant that the metaphor parallels the literal watching. The metaphor gives body to the abstract word *definition:* it makes of it some kind of plant. The next pair of phrases, which describe two restings, initially seem to move from the figurative back to the literal. That is, to wait within a certainty is a figurative act, while to rest within swags of pine trees seems perfectly literal. However, the parallelism links the two restings even as a similar construction had previously linked the two stoppings. In each case parallelism identifies the two acts with one another, stressing the relation expressed through the content of the phrases. Certainty is the result of the definition's growth, and it is to swags of pine-trees as the definition is to the hepatica. Both abstractions, indicative of mental acts, are granted a bodily form akin to natural objects that are involved in physical acts. The passage is yet a further variation on Stevens's basic theme. It relates mental and physical acts (or figurative and literal acts) by dissolving distinctions between them within its own domain.

This passage is taken from Section VII, in which it in turn parallels two other statements: "Perhaps there are times of inherent excellence" and "Perhaps there are moments of awakening." Each of these phrases introduces a series of metaphors that embody that idea. Thus in this section, as in the work as a whole, the series of greater and smaller appositional metaphors act as a cluster of "resemblances" around the phrase that introduces the section: "It feels good as it is without the giant/A thinker of the first idea."

A series of metaphors in apposition to a literal abstract statement is a consistent pattern throughout the work. In the following passage from Section IX of "It Must Be Abstract" the de-

scription of the origin of major man ("The major abstraction
is the idea of man/And major man is its exponent") follows the
literal "But apotheosis is not/The origin of major man."

> The romantic intoning, the declaimed clairvoyance
> Are parts of apotheosis, appropriate
> And of its nature, the idiom thereof.
>
> They differ from reason's click-clack, its applied
> Enflashings. But apotheosis is not
> The origin of major man. He comes,
>
> Compact in invincible foils, from reason,
> Lighted at midnight by the studious eye,
> Swaddled in revery, the object of
>
> The hum of thoughts evaded in the mind,
> Hidden from other thoughts, he that reposes
> On a breast forever precious for that touch,
>
> For whom the good of April falls down tenderly,
> Falls down, the cock-birds calling at the time.
> My dame, sing for this person accurate songs. (pp. 387–88)

A series of clauses demonstrates in what manner he comes. One
might expect that of all beings major man, as the embodiment
of the process of abstracting and the thinking of first ideas,
would not be described with metaphor. He belongs, as is made
clear by the statements that preface the description of this coming, to reason. Yet even as within these primarily abstract statements reason itself has been given a concrete form through
metaphor ("reason's click-clack, its applied/Enflashings"), so
does the description of major man consist of a series of metaphors.

The primary function of these metaphors is to make abstractions concrete (even as major man, himself, as a character in a
poem, is a personified abstraction). However, they display a
tendency to neatly balance the abstract and the concrete in the
course of their transfers. He is "swaddled in revery"; he is "ob-

ject of/The hum of thoughts evaded in the mind"; for him "the good of April" falls down tenderly. "Revery," "thoughts," and "good" are abstractions that achieve physical form, in two of the three examples, by personification. These abstractions are balanced by "swaddled," "object," and "April," each more or less concrete to begin with. Again, in the first phrase describing his coming, "Compact in invincible foils, from reason," the foils are concrete, while reason, literally abstract, is made concrete through having become an object or place from which one can come.

The section concludes with these lines:

> He is and may be but oh! he is, he is,
> This foundling of the infected past, so bright,
> So moving in the manner of his hand.
>
> Yet look not at his colored eyes. Give him
> No names. Dismiss him from your images.
> The hot of him is purest in the heart. (p. 388)

These lines suddenly take the more predictable anti-metaphor position. What is important, they announce, is "is," not "may be." Major man should neither be named nor presented with images—precisely what the lines that have preceded these have succeeded in doing. These final lines, rather, try to keep the description abstract: "so bright,/So moving in the manner of his hand" and "The hot of him is purest in the heart." The form of this section is a direct result of the problem that metaphor creates for Stevens: he can envisage a metaphysics that requires the existence of the non- or anti-metaphorical, but can write about it only with metaphor. The way in which the metaphors of this section try to balance the abstract with the concrete seems an attempt to deal, in terms of metaphor itself, with the problem.

The next example, Part IV of "It Must Change," shows how the metaphoric pattern that we have observed in more limited contexts is extended into a complete poem.

IV

Two things of opposite natures seem to depend
On one another, as a man depends
On a woman, day and night, the imagined

On the real. This is the origin of change.
Winter and spring, cold copulars, embrace
And forth the particulars of rapture come.

Music falls on the silence like a sense,
A passion that we feel, not understand.
Morning and afternoon are clasped together

And North and South are an intrinsic couple
And sun and rain a plural, like two lovers
That walk away as one in the greenest body.

In solitude the trumpets of solitude
Are not of another solitude resounding;
A little string speaks for a crowd of voices.

The partaker partakes of that which changes him.
The child that touches takes character from the thing,
The body, it touches. The captain and his men

Are one and the sailor and the sea are one.
Follow after, O my companion, my fellow, my self,
Sister and solace, brother and delight. (p. 392)

Again abstract statements ("Two things of opposite nature seem
to depend/On one another" and "This is the origin of change")
introduces metaphors that embody the concepts they express.
The totality of resemblances or metaphors creates the essence
of that which is being defined. If the structure can be envisioned
in spatial terms, then the concept, the idea of intercourse between opposites, would be in the center, with the relations that
are depicted between men and women, day and night, winter
and spring, morning and afternoon, north and south, child and
body, captain and men, sailor and sea all circling about it.

The concept itself, that change results from the dependence

of things of opposite nature upon one another, is very near to being a theory of metaphor (Stevens's metaphors), and the metaphors of the section embody that concept by showing how such relations come about and what changes are produced. Even within the introductory statements the examples that are offered—"as a man depends/On a woman, day and night, the imagined/On the real"—represent a continuum from concrete to abstract: man and woman being the most concrete, the imagined and the real, as concepts, being the most abstract, with day and night, physical and yet general, being somewhere in between. This is the nature of the interdependence with which the ensuing metaphors concern themselves. Each of the metaphors is an example of some kind of intercourse or copulation; each metaphor, in turn, carefully creates its relation between concrete and abstract. In the first—"Winter and spring, cold copulars, embrace/And forth the particulars of rapture come"—winter and spring, which embrace and bring forth issue, are embodied through personification, and yet they are further defined by an abstraction (as "cold copulars"), while their issue is identified as "the particulars of rapture." The pattern continues throughout the section. Music, embodied in that it can fall on the silence, falls as would a "sense" or a "passion." Morning and afternoon, also personified, "are clasped together"; yet other such loving couples, like North and South and sun and rain, are simultaneously described with phrases of abstraction: "an intrinsic couple", "a plural." The poet speaks of "the trumpets of solitude," another metaphoric phrase that joins a concrete with an abstract word. The technique is similar to that observed in the passage from VII of "It Must Be Abstract" (in which the truth depended upon a walk around a lake). Here the procedure is given a rationale: the supreme fiction, as well as being abstract and giving pleasure, must change; change is the product of metaphor's movement between abstract and concrete, something that has been observed throughout the whole of the poem.

This section draws to a close with additional statements of the theme that now begin to assume the nature of fiction: references to characters whose actions alone are enactments of the concept in question. Here the movement is a slight one and serves as a way of ending upon an elevated note. However, among the later sections of the poem there are entire sections that are complete extended metaphors, or total metaphors, or what Stevens calls "fiction." Section V of "It Must Change" and Sections II and III of "It Must Give Pleasure" are examples of these fictions.

V

On a blue island in a sky-wide water
The wild orange trees continued to bloom and to bear,
Long after the planter's death. A few limes remained,

Where his house had fallen, three scraggy trees weighted
With garbled green. These were the planter's turquoise
And his orange blotches, these were his zero green,

A green baked greener in the greenest sun.
These were his beaches, his sea-myrtles in
White sand, his patter of the long sea-slushes.

There was an island beyond him on which rested,
An island to the South, on which rested like
A mountain, a pineapple pungent as Cuban summer.

And la-bas, la-bas, the cool bananas grew,
Hung heavily on the great banana tree,
Which pierces clouds and bends on half the world.

He thought often of the land from which he came,
How the whole country was a melon, pink
If seen rightly and yet a possible red.

An unaffected man in a negative light
Could not have borne his labor nor have died
Sighing that he should leave the banjo's twang. (p. 393)

II

The blue woman, linked and laquered, at her window
Did not desire that feathery argentines
Should be cold silver, neither that frothy clouds

Should foam, be foamy waves, should move like them,
Nor that the sexual blossoms should repose
Without their fierce addictions, nor that the heat

Of summer, growing fragrant in the night,
Should strengthen her abortive dreams and take
In sleep its natural form. It was enough

For her that she remembered: the argentines
Of spring come to their places in the grape leaves
To cool their ruddy pulses; the frothy clouds

Are nothing but frothy clouds; the frothy blooms
Waste without puberty; and afterward,
When the harmonious heat of August pines

Enters the room, it drowses and is the night.
It was enough for her that she remembered.
The blue woman looked and from her window named

The corals of the dogwood, cold and clear,
Cold, coldly delineating, being real,
Clear and, except for the eye, without intrusion.

(pp. 399–400)

IV

We reason of these things with later reason
And we make of what we see, what we see clearly
And have seen, a place dependent on ourselves.

There was a mystic marriage in Catawba,
At noon it was on the mid-day of the year
Between a great captain and the maiden Bawda.

This was their ceremonial hymn: Anon
We loved but would no marriage make. Anon
The one refused the other one to take,

Foreswore the sipping of the marriage wine.
Each must the other take not for his high,
His puissant front nor for her subtle sound,

The shoo-shoo-shoo of secret cymbals round.
Each must the other take as sign, short sign
To stop the whirlwind, balk the elements.

The great captain loved the ever-hill Catawba
And therefore married Bawda, whom he found there,
And Bawda loved the captain as she loved the sun.

They married well because the marriage-place
Was what they loved. It was neither heaven nor hell.
They were love's characters come face to face. (p. 401)

Such fictions are not symbols, nor are they really allegories.[6]
They do, however, embody ideas; they are a way of reconciling
reality and the mind through the medium of language. They
are, to use Stevens's phrase from VI of "It Must Be Abstract,"
"An abstraction blooded, as a man by thought" (p. 385). For
example, number nine, the fiction of the blue woman, is basically
an extended metaphor standing in apposition to an unwritten
phrase to the effect that one must (or should, or can) try to

---

6. Many critics of Stevens, however, offer symbolic readings of these fictions.
Frank Dogget, for example, reads Section V, "It Must Change," in these
symbolic terms: blue stands for the imagination, green for reality, the planter
for generic man, the pineapple and the banana tree for the sexual basis of
human life, and the melon for life's origin in the womb ("This Invented
World" in Pearce and Miller, eds., *The Act of the Mind* [Baltimore, 1965],
p. 15). Writing of Section VIII of "It Must Change," Ronald Sukenick explains that Nanzio Nunzio represents reality; Ozymandias represents a fiction
that determines the conception of reality. His reading proceeds accordingly.
"Nanzio Nunzio comes prepared as 'the spouse' in order to unite with an
idea of reality that will define her aspect. She strips herself of her present
'fictive covering' so that she may assume a new one. She reveals herself as
the essence of reality, not as reality clothed by an idea of it" (*Wallace
Stevens: Musing The Obscure* [New York, 1967], p. 150). James Baird says
that Section IV of "It Must Give Pleasure" presents "a union of everlast-
ing place, of major man of human imaginings and his constant mistress. . . .
The captain is major man of the American land. The mate is his genius of
artifice, expressing his intelligence given by the earth he knows, 'the ever-
hill Catawba'" (*The Dome and the Rock: Structure in the Poetry of Wallace
Stevens* [Baltimore, 1968], p. 240).

Yet, as I have pointed out before, it is not the same thing to say that the
poem about Nanzio Nunzio and Ozymandias symbolizes the relation between
reality and "fiction" as it is to say that it is a metaphor for that relation. As
a metaphor, the fiction of Nanzio Nunzio is of equal importance with the
idea that it embodies, since the two are aspects of one thing. On the other
hand, Nanzio Nunzio as a symbol, loses her status as Nanzio Nunzio as
fiction, and becomes but the means to an end, the idea for which she stands.

see and name reality without the instrusion of the mind—in the first idea of it. The language of the fiction, unlike that of the rest of the poem, is almost entirely concrete. The play of metaphor between the abstract and the concrete is almost completely missing. The fiction is very like the common connotation of the word, a story or a play. In it the idea achieves concrete form and (to use Pound's phrase, peculiarly applicable here) goes into action. The blue woman enacts her drama, and in doing so, she acts out the thematic idea.

In each fiction subsidiary metaphors aid in its development. The story of the blue woman is especially interesting because it is another of those anti-metaphor stances which are undercut by the use of metaphor in the statement. The blue woman did not desire to make metaphors—"that feathery argentines should be cold silver" (there are those who would argue that in making the metaphors she would not make the relations have been made, anyway). Yet the depiction of her vision when it is "non-metaphoric" is full of metaphors—primarily personification, perhaps the worst sin of all. The grape leaves "cool their ruddy pulses"; the "harmonious" heat of August pines, when it enters the room, "drowses and is the night." But Stevens's own summary statement contains the motive for his use of metaphor, the fatal yet inescapable flaw. The blue woman names the corals of the dogwood "cold and clear"—"Cold, coldly delineating, being real /Clear and, *except for the eye,* without intrusion." (Italics mine.) For in human experience there is no "except for the eye," and Stevens knows this. Once the eye looks, the mind thinks. In VII of "It Must Give Pleasure" Stevens writes that "Not to impose, not to have reasoned at all,/Out of nothing to have come on major weather" is "possible, possible, possible." Yet the same section proclaims that "to find the real" is "to be stripped of every fiction except one,/The fiction of an absolute." The first idea, major weather and major man are themselves fictions. The "possible" is impossible except in a poem, which is why Stevens is a poet and not a philosopher. The poem (and especially the total metaphor, the fiction) does unite the mind and the world because it is an entity (a linguistic form) resulting from the act of the mind upon the world.

In *Notes Towards a Supreme Fiction,* as in his other poems, Stevens's attitude toward metaphor may change, but his use of it does not. Poems, as the result of the act of the mind upon the world, depend for their creation upon "the freshness of transformation"—the transfers of metaphor. Man needs metaphors to make art from the relation, the interdependence, the "war" between himself and the world, for the primary function of metaphor in Stevens's art is to effect a relation between the abstract and the concrete elements of language that is indicative of the existing situation in human experience.

Notes Towards a Supreme Fiction, one of Stevens's most extensive and mature articulations of his theories, is constructed upon a consistent pattern of metaphor. Over and over, in short language structures and in long, series of metaphors exemplify or embody abstract statements of concepts that precede them. Through their constant movement between abstract and concrete language, these metaphors point repeatedly toward Stevens's most fundamental concern: the relation of the mind and the world. The metaphors are usually a series of parallel statements, phrases in apposition to one another and to the introductory statement that they also modify. Within each section the metaphors, because of this structure, define the concept in question by acting as a totality of its "complications," or "resemblances." This form in turn extends to the larger structures of the work— the relation of each of the ten sections to their titles, also state· ments of concepts ("It Must Be Abstract," "It Must Change," "It Must Give Pleasure"), and the relation of the three parts to the title of the total work, *Notes Towards a Supreme Fiction.*

There has been a tendency in the criticism of Wallace Stevens to regard him as a philosopher, his works as a body of philosophical thought: to paraphrase his poems in order to transpose their content into the framework of his philosophical system. Yet it is precisely because a poem is more than the ideas that it expresses—and Stevens's poems make their total statement by their use of language and especially of metaphor (which is not symbol) —that such an approach is particularly inappropriate. Stevens's consistent use of poetic language—of abstract language, concrete language, and the mixed language of metaphor—must be considered along with the inconsistencies of his theoretical positions in understanding his meaning at any given moment and in responding to his poems. Poetry, as T. E. Hulme has said, is not a counter language. Nowhere is this more clear than in the poetry of Wallace Stevens.

5
Metaphor in William Carlos Williams's **Paterson**

William Carlos Williams's *Paterson* has successfully defied most critical attempts to find a structural concept which not only includes but illuminates its oddly assorted elements. Earlier in this essay I have had occasion to study several of Williams's short poems as well as his "Asphodel, That Greeny Flower." *Paterson* is Williams's most sustained work—and that work in which his use of metaphor, as I have described it, is most developed.

The five books of *Paterson* were published at intervals over a period of twelve years. They contain an assortment of material ranging from prose accounts of historical events in the New Jersey town of Paterson to excerpts from letters and shopping lists to snatches of dialogue to descriptions of tapestries and paintings to love poems. In order to provide some semblance of coherence for this material, Williams gave to his volumes several readily apparent organizational features. For example, the first four books follow the sequence of the seasons, from spring to winter. They also follow the course of the Passaic River as it moves from the falls above Paterson to the Atlantic Ocean. Each book is organized around a central feature. In order, these are the falls, the park, the library, Madame Curie and the discovery of radium, and the unicorn tapestries at New

York's Cloisters Museum. Each of the first four books is also loosely based upon one of the four elements, in the order of water, earth, fire, and air, although these tend to intermingle, so that no one element is confined to a single book. Finally, the main "actors" are the same throughout and have their counterparts in physical features of the locality in which the poem is set. There is the man, who is the city, Paterson; the woman, who is Garret Mountain; and language, which is the Passaic River.

Most discussions of *Paterson* tend to concentrate upon one or several of these organizational features, yet they are actually superficial to the structure of the poem as parts working toward a whole. It should be apparent from my brief listing that they provide neither the rationale by which a given section of an individual book proceeds to any other section nor that which relates in any profound way one book to another. Most of them do not extend at all to *Paterson V,* which, rather than an afterthought, seems to me to be a vital addition to the development and achievement of the poem. These features function, not as the basic structural principle of the poem, but rather at an introductory level as readily apprehensible guides to reading, much as the North Star points out the general direction to a traveler. They represent the literal, thematic development of the poem, but what structures the poem from moment to moment and as an inclusive principle is the pattern of metaphor that it builds. The figurative dimension of *Paterson* is concerned with other elements in the five books. Metaphors refer primarily to a branch and a bud (Book I); the flight of grasshoppers (Book II); the beautiful thing and a burning bottle (Book III); Madame Curie and the radiant gist (Book IV); and the Unicorn and the Virgin (Book V).

The function of metaphor is consistent from book to book. The poem progresses in a nonlinear fashion, by exploring the ramifications, implications, and boundaries of sets of dualities. In Book I the largest theme, to which others are connected, is the nature of man's world: hence the emphasis in this book on inner-outer, subjective-objective, idea-thing. The major theme of Book II, which moves in the external world, is that of the nature of art; its primary duality is artifact-artist. Book III (moving in the world of the mind) explores the nature of beauty, its primary duality being that of artistic form-natural form. Book IV investigates love, especially in terms of the perversion-virtue duality. Book V is of a different sort, for it is a book of reconciliation or harmony: it is the book of the imagination. In each of these books metaphor is used to establish the boundaries of the particular duality in question: both how far it can be extended in either direction and, especially, how close its two components can be brought together—can be conjoined; never melted into one another, for this would destroy the duality, but pressed together for the purpose of revelation. All of these major themes—man, art, beauty, love, and the imagination—are, besides being a part of one another, involved in any consideration of the creative act itself: what Williams calls "invention." Metaphor is most profuse in those passages in which Williams attempts to reveal in poetry the nature of the poetic act.

Book I of *Paterson* presents a nearly random arrangement of metaphors. This accords with the loose, exploratory nature of the book, in which Williams is primarily setting up his palette—establishing the themes, images, and figures with which he will fill the books to come—defining and "delineating." In the later books the metaphors tend to cluster in metaphoric passages, in which the tone is particularly lyric and intense; they contrast to long sections of more literal and more low-keyed language. When metaphors occur within the literal passages, their function usually is to echo or develop whatever has been established in the metaphoric passages.

The nonlinear movement of metaphor in *Paterson*, circling or spiraling rather like the movement in a pool when a rock has been thrown into the water, organizes its formal development. It is complemented by a linear movement, which is primarily thematic: the movement of descent. This is where Williams's use of the progress of the river, from the falls down to the sea, and the movement of the seasons, from spring "down" to winter, finds its raison d'être. Yet, for Williams the concept of descent has implications on many more levels. The books of *Paterson* descend, for example, from universals into particulars—of character, event, perception. They descend from idea into thing, abstract into concrete, and of necessity into negation and failure. Yet as Williams wrote to Marianne Moore, "At times there is no other way to assert the truth than by stating our failure to achieve it. If I did not achieve a language I at least stated what I would not say."[1] For Williams the process of artistic creation itself is one of descent, for descent is a necessary requirement of ascent.

> The descent
> > made up of despairs
> > > and without accomplishment
> > realizes a new awakening:
> > > > which is a reversal
> > of despair.

These lines are from Williams's poem "The Descent," which was first published as a passage in Book II.

The theme of descent in order to create is everywhere in Williams's work, and it has been carefully charted by J. Hillis Miller in his essay on the poet. Miller points out the existence of three "mutually incompatible" elements in Williams's poems: "the formless ground, origin of all things; the formed thing, defined and limited; a nameless presence, the 'beautiful thing' (*Paterson,* 119), there in every form but hidden by it."[2] He goes on to discuss the first movement of Williams's imagination as one of descent, of destruction, noting that "To return to the beginning is to return to the present moment, for the present is the ever-fresh origin."[3] To this effect he quotes Williams in "An Approach to

---

1. June 19, 1961, Thirwall, ed., *The Selected Letters of William Carlos Williams* (New York, 1957) p. 304.

2. *Poets of Reality* (New York, 1969), p. 328.

3. P. 337.

the Poem": "When the form has been completed, when it has at last flowered, it begins at once to become sclerotic and has to be broken down once more *to the elements*."[4] Miller notes that "The 'spring' of *Spring and All* is the rebirth of things after their annihilation. In *Paterson* the return to the beginning which leads to spring is poetically accomplished. The poem flows steadily downhill with the filthy Passaic."[5] (*Paterson V* is very much the rebirth or "spring" of *Paterson*.) In his *Autobiography* (New York, 1951) Williams wrote of the original end of *Paterson:*

> In the end the man rises from the sea where the river appears to have lost its identity and accompanied by his faithful bitch, obviously a Chesapeake Bay retriever, turns inland towards Camden where Walt Whitman, much traduced, lived the latter years of his life and died. He always said that his poems, which had broken the dominance of the iambic pentameter in English prosody, had only begun his theme. I agree. It is up to us, in the new dialect, to continue it by a new construction upon the syllables. (p. 392)

Paterson is a poem about language and poetry; at its heart is its analysis of the act and moment of creation. Its own use of language, including that of metaphor, is integrally related to Williams's aesthetic theories. These he never ceased to explicate in many essays on the subject, for he saw himself as a crusader, a man striving for over half a century to create a new kind of poetry in America.

The following passages are from two of his earliest publications, *Kora in Hell* (Boston, 1920) and *Spring and All* (Dijon, 1923), yet the ideas they contain continue throughout all of Williams's later writings. For both these reasons, therefore, they can serve as an introduction to Williams's poetics.

> Although it is a quality of the imagination that it seeks to place together those things which have a common relationship, yet the coining of similes is a pastime of very low order, depending as it does upon a nearly vegetable coincidence. Much

---

4. P. 337.
5. P. 339.

more keen is that power which discovers in things these inimitable particles of dissimilarity to all other things which are the peculiar perfections of the thing in question.

But this loose linking of one thing with another has effects of a destructive power little to be guessed at: all manner of things are thrown out of key so that it approaches the impossible to arrive at an understanding of anything. All is confusion, yet it comes from a hidden desire for the dance, a lust of the imagination, a will to accord two instruments in a duet.

But one does not attempt by the ingenuity of the joiner to blend the tones of the oboe with the violin. On the contrary the perfections of the two instruments are emphasized by the joiner; no means is neglected to give to each the full color of its perfections. It is only the music of the instruments which is joined and that not by the woodworker but by the composer, by virtue of the imagination.

On this level of the imagination all things and ages meet in fellowship. Thus only can they, peculiar and perfect, find their release. This is the beneficent power of the imagination.[6]

To redefine, to clarify, to intensify that eternal moment in which we alone live there is but a single force—the imagination.

. . . and the unique proof of this is the work of the imagination not "like" anything but transfused with the same forces which transfuse the earth—at least one small part of them.

. . . the writer of the imagination would attain closest to the conditions of music not when his words are disassociated from natural objects and specified meanings but when they are liberated from the usual quality of that meaning by transposition into another medium, the imagination.

The imagination is the transmitter. It is the changer. . . . It is the power of mutation which the mind possesses to rediscover the truth.[7]

Williams's aesthetics is a theory of the imagination, as these passages indicate. It is important to note, also, his analogy of the

6. "Prologue" to *Kora in Hell,* in *Selected Essays of William Carlos Williams* (New York, 1954) , p. 16.
7. *Spring and All,* pp. 3, 50, 92 and 92.

dance and of music and, of course, the view of figurative language that is expressed in the selection from *Kora.*

The next few remarks provide a sense of Williams's treatment of the poem itself. They are from a 1947 essay titled "An Approach to the Poem."

> So we have an object made up of words designed to have a certain effect, a rare, an elevated effect, which (apparently) cannot be obtained in any other way.

> In a sense, and this is a favorite image with me, it is a small (or large) mechanism or engine, as Saintsbury said, composed of words to do a certain job.

> All I wish to point to is that the poem in each case by its *form* creates the reality of a past age. It is not by what the poem says that we have the greatness of art. It is by what the poem has been made to *be* that we recognize it.[8]

Even Williams's *Autobiography* is in large part a vehicle for his poetic theories. In it an important set of terms in his theoretical vocabulary, "particular" and "universal," are characteristically articulated as he stresses his belief that the poet must write particularly, "as a physician works, upon a patient, upon the thing before him, in the particular to discover the universal."[9]

Williams has a great deal to say about the concept of form and measure in his essays, but he rarely deals with specific poetic techniques. Thus he says very little about metaphor, yet it is of vital importance in his own poetry. The uses to which he puts metaphor develop throughout his career until, in his longer, later poems, it becomes a primary structuring agent. Yet in all of his poetry metaphor has one basic role that remains consistent and that firmly links metaphor to his prose theories: it functions as a linguistic embodiment of the imagination. It, reflecting the imagination, redefines, clarifies and intensifies; it transmutes and changes; it enacts the power of mutation that the mind possesses

---

8. *English Institute Essays: 1947* (New York, 1965), pp. 52, 53, 56.
9. P. 391.

to rediscover the truth; it is the agent by which the writer of the imagination liberates words and objects by transposing them into another medium, the imagination. Metaphor functions, as Williams himself wrote in "A Sort of Song," to reconcile the people and the stones.[10]

As a poet worthy of scholarly consideration, Williams is only now beginning to come into his own. All but one of the full-length books that have been written about him have been published since 1964. Of all aspects of his work metaphor has received the least attention. Only Linda Wagner, in *The Poems of William Carlos Williams* (Middletown, Conn., 1964), gives the subject any significant space. Though her insights are good, they are rarely backed up by any demonstration of what she means. For example, she observes that "Important though metaphor is to the content of Williams' poems, it is even more significant as a principle of organization. All Williams' comments about the figure stress its ability to increase both the depth and the speed of the poem."[11] To which I can only agree and wish that she had provided examples. Her handling of the nature of Williams's metaphors themselves—labeling them either "transitional" or "symbolic"—is confusing and ultimately unsatisfactory. *Transitional* refers to

> the impact of consecutive images rather than any logical progression of "meaning." Like metaphor in that the reader experiences the poem through suggestion rather than didactic statement, this technique of juxtaposition makes comparisons not only with the comparative word but also without the connective.[12]

She explains symbolic metaphor as a concrete image, having almost symbolic impact, which represents an abstraction. She points out that one such image may have different referents (sparrow meaning poet, religious significance, and bravery) but that such

---

10. *The Collected Later Poems of William Carlos Williams* (New York, 1963), p. 7.
11. P. 57.
12. P. 40.

referents are not contradictory and have qualities in common. The image itself serves as nexus: "each new equivalent adds to the composite definition, reinforcing the impression derived from previous use."[13] Neither "the impact of constructive images," "concrete image," nor "symbolic impact" are definitions of metaphor. Her confusion between terms like *metaphor, image,* and *symbol* undercuts the usefulness of her observations.

More interesting than Linda Wagner's analysis of metaphor is J. Hillis Miller's denial of Williams's use of figurative language. Miller's essay on Williams in his *Poets of Reality* is the most extensive and the most perceptive examination to date of Williams's theory and technique. Yet Miller writes: "In Williams' world there are no resonances or similarities between things, no basis for metaphor. There is in fact little figurative language in his poetry."[14] This is simply not true. The only reason that I can postulate for his arriving at such a position derives from the emphasis that Miller places upon Williams's avowed concern for the particularity of an object: "its own precise edges cutting it off from other things," as Williams says.[15] It is, however, significant that one of the finest critics of Williams has such a blind spot, for it is indicative of a quality of Williams's work which, in stressing observation, objects and conciseness and minimizing rhetorical lushness and fantasy, often seems alien to the need or use of figurative language.

II

Paterson I is in every sense an introductory structure, setting forth the formal and thematic elements that will constitute the poem *Paterson*. It is subtitled "The Delineaments of the Giants" and proceeds to introduce the central characters and settings of the poem in their grandest and most monumental form—as "giants." It introduces, too, a system of techniques for delineation. From the first, metaphor is central to both themes and

---

13. P. 47.
14. P. 306.
15. P. 306.

forms. Two kinds of metaphor operate in Book I: what I shall call "thematic" or "conceptual" metaphors and "local" metaphors. The relation that exists between them is indicative of Williams's conception and subsequent development of his poem. The metaphors of Book I, both thematic and local, are consistently used to establish and explore the complex relation between the mind and the world, or between the subjective and objective worlds. This is the duality investigated in Book I, and it extends to subsidiary relations such as that between universal and particular or abstract and concrete. In each section of Book I the duality is articulated through the exploration of a prevailing theme or idea. This is first introduced at its simplest level, often by means of an image of a concrete object. Its subsequent extension and development (what I am comparing to the circling ripples around a stone) is what obliquely but nonetheless significantly controls the progression of that section and links its assorted segments to one another. Metaphor is the primary means for such extension and development.

For example, the Preface with which Book I begins devotes its three pages to an exploration of the universal-particular duality by precisely these tactics as it discusses the act of starting, or generation (starting the poem, *Paterson;* starting life and mankind; starting one man and one city—Paterson). Its underlying idea, first articulated, in the synopsis that introduces all of Book I, in the phrase *by multiplication a reduction to one,*[16] is expressed in its simplest form as the Preface commences:

> To make a start,
> out of particulars
> and make them general, rolling
> up the sum . . . (p. 11)

The arithmetical element is expanded by subsequent passages:

>   . . . Rolling
> up! obverse, reverse;

---

16. *Paterson* (New York, 1963), p. 10.

> the drunk the sober; the illustrious
> the gross; one. (p. 12)

>   (The multiple seed,
> packed tight with detail) . . .
> Rolling up, rolling up heavy with
> numbers. (p. 12)

> [a man] . . . Renews himself
> thereby, in addition and substraction,
> walking up and down. (pp. 12–13)

The act of starting is expressed poetically, in that opening statement, as *rolling up*. The repetition of this key phrase and the exploration of its references and connotations is another way of extending and developing the theme of the Preface.

> To make a start,
> out of particulars
> and make them general, rolling
> up the sum, by defective means— (p. 11)

>   Yet there is
> no return: rolling up out of chaos,
> a nine months' wonder, the city
> the man, an identity—it can't be
> otherwise—an
> interpenetration, both ways. Rolling
> up! obverse, reverse . . . (p. 12)

> Rolling up, rolling up heavy with
> numbers. (p. 12)

>   and the craft,
> subverted by thought, rolling up, let
> him beware lest he turn to no more than
> the writing of stale poems . . . (p. 13)

In each of the passages quoted, *rolling up* has a different context and reference. In the first it is a commonplace expression, another way of saying adding up. In the second it describes the physical act of birth. In the third it is the seed of life itself, moving in a gush of fluid. (Yet already—it will happen again— metaphor places this flow somewhere where the mind can also float.) In the fourth it refers to the process of artistic creativity and its motion.

Metaphor conjoins the elements of the particular-general duality by causing qualities from each, and from all supposedly separate realms, to "interpenetrate" with one another, as metaphors aid in the description of what is rolling up. The first metaphor in the preface is an explicit instance of this technique:

> . . . rolling up out of chaos,
> a nine months' wonder, the city
> the man, an identity—it can't be
> otherwise—an
> interpenetration, both ways. (p. 12)

Other metaphors continue the technique. For example, in the following sequence the seed is packed with "detail," a word more properly applicable to what is later referred to as "the craft."

> (The multiple seed,
> packed tight with detail, soured,
> is lost in the flux and the mind,
> distracted, floats off in the same
> scum) (p. 12)

(The craft, in turn, is viewed as "rolling up" in another metaphor: "and the craft,/subverted by thought, rolling up"—p. 13.) Also, the declaration that the distracted mind can float in the "same scum" as the multiple seed makes of the "flux" in which it is lost a heterogeneous place, composed of elements from supposedly separate realms.

Again, in a phrase like *Rolling up, rolling up heavy with/ numbers,* numbers, by having such weight, are depicted as both abstract and specifically concrete. In yet another metaphor the sun and man are interpenetrating identities:

> It is the ignorant sun

> rising in the slot of
> hollow suns risen, so that never in this
> world will a man live well in his body
> save dying—and not know himself
> dying; yet that is
> the design. Renews himself
> thereby, in addition and subtraction,
> walking up and down. (pp. 12–13)

The sun is personified ("ignorant"), while its act is mechanized ("rising in the slot of/hollow suns risen"); man's own life is seen to be a parallel action.

The concluding stanzas, descending to the poem *Paterson*, descend from the general and the multiple to the particular and the one. But by causing the latter to depend upon the former, they aptly illustrate the dictum "by multiplication a reduction to one."

Multiplication, here rendered in terms of the multicolored wash of seas and the divided dew, descends and is regathered into one, a particular river; that process is paralleled by a reference to the creation of life in general (shells and animalcules) and in particular (man, Paterson). This final rolling in is the action of the sea, but the phrase carries with it all of the previous meanings of rolling in, even as this description of the generation of the Passaic River cannot but connote each of the other kinds of birth—cosmic, evolutionary, individual, and mental—described in the Preface, for all of these are necessary to produce Paterson.

> Rolling in, top up,
> under, thrust and recoil, a great clatter:
> lifted as air, boated, multicolored, a
> wash of seas—
> from mathematics to particulars—
> divided as the dew,
> floating mists, to be rained down and
> regathered into a river that flows
> and encircles:
> shells and animalcules
> generally and so to man,
> to Paterson. (p. 13)

By thematic or conceptual metaphor I mean a metaphor that is composed in accordance with preconceived themes of the poem, which occurs in accordance with and in order to perpetuate this design. It is very similar to allegory, in which, as Josephine Miles says, the sense of relative position within a group or class is carried out through the other implied places.[17]

For the publication of Book III (1949) of *Paterson* Williams wrote:

> I began thinking of writing a long poem upon the resemblance between the mind of modern man and a city. The thing was to use the multiple facets which a city presented as representative for comparable facets of contemporary thought, thus to be able to objectify the man himself as we know him and love him and hate him.[18]

Williams's "Author's Note" to *Paterson* begins this way:

> *Paterson* is a long poem in four parts—that a man is himself a city, beginning, seeking, achieving and concluding his life in ways which the various aspects of a city may embody—if imaginatively conceived—any city, all the details of which may be made to voice his most intimate convictions.

"Detail and Parody for the Poem PATERSON" (a manuscript from about 1939 in the poetry collection of the University of Buffalo) begins "A man like a city and a woman like a flower—who are in love," a passage that in *Paterson I* became:

> A man like a city and a woman like a flower
> —who are in love. Two women. Three women.
> Innumerable women, each like a flower.
> > But
> only one man—like a city. (p. 15)

Initially Williams's plan for the writing of a long poem was to build it upon a thematic metaphor—man:city; woman:flower.

---

17. *Style and Proportion* (Boston, 1967) , p. 124.
18. Quoted by John Thirwall in "William Carlos Williams' 'Paterson,' " *New Directions* 17, ed. J. Laughlin (New York, 1961) : 254.

The controlling metaphor would be what tied any and all segments of the poem to one another; it would be a way to make
a long poem out of a collection of short ones.

Yet in a letter to Henry Wells, who had commented on the
poem, Williams wrote in 1953:

> I conceived the whole of *Paterson* at one stroke and wrote it
> down—as it appears at the beginning of the poem. All I had to
> do after that was fill in the details as I went along, from day
> to day. My life in the district supplied the rest. I did not
> theorize directly where I was writing but went wherever the
> design forced me to go. Many of the things you say about what
> I "thought" are true, but I did not think of them in that way.
> They were there, and I did definitely think and plan them;
> I knew what I was doing, step by step, but I was so mixed
> up with the poetic imagination that I was scarcely conscious
> of what I was about—on a theoretical level.[19]

The kind of metaphor that results from the "design" is not thematic metaphor: it is what I have called "local" metaphor. Local
metaphors occur from moment to moment during the progression
of the poem and arise from the need to express the particular
idea or describe the particular object under consideration at a
given moment. It is from these, rather than from the thematic
metaphors, that the pattern develops that most truly functions
to organize *Paterson.*

In Book I there exists a growing tension between the thematic
metaphors, with which Williams planned to structure his poem,
and the local metaphors that, he seems to have discovered through
the process of writing them, are able to support a structure of
more complex dimensions.

The giants that Williams is delineating in Book I are those
three central actors upon whom the thematic metaphors are
formed—man:city; woman:nature; and water:language, thought,
and the force of creativity. Part I of Book I begins with passages
of pure thematic metaphor.

---

19. *Selected Letters,* p. 333.

Paterson lies in the valley under the Passaic Falls
its spent waters forming the outline of his back. He
lies on his right side, head near the thunder
of the waters filling his dreams! Eternally asleep,
his dreams walk about the city where he persists
incognito. Butterflies settle on his stone ear.
Immortal he neither moves nor rouses and is seldom
seen, though he breathes and the subtleties of his
              machinations
drawing their substance from the noise of the pouring
              river
animate a thousand automatons. (p. 14)

Jostled as are the waters approaching
the brink, his thoughts
interlace, repel and cut under,
rise rock-thwarted and turn aside
but forever strain forward—or strike
an eddy and whirl, marked by a
leaf or curdy spume, seeming
to forget   . (p. 16)

And there, against him, stretches the low mountain,
The Park's her head, carved, above the Falls, by the quiet
river; Colored crystals the secret of those rocks;
farms and ponds, laurel and the temperate wild cactus,
yellow flowered   .   .   facing him, his
arm supporting her, by the *Valley of the Rocks,* asleep.
Pearls at her ankles, her monstrous hair
spangled with apple-blossoms is scattered about into
the back country, waking their dreams—where the deer run
and the wood-duck nests protecting his gallant plumage. (p. 17)

I describe such metaphors as *pure* because in them the poet is
keeping as close to his preconceived scheme of equivalences as
possible, so that his procedure approximates the method of allegory. The description of the man is meant to neatly parallel
that of the city, as the description of the female corresponds to
the mountain and the outlying hills. Yet even within such passages there are phrases that are not so neat, such as, in the description of the water as thoughts, these lines:

> Retake later the advance and
> are replaced by the succeeding hordes
> pushing forward . . . (p. 16)

> glass-smooth with their swiftness . . . (p. 16)

> split apart, ribbons; dazed, drunk
> with the catastrophe of the descent (p. 16)

These are not "neat" because they have brought in other areas of experience, complicating the figure in a way that a phrase like "Eternally asleep,/his dreams walk about the city where he persists/incognito" does not. Within the comparison of thoughts to water have been introduced battles, glass, ribbons, inebriation, and human emotions. In other words, local metaphors have interfered with the pure concept. This is because the poem cannot remain static—city, mountain, water in a suspended moment—but has begun to move and needs to follow where the "design" is taking it.

Book I explores the duality between external and internal, objective and subjective; Williams's terms for it are "idea" and "thing."

> —Say it, no ideas but in things—
> nothing but the blank faces of the houses
> and cylindrical trees
> bent, forked by preconception and accident—
> split, furrowed, creased, mottled, stained—
> secret—into the body of the light! (p. 14)

This passage itself, which occurs on the first page of Book I, offers an example of how metaphor is used to conjoin the two elements in the duality. Objects of the external world are humanized (houses have faces; trees are "secret") , bringing them nearer to the man's internal world of ideas. At the same time, ideas ("preconception") have been given a physical substance, which enables them to split, furrow, crease, mottle, and stain—to bend and fork, that is, to physically shape the objects of the external world. For Williams, speaking both philosophically and techni-

cally, there are to be no ideas but in things. Yet even in the
first expression of this important theme metaphor is the means
by which it must be explained—realized poetically.

The thematic metaphors with which the Book begins establish
the duality on a primary level. They try to directly link man
and his world (man:city; woman:mountain; language:river).
Also, with them Williams makes his first attempt at embodying
ideas in things:

> Jostled as are the waters approaching
> the brink, his thoughts
> interlace, repel and cut under,
> rise rock-thwarted and turn aside
> but forever strain forward . . . (p. 16)

> . . . Inside the bus one sees
> his thoughts sitting and standing. His
> thoughts alight and scatter— (p. 18)

Section 1 also offers an explanation for the existence of the
duality:

> The language, the language
>   fails them
> They do not know the words
>   or have not
> the courage to use them   . (p. 20)

>   —the language
> is divorced from their minds,
> the language   .   .   the language! (p. 21)

Proper use of language neither "false" nor "misunderstood" (p.
24) would lead to a diminishing of the duality, which in its most
extreme form is viewed as "divorce." All of Williams's critical
writing—and, especially, the poem *Paterson,* are to this point.
The situation about which he writes—the present human situation as he sees it—is one of divorce ("The word had been
drained of its meaning," p. 27), yet the writing of the poem is
a move toward solution.

Each of the varied prose and verse sections of Part 1 are either directly or subsequently relevant to this idea. They describe both present things—a *National Geographic* photograph of the wives of an Arab chieftan or "girls from/families that have decayed and/taken to the hills"—and past things—wondrous persons and events from historical Paterson, including a large-headed dwarf, the fall of Mrs. Sarah Cummings into the Falls, and the leaps of Sam Patch into waterfalls.

In Section 2 of Book I the real beginnings of a pattern of metaphor—local metaphors that function according to the design —are apparent. This section begins to explore the idea of "divorce" and also sets into motion ideas about an antithesis to divorce. Each is introduced through the image of a concrete object and is then expanded upon, primarily by means of the metaphors of Part 2.[20]

Divorce is rendered as "a bud forever green" as the section opens:

> a bud forever green,
> tight-curled, upon the pavement, perfect
> in juice and substance but divorced, divorced
> from its fellows, fallen low—
> Divorce is
> the sign of knowledge in our time,
> divorce! divorce! (p. 28)

Later there appear these metaphors:

> —unfledged desire, irresponsible, green,
> colder to the hand than stone,
> unready—challenging our waking (p. 28)

> certainly NOT the university,
> a green bud fallen upon the pavement its
> sweet breath suppressed . . . (p. 32)

---

20. A complete list of the metaphors of Section 2 and Section 3 can be found in Appendix B. As I have said, these metaphors are not so integrated as metaphors are to be in the later books; nevertheless a reading of the complete list yields some sense of their development and relation to one another.

Both are descriptions of the green bud. In the first it is related by metaphor to "unfledged desire"; in the second it is connected to the university. Each of these extensions, in turn, is expanded upon in subsequent metaphors. The first moves directly into a description of "Two halfgrown girls":

> Two—
>   disparate among the pouring
> waters of their hair in which nothing is
> molten—
> two, bound by an instinct to be the same:
> ribbons, cut from a piece,
> cerise pink, binding their hair . . . (p. 29)

The girls are instances of unfledged desire, and they are "disparate." Even their hair falls in separate strands; the metaphor associates it with the waterfall, which has been shown earlier to be an embodiment of divorce: "A false language pouring" (p. 24). Nevertheless, they are yet "bound by an instinct to be the same"; they bind their hair with ribbons from the same material. This instinct in the divorced for reintegration (an instinct for survival) becomes central to the poem's argument. The girls return later in the Section, crying aloud "Divorce!" The lines that precede their appearance at that point are "Divorce (the/ language stutters) /unfledged" (p. 32).

With the introduction of the university as still another manifestation of divorce Williams begins his attack on sterile learning and writing, which is to reach maximum expression in *Paterson III* ("The Library").

In Book I the antithesis of the green bud (divorce) is called "first beauty."[21] Later it will become the central preoccupation of the poem—the beautiful thing. Here Williams begins to develop the concept through images and metaphors that involve a green branch, a first wife, and another bud.

As Paterson ruminates upon his poem and its themes in Part

---

21. The Preface to Book I begins with these lines: " 'Rigor of beauty is the quest. But how will you find beauty when it is locked in the mind past all remonstrance?' " (p. 11).

2 he is, as he says, "watching": standing on the embankment, watching the river.

> —and watch, wrapt! one branch
> of the tree at the fall's edge, one
> mottled branch, withheld,
> among the gyrate branches
> of the waist-thick sycamore,
> sway less, among the rest, separate, slowly
> with giraffish awkwardness, slightly
> on a long axis, so slightly
> as hardly to be noticed, in itself the tempest:
> Thus
> the first wife, with giraffish awkwardness
> among the thick lightnings that stab at
> the mystery of a man: in sum, a sleep, a
> source, a scourge .
> on a log, her varnished hair
> trussed up like a termite's nest (forming
> the lines) and her old thighs
> gripping the log reverently, that,
> all of a piece, holds up the others—
> alert: begin to know the mottled branch
> that sings   . (pp. 31–32)

The first wife is the first of the nine women of an African chieftain. She appeared in Part I as last in a "descending scale of freshness," as "supporting all the rest growing/up from her"; all the wives are, like branches, "astraddle a log, an official log to/ be presumed." In Part 2 her reappearance is a direct repercussion of the description of a branch by the river edge. The word "thus" links branch and wife; so, more emphatically, does the vocabulary used to describe her. Like the branch, she, too, moves with "giraffish awkwardness"; the log gripped by her thighs is "all of a piece," a phrase that next occurs in a subsequent passage about the branch. The reintroduction of the wife is followed by the metaphor of the university as a green bud, the reappearance of the two sisters crying, "Divorce!", and then the second description of the swaying branch.

While

> the green bush sways: is whence
> I draw my breath, swaying, all of a piece,
> separate, livens briefly, for the moment
> unafraid   .   . (pp. 32–33)

The reason for connecting the green branch and the first wife, and for describing them at all, is made apparent in the long sequence of metaphors that follows:

> Which is to say, though it be poorly
> said, that there is a first wife
> and a first beauty, complex, ovate—
> the woody sepals standing back under
> the stress to hold it there, innate
>
> a flower within a flower whose history
> (within the mind) crouching
> among the ferny rocks, laughs at the names
> by which they think to trap it. Escapes!
> Never by running but by lying still—
>
> A history that has, by its den in the
> rocks, boles and fangs, its own cane-brake
> whence, half hid, canes and stripes
> blending, it grins (beauty defied)
> not for the sake of the encyclopedia.
>
> Were we near enough its stinking breath
> would fell us. The temple upon
> the rock is its brother, whose majesty
> lies in jungles—made to spring,
> at the rifle-shot of learning: to kill   (p. 33)

It is to say that there is a first wife and a first beauty, which is, in turn, a flower—a bud. The qualities shared by branch and wife both viewed as organic entities, as sources for potency, as moving alone to a special rhythm—are even more clearly manifested in the metaphor that makes of first beauty a bud—complex, ovate, and innate. Yet later in the passage the wild first beauty is explicitly shown to be the enemy of "the rifle shot of learning"

(the university, which is a green bud fallen upon the pavement).
Both, then, are buds; the latter, however, has fallen and been
separated from the living plant, "forever green" and "tight-
curled." (It was relevant that in the passage about the two girls
one of them had in her hand "a willow twig pulled from a low/
leafless bush in full bud.") Metaphor, by asserting that both are
buds, indicates shared qualities is well as differences; this recalls
the earlier line, "two, bound by an instinct to be the same."

Other phrases in the section continue to express this idea:
"parallel but never mingling" and "one unlike the other, twin/
of the other, conversant with eccentricities/side by side . . .
vergent" (p. 37). It is in many respects an expression of the
theory behind Williams's use of metaphor in *Paterson*. Divorce
is the universal condition; however, the separated yearn for unity,
which is ideally possible but consistently difficult to attain. The
mind is divorced from the world, which leads to countless subsequent dualities.

As Section 2 continues, its metaphors occur within discussions
of divorce and lists of objects and entities from "separate worlds,"
yet they consistently display the characteristics mentioned above:
they tend to conjoin the elements of dualities even as they announce the existence of those dualities. In most cases this is
achieved by making things of ideas (". . . the whole din of fracturing thought/as it falls to nothing upon the streets," p. 34)
or by bringing things closer to ideas—to the human mind—primarily through the personification of objects. The following example combines both, for events are personified while language
is objectified. Their dance is an enactment of what is at once
the seemingly irrevocable connection and separation of events
and language.

> The vague accuracies of events dancing two
> and two with language which they
> forever surpass . . . (p. 34)

This is also the form of the metaphors in the next passage, perhaps the most eloquent statement in Section 2 of the condition

it is constantly attempting to describe. Air and water are personified: they are "brother to brother"; water curls; air observes and
brings in rumors; water soothes the air as it "drives in . . . fit-
fully." On the other hand, the mind touches (as do air and
water, "counter-current," "parallel but never mingling"), and
eccentricities are said to be "side by side."

> And the air lying over the water
> lifts the ripples, brother
> to brother, touching as the mind touches,
> counter-current, upstream
> brings in the fields, hot and cold
> parallel but never mingling, one that whirls
> backward at the brink and curls invisibly
> upward, fills the hollow, whirling,
> an accompaniment—but apart, observant of
> the distress, sweeps down or up clearing
> the spray—
>
>   brings in the rumors of separate
> worlds, the birds as against the fish, the grape
> to the green weed the streams out undulant
> with the current at low tide beside the
> bramble in blossom, the storm by the flood—
> song and wing—
>
>   one unlike the other, twin
> of the other, conversant with eccentricities
> side by side, bearing the water-drops
> and snow, vergent, the water soothing the air when
> it drives in among the rocks fitfully— (pp. 36–37)

In Section 3 of Book I the duality between thought and thing
is being probed, primarily in terms of the relation between
physical and mental acts.

In Part 3 Paterson has become a particular human being,
identified (although not yet named) as Dr. Paterson. He picks
up hairpins, smells his hands, rolls his thumb about the tip of
his left index finger—and he goes on thinking. His thoughts are
concerned with facts and details—of death and of living, of the

past and of the present. Especially, prose and verse juxtapose details of the wondrous deaths from Paterson's past against details of present-day life in Paterson.

In this section, shorter than the others in Book I, there is perhaps the greatest contrast in language. The details and facts are rendered in language that is spare and precise:

> He descried
> in the linoleum at his feet a woman's
> face, smelled his hands,
> strong of a lotion he had used
> not long since, lavender,
> rolled his thumb
>
> about the tip of his left index finger . . . (pp. 41–42)

> Cornelius Doremus, who was baptized at Acquackonock
> in 1714, and died near Montville in 1803, was possessed
> of goods and chattels appraised at $419.58 1/2. He
> was 89 years old when he died, and doubtless had turned
> his farm over to his children, so that he retained
> only what he needed for his personal comfort:
> 24 shirts at .82 1/2 cents, $19.88: 5 sheets, $7.00:
> 4 pillow cases, $2.12: 4 pair trousers, $2.00:
> 1 sheet, $1.37 1/2: a handkerchief, $1.75: 8 caps, .75
> cents: 2 pairs shoebuckles and knife, .25 cents . . . . (p. 45)

> Things, things unmentionable,
> the sink with the waste farina in it and
> lumps of rancid meat, milk-bottle tops . . . (p. 51)

As Section 3 begins, the careful descriptions of Dr. Paterson's activities are juxtaposed (the series of colons are significant, as they usually are in this poem) against the simultaneous actions of his thoughts.

> . . . of
> earth his ears are full, there is no sound
>
> :And his thoughts soared

> to the magnificence of imagined delights
> where he would probe
>
> as into the pupil of an eye
> as through a hoople of fire, and emerge
> sheathed in a robe
>
> streaming with light. What heroic
> dawn of desire
> is denied to his thoughts?
>
> They are trees
> from whose leaves streaming with rain
> his mind drinks of desire : (p. 42)

The imaginative excess of this passage is emphasized because of its proximity to acts such as picking hairpins and smelling hands. Not only are thoughts given a physical form that allows them to soar and to have desires that may be either denied or granted them, but they actually become trees. Further, his mind, an animal of some kind, drinks of desire from the leaves of the tree, thought (desire manifests itself in heroic dawns) and he himself can both probe the magnificence of imagined delights and emerge sheathed in a robe streaming with light. Earlier in Book I Williams had written of "The vague accuracies of events dancing two/and two with language which they/forever surpass"; the doctrine of "no ideas but in things" itself tacitly places superiority with the things. The whole of *Paterson* is an attack on thought and language that are divorced from the world of actuality. But the problem is not this simple, as Williams's theory of the imagination and this Section of Book I demonstrate, for in this passage metaphors emphasize that mental acts may have greater significance and dimension than physical acts. Metaphor must do this (the passage is a composite of extravagant metaphors) , for metaphor is the linguistic embodiment of the imagination, which alone can bridge the gap between idea and thing.

The most extreme metaphor in this passage is, in the lines that immediately follow it, extended into a conceit. If thoughts are trees, then undeveloped thought, or youth, is a twig; the mature man, Paterson, is the mature tree.

> Who is younger than I?
>   The contemptible twig?
> that I was? stale in mind
>   whom the dirt
>
> recently gave up? Weak
>   to the wind.
> Gracile? Taking up no place,
> too narrow to be engraved
>   with the maps
>
> of a world it never knew,
>   the green and
> dovegrey countries of the mind.
>
> A mere stick that has
>   twenty leaves
> against my convolutions.
>   What shall it become,
>
> Snot nose, that I have
>   not been?
> I enclose it and
>   persist, go on.
>
> Let it rot, at my center.
>   Whose center?
> I stand and surpass
>   youth's leanness.
>
> My surface is my self.
>   Under which
> to witness, youth is
>   buried. Roots?
>
> Everybody has roots. (pp. 42–44)

Within the conceit are supplementary metaphors. One of them, in particular, once more grants a significant status to the mental world. The young tree is weak, small, and "too narrow" to have (to translate) undergone complex mental experiences. The metaphor speaks in terms of his (its) not having been engraved with the maps of "the green and dovegrey countries of the mind." But again, the manner in which metaphor makes such an assertation is by depicting that "world" as a physical one, even as it had previously done in Section 2 in the description of the first beauty, which lived (within the mind) in a den among ferny rocks. Metaphor's ability to explore dualities lies precisely in its power to transpose qualities and characteristics, and the method of metaphor seems to be the answer to the prose question that introduces the Preface to Book I: " 'Rigor of beauty is the quest. But how will you find beauty when it is locked in the mind past all remonstrance?' "

Another important aspect of the metaphor of twig and tree is its resolution:

> My surface is myself.
> Under which
> to witness, youth is
> buried. Roots?
>
> Everybody has roots.

The statement that "my surface is myself" has several meanings. First, that the self is what one is at present, not what one has been—or will be, presumably. Also that one is one's actions (the surface), yet these acts are not independent from what is "under" them—roots (the inner world?). The passage ends with a cliché phrase—a "dead" metaphor—"Everybody has roots." One thing that the long extended metaphor has done is to resurrect that metaphor and to develop its meanings—meanings of roots.

The section continues into another repudiation of the university and what it stands for as the goal of life.

> We go on living, we permit ourselves
> to continue—but certainly
> not for the university, what they publish

> severally or as a group: clerks
> got out of hand forgetting for the most part
> to whom they are beholden.

> spitted on fixed concepts like
> roasted hogs, sputtering, their drip sizzling
> in the fire

> Something else, something else the same. (p. 44)

Its members are clerks got out of hand—they are spitted on fixed concepts like hogs, and they drip and sputter into the fire. The metaphor in the third stanza is an ironic way of asserting the discrepancy in the university between ideas and things, using the same technique that Williams has employed throughout the Book. The making of ideas (fixed concepts) into things (skewers) produces a very physical scene of blood and fire, the very opposite of the dry intellectual pursuits of the university, which we know to be divorced from reality, a "green bud fallen upon the pavement."

Later in the section, Paterson, standing along the river, looking upon the factories, is concerned once again with the nature of his own thoughts.

> What can he think else—along
> the gravel of the ravished park, torn by
> the wild worker's children tearing up the grass,
> kicking? screaming? A chemistry, corollary
> to academic misuse, which the theorem
> with accuracy, accurately misses   .   .

> He thinks: their mouths eating and kissing,
> spitting and sucking, speaking; a
> partitype of five   .

> He thinks: two eyes; nothing escapes them,
> neither the convolutions of the sexual orchid
> hedged by fern and honey smells, to
> the last hair of the consent of the dying.

> And silk spins from the hot drums to a music
> of pathetic souvenirs, a comb and nail-file
> in an imitation leather case—to
> remind him, to remind him! (p. 49)

Again, the metaphors that occur in the third stanza function to include mental acts in the totality of an experience and to underline their importance. In the first of the two stanzas beginning "He thinks:", the citizens of Paterson are considered as grossly physical segments. Sister M. Bernetta Quinn links this stanza with the following one in her comment:

> Since there are no ideas but in things, Paterson thinks of mouths eating, kissing, spitting, sucking, speaking; of eyes; of silk-producing machines; of pathetic souvenirs such as a comb and nail-file in an imitation leather case, or a photograph holder.[22]

Misconstruing the complexity of a concept like *no ideas but in things*, Sister Quinn also misconstrues the things, such as the silk-producing machine, of the second passage. The silk-producing machine is not a literal thing but a metaphor for the process of life; metaphors, too, are the sexual orchid, the hot drums, and the music of pathetic souvenirs. Yet to be able to talk about death and life, even among factory workers, words like "eating," "kissing," or "spitting," which isolate physical acts, are insufficient to represent the whole. The metaphors are an imaginative extension of the experience. Albeit these thoughts are expressed in terms of physical objects, they are not those objects at which Paterson is actually looking. In this sense the process of metaphor is also an abstracting one, abstracting orchid out of kissing to reveal a fuller meaning.

Paterson continues to think about and describe the life he sees as he drives out to the suburbs or peers in tenement windows, but he concludes his series of factual details with the observation that things unmentionable have

---

22. *The Metaphoric Tradition in Modern Poetry* (New Brunswick, N.J., 1955) , p. 105.

> here a tranquility and loveliness
> Have here (in his thoughts)
> a complement tranquil and chaste.   (p. 51)

The last verse sequence in Section 3 is the following:

> Thought clambers up,
> snail like, upon the wet rocks
> hidden from sun and sight—
>   hedged in by the pouring torrent—
>
> and has its birth and death there
> in that moist chamber, shut from
> the world—and unknown to the world,
> cloaks itself in mystery—
>
>   And the myth
> that holds up the rock,
> that holds up the water thrives there—
> in that cavern, that profound cleft,
>   a flickering green
> inspiring terror, watching   .   .
>
> And standing, shrouded there, in that din,
> Earth, the chatterer, father of all
> speech   .   .   .   .   (pp. 51–52)

This return to the thematic metaphor of the opening pages of Book I is nowhere pure; it is complicated by both the techniques of metaphor and the ideas that Williams has been developing throughout the book. Sister Bernetta's reading of the passage entirely within its thematic framework reveals, by what it omits, wherein the complications are to be found.

> The first book closes with Thought, personified, climbing up like a snail on the wet rocks of the cavern behind the Falls. Earth is not only our mother, but the father of all speech (Pater*son*), the chatterer (Paterson is often spelled Patterson), a chamber private as a skull to which the world has no access and from which man cannot truly know the world. The torrent (the language) pours down before it, hiding it from sun and sight. In the cavern resides the force that gives reality

to all external phenomena. .... Time, in the traditional symbol of the serpent, is the fact that makes real the physical universe.[23]

The chamber being described is not only, as Sister Bernetta says, "private as a skull"—it is the skull, for surely the passage can be read as yet another of Book I's descriptions of "the green and/dovegrey countries of/the mind." Is not the mind the place where thought clambers—a "moist chamber" that is actually "shut from/the world"? The "pouring torrent" is at once literally the falls and metaphorically language (water described metaphorically as language) and literally language and metaphorically the falls (language described metaphorically as water). In this passage metaphor conjoins the elements of the external-internal duality by balancing them. Through metaphor the mental act is a physical one, even as the physical act is a mental one (i.e., an instance of a thematic metaphor). As always, in its technique of making things of ideas and ideas of things, it communicates simultaneously the existence of the divorce and the tendency—and route—toward union. In this final description of the falls with which the book began, the "giants" of Williams's thematic metaphors reappear—here referred to as Earth, Thought, and "the myth"—but the metaphors that depict them follow the techniques Williams has begun to use with his local metaphors. Already, in this way, the poem has come a great deal closer to creating "the resemblance between the mind of man and a city."

Paterson I reveals a poet at work learning how to write his poem. In the process of setting up his palette—of setting forth what are to be the ingredients of his long poem, its characters and themes—he seems to discover a method for putting them into action. The method involves metaphor: specifically, local metaphors that form patterns that can structure such a varied and heterogeneous work. His original plan, involving the use of thematic or conceptual metaphors to draw together the poem's many segments, is modified as it becomes apparent that such

---

23. Pp. 105–6.

metaphors work at one level only and cannot handle the many subtle dimensions in which the poem needs to move.

Paterson I is concerned with man's relation to his world. It sees the mind as cut off, or divorced, from the world, primarily because of the improper use of language. Man's imagination has the power to bridge the gap, but it needs language, as its agent, to accomplish this. Each of the sections of Book I explores the existing dualities that result from this divorce, such as that between general and particular, objective and subjective, concrete and abstract, physical and mental. Williams himself articulates the problem with his terms *idea* and *thing*. He announces that in *Paterson* there are to be "no ideas but in things," which on its simplest level means that he will refrain from abstract (hence empty and meaningless) statements, but will rather embody his concepts in things—in objects, people, and events. As he proceeds it becomes apparent that metaphor is the primary agent for the making of ideas into things, because, literally, the two are separate. Also, as the poem proceeds, the complexities involved in such a notion begin to emerge, as Williams explores in greater detail the nature of both ideas and things. Section 2 reveals the need for—and route toward—unity inherent in every instance of divorce. In language, metaphor can accomplish this by at once conjoining but never merging the elements of any duality or divorce. Section 3 reveals the importance of ideas— mental acts—to experience. Here metaphor embodies them in things, but things that are the creation of the imagination. By the time Williams returns to thematic metaphor at the conclusion of the book, his poem has begun to move, to go where the design forced him to go, so that the basically static nature of the thematic metaphor has been reinforced by the added dimensions achieved by local metaphor.

III

In the next three books Paterson explores his world. In Book II, "Sunday in the Park," he takes a walk in the park outside of the city and observes the activities of the citizens there. In Book III, "The Library," he enters the Paterson public library and reads, exploring mankind through the written words it has produced. These two books may be seen as separate extensions of the fundamental duality around which Book I was structured: that of internal-external; subjective-objective; idea-thing. Book II investigates the external world; Book III investigates the internal world. Book IV is perhaps the most fragmented in that, although its three sections are bound together thematically, they have different settings. The first section is almost a playlet, set in New York City. The others range in time and space, for they have begun to inhabit the spaces of memory. This book may be said to explore the implications and results of the subjective-objective duality.

In Book II Williams explores the duality of artifact and artist intensively in three metaphoric passages, one occurring in each of the three sections into which the book is divided. In Section 1 he uses a specific experience that Paterson undergoes in the park, the sight of the intermittent flight of grasshoppers, to discuss the creative process itself, involving the grasshoppers as subject matter, a stone grasshopper as artifact, and the mind of the artist, his imagination. The metaphors in this long sequence establish the underlying relations among the three and in this way explore the duality. In Section 2 the metaphoric passage is a prayer, in yet another depiction of artist and artifact, which concentrates upon the female aspect of the rock, or artifact, as opposed to the maleness of the artist. In Section 3 the metaphoric passage discusses the opposite of the creative act, or the element of descent in the subsidiary duality of ascent and descent. Throughout the remainder of these sections other kinds of action and language reinforce the movement of the major metaphoric passages.

Book II opens with the following lines, which serve as an introduction to its themes:

Outside

<pre>
                    outside myself
                                    there is a world,
        he rumbled, subject to my incursions
        —a world
                        (to me) at rest,
                                which I approach
        concretely—
                        The scene's the Park
                        upon the rock,
                        female to the city
        —upon whose body Paterson instructs his thoughts
        (concretely)
                            —late spring,
                    a Sunday afternoon! (p. 57)
</pre>

Paterson spends Book II in approaching, concretely, the world outside himself by observing the citizens who are seeking pleasure in the park. The connection between sex and language, love and poetry, a thematic concern in Book II, is revealed in this opening passage—"upon whose body Paterson instructs his thoughts/(concretely)." Both are versions of the creative act. Here and earlier in this passage the word *concretely* already carries several important meanings: it refers both to the fact that Paterson will physically join the citizens (he will not only think, but walk, so that great emphasis is placed upon the physical fact of his walking) and also to the essence of the rock, itself, upon which the scene is laid and around which it is structured. The rock is "female to the city."

Paterson walks throughout Book II. Early in Part 1 the first long metaphoric passage occurs.

<pre>
        Walking—
                he leaves the path, finds hard going
                across-field, stubble and matted brambles
                seeming a pasture—but no pasture   .
                —old furrows, to say labor sweated or
                had sweated here   .

                                            a flame
        spent.
</pre>

              The file-sharp grass   .

When! from before his feet, half tripping,
picking a way, there starts   .
              a flight of empurpled wings!
—invisibly created (their
jackets dust-grey) from the dust kindled
to sudden ardor!

              They fly away, churring! until
their strength spent they plunge
to the coarse cover again and disappear
—but leave, livening the mind, a flashing
of wings and a churring song   .

AND a grasshopper of red basalt, boot-long,
tumbles from the core of his mind,
a rubble-bank disintegrating beneath a tropic
downpour
Chapultepec! grasshopper hill!

—a matt stone solicitously instructed
to bear away some rumor
of the living presence that has preceded
it, out-precedented its breath   .

These wings do not unfold for flight—
no need!
the weight (to the hand) finding
a counter-weight or counter buoyancy
by the mind's wings   .

He is afraid! What then?
Before his feet at each step, the flight
is renewed. A burst of wings, a quick
churring sound   :

              couriers to the ceremonial of love!

—aflame in flight!
              —aflame only in flight!

                    No flesh but the caress!

He is led forward by their announcing wings. . . .
(pp. 61–63)

[prose section]

his mind a red stone carved to be
endless flight   .
Love that is a stone endlessly in flight,
so long as stone shall last bearing
the chisel's stroke   .

.   .   and is lost and covered
with ash, falls from an undermined bank
and—begins churring!
AND DOES, the stone after the life!

The stone lives, the flesh dies
—we know nothing of death.

—boot long
window-eyes that front the whole head,
Red stone! as if
a light still clung in them   .

Love

combating sleep
———————————
the sleep
piecemeal   (pp. 63–64)

In this long passage, metaphor—much as it did in many of
Williams's short poems—renders the complexity and fullness of
a moment of perception. The difference now is that this perception is no longer isolated in time and space from any other
perceptions or experiences. Rather, it is a section of a long
poem, composed of many such experiences. Even without the
transfers of metaphor the experience is rich in associations and
meanings. Not one metaphoric "leap" but a succession of metaphors are necessary here to reveal the full significance of the
experience. These metaphors order the passage much as a trip-
tych painting orders its components—by presenting a simultaneous spatial balancing, rather than a sequential development
(the ripples on the pond). Metaphor, using a vocabulary of

wings, flame, and stone, creates a structure of "interpenetrating realities," each one representing an aspect of a total concept and incomplete in itself.

The perception is that of the rising and falling motion of grasshoppers, moving before his feet as he walks.[24] Williams finds

---

24. Sister Bernetta, describing this passage, writes that Paterson

is led forward by the intermittent flights of grasshoppers. Next follow images that are protean indeed; uniting stasis and motion, his mind is shown metamorphosing into a carved red stone in flight (which also incorporates the woman in her role as the red rock of the Park), then into a live grasshopper. . . . Love, another meaning attributed to the stone, is the only force strong enough to break the power of that sleep which prevents wholeness, the creative act here being identified with love as one of its manifestations.

In the poetic statement, "The stone lives, the flesh dies," Williams wishes to indicate how art outlives man. (p. 107)

Sister Bernetta's terms, such as *incorporates, another meaning attributed, manifestations,* and of course, *metamorphosing,* point to what is indeed the protean character of the entire passage. Yet metamorphosis is not metaphor, and both have a place in *Paterson.* Sister Bernetta identifies metamorphosis—"a striking alteration in appearance, character or circumstances . . . a passing from one form or shape into another" (p. 3) —as that agent by which the modern poet transcends "the boundaries of matter" (p. 13). She sees many functions for metamorphosis in modern poetry, viewing it as a way of giving bodies to ideas and emotions "from which gift springs their power to appeal to men in human terms" (p. 44); as verbal equations for contemporary emotional situations (p. 5); as "descriptive of the natural world and the way in which that world is known" (p. 8); and in its highest finite forms, as "baptism and its culmination, the resurrection of the body to glory" (p. 12). A problem with her approach is that, even in the above statements, she does not discriminate between "the metamorphic principle" and the use in modern poetry of ancient metamorphoses or the creation of new ones. Her conclusions about the latter are more accurate than these about the former, for it is when she is discussing the metamorphic principle that she often confuses its characteristics with those of metaphor, as her description of the grasshopper sequence indicates. Thus she is correct in identifying Williams's creation of Paterson as a new myth "in which a super-human character adopts identity after identity while yet retaining a recognizable self. Such a character is Paterson, a modern god of place" (p. 8). However, she ignores Williams's expressed desire that the "perfections" of "the two instruments" be emphasized by the joiner, rather than the blending of the tones of the oboe with the violin. Metaphor, by setting up a relation, by being a "partial yet double statement" (Josephine Miles, *Style and Proportion,* p. 127), results in simultaneity rather than fusion. Shapes shift, but they never dissolve or merge. Nevertheless, the distinction between the principle of metamorphosis and metamorphoses is a good clue to the nature of the distinction that I have made between Williams's thematic metaphors and his local ones. The former are very close to being metamorphoses; the latter are very far.

The grasshopper sequence is a good example of the metaphoric principle (Williams's) in operation, in which meaning derives from spatial simultaneity.

in his experience of the flight of grasshoppers elements that reveal something about the relation of artifact to artist, art to life. Each metaphor used clarifies Williams's statement of his ideas by adding another form—and dimension—to the experience itself.

In Book I metaphor created a pattern with which there might be no ideas but in things. Here the now-familiar pattern is put to use for purposes beyond the simple enactment of that dictum. The following is a list of the specific instances of metaphor with which this passage is formed. The words in parentheses are the subjects of metaphors where they are not self-explanatory from the text.

	1) old furrows, to say labor sweated or /had sweated here
(labor)	2) a flame,/spent
	3) the file-sharp grass
(a flight of wings)	4) invisibly created/. . . from the dust
"	5) kindled/to sudden ardor
(grasshoppers)	6) leave, livening the mind, a flashing /of wings and a churring song
	7) AND a grasshopper of red basalt, boot long,/tumbles from the core of his mind,/a rubble-bank disintegrating beneath a/tropic downpour
	8) —a matt stone solicitously instructed/ to bear away some rumor/of the living presence that has preceded/it, out-precedented its breath .
(these wings)	9) the weight (to the hand) finding/a counter-weight or counter buoyancy/ by the mind's wings .
(wings)	10) couriers to the ceremonial of love
"	11) aflame in flight!/aflame only in flight!
	12) their announcing wings

13) his mind a red stone carved to be/ endless flight   .

14) Love that is a stone endlessly in flight

(the stone)   15) and—begins churring!/AND DOES, the stone after the life!

16) The stone lives, the flesh dies

17) window-eyes

18) Love/combating sleep

19) the sleep/piecemeal

As we have come to expect, *ideas* are constantly rendered through metaphor as things, and *things* are personified. Clear examples of the former are numbers seven, in which the core of his mind becomes a physical place from which a stone grasshopper can tumble, and nine, in which the mind has wings that have weight or buoyancy (is thus, we know from the context, a grasshopper). Abstractions are also versions of ideas, as in number fourteen, in which love is a stone. Number ten is a good example of the personification of things; through metaphor wings become couriers. Again, in number eight, a stone is instructed to bear away some rumor. In addition, many of these metaphors conjoin one thing to another thing, as in eleven, in which wings, being aflame, are wood or fire, and in number seventeen, in which eyes are windows. This constant shifting of qualities and characteristics accomplishes several purposes. It links labor, flames, wings, stones, the mind, love, and messengers each to the other in a succession of pairings, so that what emerges is a perception of the interpenetration of these things. Labor is a flame; grasshopper wings are a flame; a flame is love. The mind is a place. The stone is a messenger. The mind is a grasshopper. Grasshopper wings are messengers and flames. The mind is a stone grasshopper. Love is a stone grasshopper. The stone grasshopper is a live one.

The duality being explored is that between artist and artifact, which is yet another version of the basic idea-thing relation.

Here however, the object involved is something that the mind has itself created. This is why the investigation of the boundaries between inner and outer is so especially crucial, and why Williams is at great pains to try to break down these boundaries (through metaphor) in order to show ways in which each must of necessity (that the creative process take place) interpenetrate with the other.

Even before the grasshoppers have been sighted, metaphor links the once-fertile pasture, a woman's act of giving birth, and the flaring and extinguishing of a flame: "—old furrows, to say labor sweated or/had sweated here   ./a flame,/spent." When the grasshoppers do rise, then fall, they too are flames—love flames, as "empurpled," "kindled," and "ardor" reveal. Yet even after they have disappeared from sight, they remain; they leave their flashing wings and churring song "livening the mind." The afterimage (in the mind) is rendered as a continuation of the physical event.

The next sequence, from "AND a grasshopper of red basalt" to "the mind's wings," begins weaving together wings, stone, birth, love, flame, earth, and mind into a single narrative. This sequence is a series of appositional phrases, phrases never connected by words of cause or effect, only by commas, dashes, exclamation points, or no punctuation at all. At the heart of the passage is "Chapultepec!" Chapultepec is the name of a rocky hill outside of Mexico City and also of the palace, gardens, park, and museum built upon it. Chapultepec, therefore, has a kinship with the park in which Paterson is walking, it, too, being built upon a rock. Chapultepec, especially, is a type for art built from rock, with its magnificently fashioned palaces and gardens and its national museum, which contains stone relics of a "dead" culture, made by dead men. "Chapultepec" means "grasshopper hill" in the Nahautl language. Thus Chapultepec is a stone grasshopper, which is a work of art.

The two stanzas that precede and follow the exclamation, "Chapultepec! grasshopper hill!" make of the mind a place, then personify the stone artifact. The appositional structure of the clause, "a rubble-bank disintegrating beneath a/tropic downpour," makes it appear to modify "the core of his mind." The rubble-bank under the tropic downpour also seems to be (there is no punctuation between it and the Chapultepec phrase) the grasshopper hill, so that metaphor indicates that the mind is Chapultepec itself (Chapultepec as a type of art built from rock). Conversely, the stone image (a stone grasshopper), because it has been "solicitously instructed/to bear away some rumor" and even more significantly because "breath" has been granted to it (the "living presence that has preceded it" has "outprecedented its breath"), is bequeathed some of the life of its creator.

The following stanza announces that these (the stone) wings do not unfold for flight; there is "no need!"—no need because of the existence of a counter-weight or counter buoyancy: the mind's wings, which presumably do unfold for flight. Here Williams is positing the necessity and existence of not two but three sets of wings in the creative process: the wings of the observed grasshopper, stone wings, and the mind's wings. (These can be interpreted as object, work of art, and imagination. Once again it is the imagination that mediates, here between object and artifact, as a counter-buoyancy. Its "flight" is its movement, necessary to the creative process.)

The process is a recurrent one: "at each step, the flight/is renewed." The next series of short metaphors, making the "announcing" wings "couriers to the ceremonial of love," describing them as "aflame in flight," reinforces the association of the wings—and, by implication, the creative process—with love that was begun earlier in the passage when the wings were described as "invisibly created/. . . from the dust kindled/to sudden ardor." Now they are again flames and also couriers that announce; in other words, they, like the stone in an earlier stanza, are personified because they are viewed as message-carrying (in the earlier lines they bore rumors). Love, as was indicated in the opening description of the furrows where labor sweated (a flame, spent) is also an aspect of the creative process; hence, labor is also a flame.

After a prose interruption (this celebration of integrated form juxtaposed against a statement from Paterson's unhappy poetess correspondent concerning her personal state of "divorce," discussed in terms of inner and outer, reality and unreality) the final complexities of the experience are set forth.

His mind is a red stone (the artifact, a stone grasshopper); love is also a stone. Both are "endlessly in flight." Both the flight (the creative process—the movement of the imagination that results in an artifact that then communicates something of its creator) and its endlessness are emphasized here and as the stanza continues. It says that the process is endless so long as the stone, bearing the chisel's stroke, shall last; and it does— lost, covered, it yet "falls from an undermined bank/and—begins churring!" The "dead" stone becomes a "live" grasshopper, by virtue of falling from the bank of the mind. In this way "The stone lives, the flesh dies/—we know nothing of death."

Williams has used metaphor to express the complex meaning inherent in a moment of perception. On the next page he generalizes upon the same ideas, and the result is an eloquent contrast to the grasshopper sequence. Here language, concrete but almost entirely literal, states a general truth.

> Without invention nothing is well spaced,
> unless the mind change, unless
> the stars are new measures, according
> to their relative positions, the
> line will not change, the necessity
> will not matriculate: unless there is
> a new mind there cannot be a new
> line, the old will go on
> repeating itself with recurring
> deadliness: without invention
> nothing lies under the witch-hazel
> bush, the alder does not grow from among
> the hummocks margining the all
> but spent channel of the old swale,
> the small foot-prints
> of the mice under the overhanging
> tufts of the bunch-grass will not
> appear: without invention the line

> will never again take on its ancient
> divisions when the word, a supple word,
> lived in it, crumbled now to chalk. (p. 65)

Again all forms of creativity (invention) are linked—cosmic,
physical, mental—for all are manifestations of the same force
and must not be divorced from one another. Only in the final
lines does a metaphor occur, used once again to assert one of
Williams's firm beliefs, that words are things.

In the remainder of Section 1 Paterson, wandering through
the park, observes it and its inhabitants: "a park, devoted to
pleasure: devoted to . grasshoppers!" (p. 66). In almost every
scene he sees an unresolved tension (or divorce) between
natural impulse and some form of blockage:

> Minds beaten thin
> by waste—among
> the working classes SOME sort
> of breakdown
> has occurred . . . (pp. 66–67)

Thus a reference to the grasshopper sequence takes on a de-
graded form:

> their pitiful thoughts do meet
>
> in the flesh—surrounded
> by churring loves! Gay wings
> to bear them (in sleep)
>
> —their thoughts alight,
> away . . . (p. 67)

Williams's comment on the situation is succinctly expressed in
lines that occur after he has compared the sight of an old lady
dancing to "the peon in the lost/Eisenstein film drinking/from
a wine-skin with the abandon/of a horse drinking/. . . Heavenly
man!" He points to "the leer, the cave of it/the female of it
facing the male, the satyr" and concludes:

Rejected. Even the film
suppressed : but . persistent (p. 74)

Section 2 immediately announces its thematic extension of
Section 1: "Blocked./(Make a song out of that: concretely)."
In Section 2 Paterson hears the haranguing, monotonous evange-
list address an audience of a few children. His theme is the evil
of money. The prose passages provide a counter-melody with
their Pound-esque indictment of the Federal Reserve System,
initiated by Hamilton, who "had been impressed by the site of
the Great Falls of the Passaic . . ." (p. 87). The "Federal Reserve Banks constitute a Legalized National Usury System, whose
Customer No. 1 is our Government" (p. 91). Suddenly, after
many pages of this, a new tone is heard:

If there is subtlety,
you are subtle. I beg your indulgence:
no prayer should cause you anything
but tears. I had a friend . . .
let it pass. I remember when as a child
I stopped praying and shook with fear
until sleep—your sleep calmed me—

You also, I am sure, have read
Frazer's Golden Bough. It does you
justice—a prayer such as might be made
by a lover who
appraises every feature of his bride's
comeliness, and terror—
terror to him such as one, a man
married, feels toward his bride—

You are the eternal bride and
father—quid pro quo,
a simple miracle that knows
the branching sea, to which the oak
is coral, the coral oak.
The Himalayas and prairies
of your features amaze and delight—

Why should I move from this place

where I was born? knowing
how futile would be the search
for you in the multiplicity
of your debacle. The world spreads
for me like a flower opening—and
will close for me as might a rose—

wither and fall to the ground
and rot and be drawn up
into a flower again. But you
never wither—but blossom
all about me. In that I forget
myself perpetually—in your
composition and decomposition
I find my   .   .
                                    despair! (pp. 92–93)

J. Hillis Miller describes the beautiful thing of Book III
(the "first beauty" of Book I) as a "hidden flame":

present in the ground but invisible, and present too in every
form but covered up as soon as the form gets fixed in a shape.
Only in the moment when the flower rises from the ground
is a brief glimpse of the presence released. For this reason
validity lies in the process of flowering and not in the flower
full blown.[25]

This is what Williams is talking about in his prayer. Its recipient
is surely a woman, probably his mother (". . . I remember when
as a child/I stopped praying and shook with fear/until sleep—
your sleep calmed me—") and as such, the female principle.
For Williams the beautiful thing (the essence of beauty) is
often depicted as a woman. This emphasizes the sexual nature
of the creative act. With metaphor woman, goddess, earth, sea,
flower, and work of art can be conjoined, in that the same
principle or essence informs them all (the rock is "female to
the city"). She is goddess, as "the eternal bride and/father . . .
/a simple miracle that knows/the branching sea, to which the
oak/is coral, the coral oak." As earth, her features are seen as

---

25. P. 332.

"Himalayas and prairies." As flower (a very special flower, because it is also woman, goddess, and work of art) she never withers, but blossoms all about him. Discussing her "composition and decomposition," Williams sees her as a work of art, while at the same time he is referring also to her aspects of flower and earth. The tone of this prayer, which picks up the confidence of the grasshopper passage, stands in direct contradiction to that of the rest of Section 2, both the historical material and the "sermon" (also blocked) that precede it and the section of a letter from the poetess C. that follows it, concluding the Section.

Section 3 begins by briefly and perhaps ironically proposing an alternate role for the rock: not the generative principle or the achieved artifact but "the N of all equations," "the blank," "the nul"—total negation. Yet the nul, since it is absolute, is in its own way "positive." The enemy, we should remember, is not death, but blockage and divorce. Thus the spare "nul" poem, which ends with death, moves quickly into birth and a new form and tempo:

> Look for the nul . . .
>
> that's past all
> seeing
>
> the death of all
> that's past
>
> all being   .
>
> But Spring shall come and flowers will bloom
> and man must chatter of his doom   .   . (p. 95)

These lines in turn move immediately into a much more serious and profound exploration of the same themes, descent and defeat (echoing the first couplet of the nul poem, "Look for the nul/defeats it all") .

The descent beckons
         as the ascent beckoned
                Memory is a kind
of accomplishment
         a sort of renewal
                even
an initiation, since the spaces it opens are new
places
         inhabited by hordes
                heretofore unrealized,
of new kinds—
         since their movements
                are towards new objectives
(even though formerly they were abandoned)

No defeat is made up entirely of defeat—since
the world it opens is always a place
         formerly
                unsuspected. A
world lost,
         a world unsuspected
                beckons to new places
and no whiteness (lost) is so white as the memory
of whiteness   .

With evening, love wakens
         though its shadows
                which are alive by reason
of the sun shining—
         grow sleepy now and drop away
                from desire   .

Love without shadows stirs now
         beginning to waken
                as night
advances.

The descent
         made up of despairs
                and without accomplishment
realizes a new awakening :
                which is a reversal
of despair.

> For what we cannot accomplish, what
> is denied to love,
>   what we have lost in the anticipation—
>   a descent follows,
> endless and indestructible   . (pp. 96–97)

This passage is Williams's explanation for the descent of the grasshoppers, which both follows and prefaces each ascent in an "endless flight." Descent and ascent form yet another duality; now Williams investigates the former element as he has the latter. Its metaphors find, once again, a physical landscape within the mind: "the spaces it opens are new/places/inhabited by hordes/hithertofore unrealized." It is inhabited, especially, by Love, an abstraction personified, stirring and beginning to waken. Love's awakening in these new places is compared to (because it has embodied) the possible consequence of descent and despair—a "new awakening: which is a reversal of despair." This is, in other words, the process of creation. (Love's association with the ascent—the kindling and burning of a flame—has already been described in Book II.) The specific role of memory as an agent of descent is mentioned here for the first time. Williams's ultimate understanding of this insight leads to the final and altered form that *Paterson* achieves.

In Section 3 the park closes, the citizens leave, the moon rises, and the lovers in the park are once again the two giants, "He" and "She." This attempt to return to the realm of thematic metaphor (a technique that Williams utilizes in the conclusion to each of the first four books of *Paterson*) seems to me to be the least fully realized here. For example, the usual tension between thematic and local metaphor is absent. Williams is perhaps trying too hard to make language and form adhere to idea (to be worn out). Most of the dialogue simply repeats essential themes—"—divorced"; "and leaped (or fell) without a/language, tongue-tied"; "—the language is worn out," and the book fades to a close with a long (eight-page) extract from the unhappy C.

In summary, the Paterson of Book II, now a human character, takes a walk in the park outside the city. Thematic metaphor, which is used only at the beginning and the end of the book, sets up the underlying idea:

> The scene's the Park
> upon the rock,
> female to the city
> —upon whose body Paterson instructs his thoughts
> (concretely)   (p. 57)

Williams is concerned here with Paterson's relation to the rock. The rock is female to the city, and more—it becomes a type for the work of art, with Paterson functioning as artist. Thus male-female and artifact-artist relations are connected throughout the book as Paterson observes the citizens of Paterson making love in the grass and thinks about his own role as writer of the poem. Love and art are both manifestations of the creative process.

The patterns of metaphor of Book I functioned to demonstrate the several complexities involved in Williams's program of "no ideas but in things." In Book II, continuing this basic form, the metaphors cluster in long metaphoric sequences. "No ideas but in things" is, among other things, a statement about the creative process itself, so that by making ideas into things and things into ideas (personifying them), metaphors by their very form indicate something about the process. In addition, in this book Williams has the metaphors build from one another in each sequence, especially in the grasshopper passage, so that the statement results from the composite of metaphoric transfers viewed in their totality, what I have called their "spatial simultaneity." In exploring the duality of artist-artifact, Williams is trying to show how its elements ought to interpenetrate one another in an organic relation. His metaphors do this, yet each of the three long metaphoric passages are instances of his thoughts. All about him he observes the opposite of this fluid exchange of life and meaning: natural impulses are "blocked." And yet, even as in Book I Williams recognized the inherent desire of the divorced for unity, so here his comment on the overwhelming occurrence of rejection and suppression ends with "but . persistent." In Book II the prime example of the persistence toward creation is the thoughts of Paterson, expressed through patterns of metaphor.

IV

Whereas *Paterson I* was concerned with man's relation to his world, and *Paterson II* was concerned with man's relation to his work (man as artist and work as art), *Paterson III* is concerned with the relation of world and work. An exploration of the nature of beauty involves the duality between natural form and artistic form, between the beautiful thing and the book. Here Williams is dealing with what, at the outset, seems an insurmountable paradox. Books (the output of universities) represent staleness, stagnation, and death; they "enfeeble the mind's intent"; they are the prisons of "dead men's dreams." The beautiful thing, on the other hand, is characterized by her vital aliveness and her femaleness. Book III describes a series of encounters with women who embody her: vulgar, drunk, smelling "like a whore," in a white lace dress with "a busted nose." The two could not be more separate. This is how James Guimond, in *The Art of William Carlos Williams*, reads Book III:

> As Book III continues, the poet does more than destroy his own "words." By reading a "leaden flood" of "rubbish" he drives himself to revolt against the entire principle of books, the entire humanistic tradition of relating the living to the past. By forcing himself to read meaningless, dead books, Paterson's mind is driven to reveries about their antithesis: the "Beautiful Thing," the young woman he worships at the end of Part 2 of Book III. She lives in the squalor of the totally immediate, illiterate present. . . .
> Paterson's reveries about the Beautiful Thing cause him to decry "all books/that enfeeble the mind's intent." Her "vulgarity of beauty surpasses" all the books' "perfections" (III, ii, 145). He rejects the entire library as worthless because it contains nothing of her, and, in his mind, consigns it to flames of destruction like those that destroyed Paterson in 1902. Thus.

when Paterson rejects his erudition, the "library is muffled and dead" and the reign of the dead over the living is ended (III, ii, 140) .[26]

Yet Guimond is only partially accurate. For Williams's over-riding concern throughout all of *Paterson* is "the craft," the writing of books. His goal is not, as Guimond says later, "to appreciate the drunken, totally immediate lives of the Beautiful Thing and persons like her" (p. 191) . He wants to make poems from what he sees; to release the beautiful thing through words.

If Williams is interested in destruction ("Blow! So be it. Bring it down! So be it. Consume/and submerge! So be it. Cyclone, fire/and flood. So be it." p. 120) , it is for this purpose. As he writes in "An Approach to the Poem":

> *Everything* has to be broken down, not cynically,
> not without a deep sense of its old dignity, to
> get at the essential; the *formal* unit in its purity
> (that has been tied into now partially meaningless
> configurations by old languages) ; a rebellion on
>
> new (refreshed) formal lines:
> We must break down
>   the line
>   the sentence
> to get at the unit of the measure in order to
> build again. (p. 57)

In Book III the beautiful thing has other forms besides the whorish woman or women whom Paterson loves, forms that are created with metaphors. It is these aspects of the beautiful thing which Guimond, and any reading like his, overlooks. The metaphors for the beautiful thing, as I shall show, are what counteract the paradox; they indicate how beauty can entail both natural and artistic form.

Book III opens with a poem about a locust tree. Spare in form and statement, it is very like many small Williams poems about trees and flowers, except for one glaring difference. This

---

26. (Urbana, 1968) , pp. 190–91.

poem does not simply present or reveal the tree—it "loves" the tree and it is concerned about the "cost" of such a love. The question, "How much?" and the answer, "So much" and "heavy cost" entwine themselves about the tree.

Love of the locust tree is an instance of the love (for the most part, an unsatisfied lust) for beauty that is the poet's concern throughout Book III.

To understand this—to define and explore the nature of beauty—it is necessary for Paterson to descend into his own mind in this book, even as, in Book II, he had descended into concreteness, into the particulars of experience, in order to understand something of the nature of the creative process. Now Paterson is "Spent from wandering the useless/streets these months"; "something/has brought him back into his own/mind." For even though the beautiful thing is contained within external or natural form (the locust tree), it is through the work of the mind (resulting in artistic form) that it can be released and revealed.

The beautiful thing appears only after Paterson has entered his mind. It is wind that has brought him there.

> A cool of books
> will sometimes lead the mind to libraries
> of a hot afternoon, if books can be found
> cool to the sense to lead the mind away.
>
> For there is a wind or ghost of a wind
> in all books echoing the life
> there, a high wind that fills the tubes
> of the ear until we think we hear a wind,
> actual   .
>
> to lead the mind away.
>
> Drawn from the streets we break off
> our minds' seclusion and are taken up by
> the books' winds, seeking, seeking
> down the wind
> until we are unaware which is the wind and

which the wind's power over us   .

                    to lead the mind away

and there grows in the mind
a scent, it may be, of locust blossoms
whose perfume is itself a wind moving

                    to lead the mind away

through which, below the cataract
soon to be dry
the river whirls and eddys

                         first recollected. (p. 118)

At first the wind in all books, as a mental wind, is contrasted
to an "actual" wind. It may be a ghost; it is an echo; yet it has
power enough to make us think it is an actual wind and power
enough to "actually" fill the tube of the ear. In the next stanza
the wind is more active, and the distinction between mental and
actual is lessening. We are "taken up by/the books' winds," we
seek "down the wind," and ultimately we do not distinguish—
not between the mental wind and the actual wind—but between
the wind and its power over us "to lead the mind away." In
this stanza we (and Paterson) enter the mental world, so that
it can no longer be seen as figurative—that is, opposed to something else that is literal. In the next stanza the locust tree enters
the mental world, but as a "scent" or "perfume." As such—its
perfume "is itself a wind"—it assists in leading the mind away.
    In this world it is inevitable that we encounter the river and
waterfall of Paterson.

                Spent from wandering the useless
                streets these months, faces folded against
                him like clover at nightfall, something
                has brought him back to his own
                                        mind   .

                    in which a falls unseen

> tumbles and rights itself
> and refalls—and does not cease, falling
> and refalling with a roar, a reverberation
> not of the falls but of its rumor
> > unabated (pp. 118–19)

The reference to the waterfall here is neither thematic nor local metaphor: it is not metaphor at all. In Book I, where Williams was involved in studying the the relation between subjective and objective, and in moving his poem back and forth between both realms, metaphor was consistently used, as I have said, to explore those areas where the two come closest together. Thus metaphor would often describe a landscape of the mind. This landscape—"the green/and/dovegray countries of/the mind" —was metaphoric because only metaphor, the embodiment in language of the imagination, can join idea and thing. In Book III something else is happening. For the purposes of an exploration of the nature of beauty the external world has been dispensed with. Slowly, gradually, the mind has been led away, into itself; at this moment in *Paterson* only the mental world exists. Metaphor, used throughout *Paterson* to deal with the moment of contact between two elements of a duality, is not now concerned with the landscape of the mind, for now that is literal and physical. Metaphor is for the relation between natural and artistic form: it is for the beautiful thing.

The first metaphor for the beautiful thing immediately follows this evocation of the falls, and the movement and sound of the water continue throughout the passage.

> > Beautiful thing,
> my dove, unable and all who are windblown,
> touched by the fire
> > and unable,
> a roar that (soundless) drowns the sense
> with its reiteration
> > unwilling to lie in its bed
> and sleep and sleep, sleep
> > in its dark bed. (p. 119)

Metaphor allies the beautiful thing with wind, fire, and water,

the elements that in Book III are seen as counteracting the forces
of blockage and divorce that are specifically called upon to
destroy the library. As a "roar that (soundless) drowns the sense
/with its reiteration" the beautiful thing is connected with the
falls and its motion of falling, righting itself and refalling. This
kind of movement was shown in Book II to be the movement
of creation or invention; its "reverberation" is that movement
within the mind. The concept becomes even clearer when the
following passage appears almost directly after the description
of the beautiful thing.

> Books will give rest sometimes against
> the uproar of water falling
> and righting itself to refall filling
> the mind with its reverberation
> > > shaking stone. (p. 119)

Here "books" represent the opposite of the roar of the life-giving
creative process; they give rest against it. Finally, the beautiful
thing, as something unwilling and unable to lie in its dark bed
and sleep, is in yet another way allied with the proper kind of
writing—alive, not "stale," for these lines echo an earlier sequence
from the Preface to Book I:

> > and the craft,
> subverted by thought, rolling up, let
> him beware lest he turn to no more than
> the writing of stale poems . . .
> Minds like beds always made up,
> > > (more stony than a shore)
> unwilling or unable. (p. 13)

The next two metaphors for the beautiful thing call it, once
again, "a dark flame,/a wind a flood—counter to all staleness"
(p. 123) and also "the cost of dreams" (p. 124). The context
within which these metaphors occur offers both a detailed description of the problem and a move toward solution.

The province of the poem is the world.

when the sun rises, it rises in the poem
and when it sets darkness comes down
and the poem is dark   .

and lamps are lit, cats prowl and men
read, read—or mumble and stare
at that which their small lights distinguish
or obscure or their hands search out

in the dark. The poem moves them or
it does not move them.   Faitoute, his ears
ringing . no sound . no great city,
as he seems to read—

                              a roar of books
from the wadded library oppresses him
                                          until
his mind begins to drift .

                    Beautiful thing:

                            —a dark flame,
a wind, a flood—counter to all staleness.

Dead men's dreams, confined by these walls, risen,
seek an outlet. The spirit languishes,
unable, unable not from lack of innate ability—

                    (barring alone sure death)

but from that which immures them pressed here
together with their fellows, for respite .

Flown in before the cold or nightbound
  (the light attracted them)
                        they sought safety (in books)
but ended battering against glass
                        at the high windows

The Library is desolation, it has a smell of its own
of stagnation and death   .

                    Beautiful Thing!

—the cost of dreams. (pp. 122–24)

Williams is offering the poem itself as the contrast to the stale, closed tomb of dead men's dreams, the Library. The poem is fresh and open; it is life itself.

> When the sun rises, it rises in the poem
> and when it sets darkness comes down
> and the poem is dark   . (p. 122)

He is trying to show how words can escape the fate of the books in the Library. At the start of Section 3 he will write in prose: "Only one answer: write carelessly, so that nothing that is not green will survive" (p. 155). The use of metaphor in this passage makes the point, too, by insisting that the world of the poem is the real world. (The poem stands halfway between the mind and the external world; here Williams is emphasizing its vital connection with the latter.) The lines reiterate his view of the true poem, the "work of the imagination not 'like' anything but suffused with the same forces which transfuse the earth—at least one small part of them."

Paterson, his own spirit languishing in the Library's desolation and stagnation, calls again upon the beautiful thing, identifying her as "the cost of dreams." This "cost" is, as before, the cost of loving the locust tree. To love the locust tree is to try to write about it—to release, by writing, its essential beauty. Thus Williams wrote in the Prologue to *Kora in Hell:*

A poet witnessing the chicory flower and realizing its virtues of form and color so constructs his praise of it as to borrow no particle from right to left. He gives his poem over to the flower and its plant themselves, that they may benefit by those cooling winds of the imagination which thus returned upon them will refresh them at their task of saving the world. (XIII, 3, p. 17)

The "dreams" are those of dead men. Metaphor has made moths of these dreams, which were attracted by the light (and safety)

of books, but which now have flown up to the library's high
windows and batter against them, trying to escape. Ideas, once
again, are things; the purpose behind this particular manifestation of the technique seems to be to thereby relate the moth-
dreams to the grasshoppers of Book II. The rising movement
of the grasshoppers represented the ongoing motion of the creative process; the moth's movement indicates the very opposite,
and yet it is almost the same motion. The two are allied as
well as distinct, for the impulse of the dead men's dreams was
similar. The tragedy occurred later, in the writing itself.

Nothing "green" survives of poems (put into books and
libraries) that are treated as tradition, history, and fact. They
are completely divorced from the locust and cannot release the
beautiful thing. The imagination of the poet has been castrated.
Yet, even as this long sequence ends on a note of seeming despair, with the mind of Paterson fading, flying off, and joining
the dreams of dead men as they continue to batter against
the high windows and shriek as furies, the imagination is described, in almost the same breath, as "impotent" and unable
to be destroyed—"the life will not out of it."

> (They do not yield but shriek
>   as furies,
> shriek and execrate the imagination, the impotent,
> a woman against a woman, seeking to destroy
> it but cannot, the life will not out of it)
>
> A library—of books! decrying all books
> that enfeeble the mind's intent
>   Beautiful thing! (p. 125)

Metaphors for the beautiful thing have related it to both the
elements themselves, the fundamental forces of natural form,
and also to the writing process and its effect on the poet. In
the final metaphors of Section 1 it is invoked in the form it
assumes as it is being released by the poem from the natural
object; it is called the "radiant gist." (Later this image will be
expanded, as Williams devotes much of Book IV to a discussion

of Madame Curie and her discovery of radium. As J. Hillis
Miller writes, "The presence of beauty in things is like radium
in inert uranium ore. As the radioactive metal turns to lead, a
luminous energy is given forth. . . . This image expresses Williams's intuition perfectly."[27])

> —the voice rises, neglected
> (with its new) the unfaltering
> language. Is there no release?
>
> Give it up. Quit it. Stop writing.
> "Saintlike" you will never
> separate that stain of sense,
>   an offense
> to love, the mind's worm eating
> out the core, unappeased
>
> —never separate that stain
> of sense from the inert mass. Never.
> Never that radiance
>
>   quartered apart,
> unapproached by symbols
>
> Doctor, do you believe in
> "the people," the Democracy? Do
> you still believe—in this
> swill-hole of corrupt cities?
> Do you, Doctor? Now?
>
>   Give up
> the poem. Give up the shilly-
> shally of art.
>
>   What can you, what
> can YOU hope to conclude—
> on a heap of dirty linen?
>
>   —you
> a poet (ridded) from Paradise?

27. P. 334.

Is it a dirty book? I'll bet
it's a dirty book, she said.

　　Death lies in wait,
a kindly brother—
full of the missing words,
the words that never get said—
a kindly brother to the poor.
The radiant gist that
resists the final crystallization

　.　in the pitch-blend
the radiant gist　.　(pp. 131–33)

The metaphors are contained within an attack on the poet—
now a specific poet, Dr. Paterson—an attack, once again, upon
the significance of the poem. The sequence is built upon a
contrast between the poet's material and the transcendence that
art can achieve, through the release of the beautiful thing, between "a heap of dirty linen," "this swill-hold of corrupt cities,"
"the inert mass" and "that radiance/quartered apart,/unap-
proached by symbols." The poet is admonished to "Give up the
shilly-/shally of art" and asked, "Is it a dirty book?", yet he
speaks of "The radiant gist that/resists the final crystallization."
The two stanzas that contain these references to the radiant
gist juxtapose the two poles of this aspect of the duality—brute
physicality and transcendence—in a most extreme form. Each
is a series of appositional phrases, so constructed that it is difficult to tell which modifies which. Thus in the first we are given
the following:

that stain of sense
an offense to love
the mind's worm eating out the core, unappeased
that stain of sense
that radiance quartered apart, unapproached by symbols

If all or even some of the phrases that precede it are metaphors
for the radiant gist, then the function of these metaphors must

be to show that beauty involves all of these disparate qualities. More important, process is shown to be essential to its nature, for in that passage the poet is speaking of separating that stain of sense from the inert mass—of releasing the essence of beauty from its enmeshment in physical form.

The second mention of the radiant gist concludes another series of phrases:

> Death lies in wait
> a kindly brother
> full of the missing words
> the words that never got said
> a kindly brother to the poor
> The radiant gist that resists the final crystallization

Is the radiant gist death, or is death the "final crystallization"? Is death, perhaps, the ultimate poem ("full of the missing words /the words that never got said")? Or is it the poem which, alone, can survive death? The structure of the passage makes all of these possible; its significance lies in the interdependence of such possibilities.

The metaphors of Section 1 offer a series of definitions of the beautiful thing. It is wind, fire, and water; it is the cost of dreams; it is the radiant gist. It is at once the fundamental forces of natural form, the implication of the writing process, and the result of that process—the release of transcendent beauty through the achievement of artistic form. These metaphors function primarily to name or identify by means of the copula. Only as the section comes to a close does a sense of the verb, of the necessity of the process, manifest itself, when Williams speaks of separating the stain of sense from the inert mass, or of the radiant gist resisting the final crystallization. In Section 2 this is to become central, even as Section 2 is really the center of *Paterson*. Having identified the beautiful thing through both literal language and metaphor, Williams now attempts to describe it in action, to write of the actual moment of release of the beautiful thing.

The flame becomes, in Section 2, the sign for that moment

of release. Section 2 is a poem about fire. Its opening pages are devoted to an exploration, primarily by means of metaphor, of the nature of the flame. At the center of the Section the flame goes into action—the library burns; and at the heart of those pages is a metaphoric sequence that is perhaps the most intricate use of metaphor in *Paterson*. This is followed by a return to the beautiful thing in the closing pages of Section 2.

In the following list of metaphors, to write is a flame; so, too, are the conditions from which writing should be a relief. Flames make the day night. The poet feeds on the flames. Yet the flames have a requirement, a belly of their own that destroys. Primarily, the flame is the physical manifestation of the idea of action; although action seems to require destruction, we know from the previous sections of the poem that destruction is necessary to creation.

> . . . They have
>
> maneuvered it so that to write
> is a fire and not only of the blood. (p. 137)
>
> . . . The writing
> should be a relief,
>
> relief from the conditions
> which as we advance become—a fire,
>
> a destroying fire. (p. 137)
>
> The night was made day by the flames, flames
> on which he fed—grubbing the page
> (the burning page)
> like a worm—for enlightenment
>
> Of which we drink and are drunk and in the end
> are destroyed (as we feed). But the flames
> are flames with a requirement, a belly of their
> own that destroys—as there are fires that
> smolder
> smolder a lifetime and never burst
> into flame (pp. 141–42)

The other metaphors in the passages that precede the introduction of the bottle deal primarily with books, personifying
them:

> Breathless and in haste
> the various night (of books) awakes! awakes
> and begins (a second time) its song, pending the
> obloquy of dawn   .
>   It will not last forever
> against the long sea, the long, long
> sea, swept by winds, the "wine-dark sea"   . (p. 140)

>   And there,
> in the tobacco hush : in a tepee they lie
> huddled (a huddle of books)
>   antagonistic,
>   and dream of
>
> gentleness—under the malignity of the hush
> they cannot penetrate and cannot waken, to be again
> active but remain—books
>   that is, men in hell,
> their reign over the living ended (p. 140)

A small passage, inserted within the discussion of flame and
fire, recalls and reintroduces the major concerns (and dualities)
of the previous books—inner-outer, artist-artifact, reminding us
of their involvement in the crucial moment with which Williams
will soon deal.

> Clearly, they say. Oh clearly! Clearly?
> What more clear than that of all things
> nothing is so unclear, between man and
> his writing, as to which is the man and
> which is the thing and of them both which
> is the more to be valued (p. 140)

As the flames begin, at first the poet wishes only to describe
their beauty. They are *like* a mouse, a red slipper, a star, a
geranium, a cat's tongue, or—thought; but thought *is* a leaf, a
pebble, and an old man out of a story by Pushkin. (Again we

are reminded of our present environ—all this is taking place within the mind.) The poet notices, enthusiastically, how the fire is beginning to take effect.

Ah!

. an old bottle

mauled (p. 141)

The bottle is to become another central image of the poem— the antithesis of the green bud upon the pavement. The bottle, locked in a sexual embrace with the flame, represents both the beautiful thing and the poem in which it is manifested, for its moment of consummation with the fire embodies the moment in which the poet, through his poem, releases (if only for a moment) the beautiful thing, the radiant gist, from the matter, the object in which it has been imprisoned. In that single moment all are united.

An iron dog, eyes

aflame in a flame-filled corridor. A drunkenness
of flames. So be it. A bottle, mauled
by the flames, belly-bent with laughter:
yellow, green. So be it—of drunkenness
survived, in guffaws of flame. All fire afire!
So be it. Swallowing the fire. So be
it. Torqued to laughter by the fire,
the very fire. So be it. Chortling at flames
sucked in, a multiformity of laughter, a
flaming gravity surpassing the sobriety of
flames, a chastity of annihilation. Recreant,
calling it good. Calling the fire good.
So be it. The beauty of fire-blasted sand
that was glass, that was a bottle: unbottled.
Unabashed. So be it.

An old bottle, mauled by the fire
gets a new glaze, the glass warped
to a new distinction, reclaiming the
undefined. A hot stone, reached
by the tide, crackled over by fine

lines, the glaze unspoiled   .
Annihilation ameliorated: Hottest
lips lifted till no shape but a vast
molt of the news flows. Drink
of the news, fluid to the breath.
Shouts its laughter, crying out—by
an investment of grace in the sand
—or stone: oasis water. The glass
splotched with concentric rainbows
of cold fire that the fire has bequeathed
there as it cools, its flame
defied—the flame that wrapped the glass
deflowered, reflowered there by
the flame: a second flame, surpassing
heat   .

Hell's fire. Fire. Sit your horny ass
down. What's your game? Beat you
at your own game, Fire. Outlast you:
Poets Beats Fire at Its Own Game! The bottle!
the bottle! the bottle! the bottle! I
give you the bottle! What's burning
now, Fire?

The Library? (pp. 142–43)

In all of the first stanza there is no complete sentence. This form is itself a means of arresting the action, the moment. Noun phrases and assorted modifying, participial phrases circle around the bottle. Of these phrases the majority are metaphoric: "a drunkenness of flames"; "mauled by the flames"; "belly-bent with laughter"; "of drunkenness survived"; "in guffaws of flame"; "Torqued to laughter by the fire"; "swallowing the fire"; "chortling at flames sucked in"; "a multiformity of laughter"; "a flaming gravity surpassing the sobriety of flame"; "a chastity of annihilation"; "recreant"; "unbottled"; "unabashed." Both bottle and flame are personified—experiencing drunkenness and laughter. Now verbs are especially prominent. Of the fourteen metaphors, ten contain and stress verbs. These verbs are primarily either past or present participles. These, because of their very form, describe action, but action that is in some way arrested. The bottle is both acted upon and acting, and all verbs are violent ones: "mauled" and "torqued"; "swallowing" and "chortling." Yet amid this violent action are recurrent phrases of abstraction—"a multiformity of laughter"; "a flaming gravity surpassing the sobriety of flames"; "a chastity of annihilation"— and a profusion of abstract nouns like "drunkenness," "laughter," "multiformity," "gravity," "sobriety," "chastity," and "annihilation," used as if they were concrete. For this passage, too, presents Williams's familiar pattern of making ideas into things and things into ideas (the personification of bottle and flame). Here the ideas, the abstract concepts, have not had to be transformed into things; rather, they are simply named and treated as if they were things. Abstractions like "drunkenness" or "laughter" indicate all instances of their subject matter; used so persistently and strikingly in this description of a very specific event, they function to involve the universal in this particular, which is, as we know, of universal significance. The response of laughter to destruction, what the whole stanza has been describing, is an indication of what is to come in the next, for the destruction will initiate creation. The stanza concludes with a line of implication that points out the release of the beautiful thing with "unbottled./Unabashed."

The second stanza is yet more intricate. The first stanza depicted the moment of contact, encounter, penetration; the second attempts to render the extension of the moment into consummation. Now there are four components to the event being described: the subject (the bottle); the agent (the fire); the action and its result. Over and over in this stanza the action is presented, each time by means of new metaphors for each of the components, until the final line, which binds the whole together, can be reached. Thus the subject is given five times— an "old bottle"; "the glass"; a "hot stone"; "hottest lips"; and "the glass." The action of the flame upon it (always in participial phrases) is described as mauled by the fire; warped to a new distinction; reached by the tide; crackled over by fire lines; lifted;

splotched. The bottle, too, acts; it gets, flows, shouts. The result of acting and being acted upon is a new glaze; it is "the glaze unspoiled"; "no shape but a vast molt of the news"; "drink of the news"; "Fluid to the breath"; "concentric rainbows/of cold fire that the fire has bequeathed/there as it cools." There are again phrases of explication: "reclaiming the undefined"; "annihilation ameliorated"; "by/an investment of grace in the sand /—or stone: oasis waters." The recircling over object and event by means of continually paralleling syntactic form is a means of exploring their particularity. On the other hand, phrases and words like "hottest lips," "tide," "molt," "the news flows," "drink of the news," as well as "grace" or "oasis"—all transfers of metaphor—are what extend, through implication and relation, the particular into the universal. Here the technique is similar to that used in the initial Preface to Book I, which was also especially concerned with the particular-universal duality. Again, the expansion and development of one idea is achieved through metaphors that cause qualities from supposedly different realms to "interpenetrate."

Such meticulous probing of each aspect of the duality is necessary in order for the final lines of the stanza to be reached. In these lines occurs the creation, or release, of a second flame (beauty) which makes the passive active and the active passive. The flame that wrapped the glass is now deflowered, then reflowered, by the second flame, one which surpasses heat. Destruction has resulted in invention through the mutual imposition and discovery of new form: the beautiful thing has been freed; the revelation has occurred.

But it is immediately over, as the tone and manner of the final stanza indicates. Yet it did (and can) happen; that the third stanza tells us, too.

In the pages that follow the description of the bottle, other metaphors (as in the following sequence) offer still more "examples" that refer to that central experience.

> How shall I find examples? Some boy
> who drove a bull-dozer through

> the barrage at Iwo Jima and turned it
> and drove back making a path for the others—
>
> Voiceless, his
> action gracing a flame
>
> —but lost, lost
> because there is no way to link
> the syllables anew to imprison him
>
> No twist of the flame
> in his own image : he goes nameless
> until a Nike shall live in his honor—
>
> And for that, invention is lacking,
> the words are lacking:
>
> the waterfall of the
> flames, a cataract reversed, shooting
> upward (what difference does it make?)
>
> The language, (pp. 145–46)

Again, the metaphors are all of the flame: "voiceless, his/action gracing a flame"; "No twist of the flame/in his own image"; "the waterfall of the/flames, a cataract reversed." The idea here is that action is lost if it does not become a flame; that is, if it cannot be expressed. For the flame (its true revelation) is released through the expression of it (the language).

Yet another flame metaphor, also hearkening back to the bottle passage, indicates how that experience may be seen as the answer to the question asked earlier in literal language: "which is the man and/which is the thing and of them both which/is the more to be valued" (p. 140).

> Rising, with a whirling motion, the person
> passed into the flame, becomes the flame—
> the flame taking over the person (p. 146)

In other words, the duality, at that particular moment (and that moment only) is collapsed into the sought-after unity.

Most characteristic of the metaphors of the concluding pages, though, is their return to the invocation (and evocation) of the beautiful thing.

> Beautiful thing! aflame   .
>
>   a defiance of authority
> —burnt Sappho's poems, burned
> by intention (or are they still hid
> in the Vatican crypts?)   :
>   beauty is
> a defiance of authority   : (p. 144)
>
>   Beautiful thing, your
> vulgarity of beauty surpasses all their
> perfections!
>
>   Vulgarity surpasses all perfections
> —it leaps from a varnish pot and we see
> it pass—in flames!
>
>   Beautiful thing
>
> —intertwined with the fire. An identity
> surmounting the world, its core—from which
> we shrink squirting little hoses of
>   objection—and
> I along with the rest, squirting
> at the fire
>   Poet. (p. 145)
>
>   But you are the dream
> of dead men
>
>   Beautiful Thing!
>
> Let them explain you and you will be
> the heart of the explanation. Nameless,
> you will appear
>   Beautiful Thing
> the flame's lover— (p. 148)
>
>   —a flame,
> black plush, a dark flame. (p. 154)

These metaphors, too, are dependent upon the bottle experience. In each of them the beautiful thing is also the flame, for it reaches its fullest identity at the moment of its release, by the poem, from the physical object. These metaphors are like a summary of the aspects of the flame, and of the beautiful thing, which have been described thus far. The beautiful thing is "a defiance of authority," reminding us yet again of the reason for the necessity of destruction. It is vulgar, thus surpassing all perfections. The bottle experience is described once again, as the vulgar beauty is seen to leap from a varnish pot and pass—"in flames!" It is "intertwined with the fire"; "an identity surmounting the world." At the moment of release, as the long bottle passage has shown, words like "identity" and "intertwined" can be used; this is the only moment when dualities are dissolved. Finally, it is "the dream of dead men"; "the flame's lover"; "a flame/black plush, a dark flame." These metaphors recapitulate in capsule form Section 1's discussion of the library and its imprisoned dreams of dead men and Section 2's description of their release through a moment of interpenetration and creation that is clearly akin to the sexual. It concludes with the flame itself. In form these metaphors have returned to naming through copula or apposition and have all but relinquished (the primary exception is the second passage) the active verb.

Section 3 is the book of water and flood, which descends to the mud of the river bottom, not only to the divorce of language from object but to the depths of inarticulateness. The beautiful thing is no longer invoked here. Yet now that we know who she is, we know why this part of the poem must render the total descent and destruction that is necessary in order to begin again. In this brief section metaphor serves to remind us of the fact that we are still within the mind:

> . . . The stream
> grows leaden within him, his lilies drag. So
> be it. Texts mount and complicate them-
> selves, lead to further texts and those

> to synopses, digests and emendations. So be it.
> Until the words break loose or—sadly
> hold, unshaken. Unshaken! So be it. For
> the made-arch holds, the water piles up debris
> against it but it is unshaken. They gather
> upon the bridge and look down, unshaken.
> So be it. So be it. So be it. (p. 156)

Metaphor accompanies the many references to water, flood, and mud, even as it did those to wind and fire in Sections 1 and 2. These include

1) The sullen leaden flood, the silken flood
   —to the teeth
                       to the very eyes (p. 157)

2) tense with the wine of death
                                           downstream
   on the swift current   : (p. 158)

3) —the water at this stage no lullaby but a piston,
   cohabitous, scouring the stones   . (p. 163)

4) If it were only fertile. Rather a sort of muck, a detritus,
   in this case—a pustular scum, a decay, a choking
   lifelessness—that leaves the soil clogged after it,
   that glues the sandy bottom and blackens stones—so that
   they have to be scoured three times when, because of
   an attractive brokenness, we take them up for garden uses.
   An acrid, a revolting stench comes out of them, almost one
   might say a granular stench—fouls the mind   .

   How to begin to find a shape—to begin to begin again,
   turning the inside out : to find one phrase that will
   lie married beside another for delight   .   ?
   —seems beyond attainment   . (p. 167)

Here it is no longer a case of metaphor making either idea of thing or thing of idea. Each metaphoric reference to water and especially to mud conjoins it with some other thing or object. This technique reflects Williams's endeavor to point out in

Section 3 that this is descent in the fullest sense ("FULL STOP"); the mud is in no way alive.

> When the water has receded most things have lost their
> form. They lean in the direction the current went. Mud
> covers them
>
>   —fertile (?) mud.
> If it were only fertile . . . (p. 167)

These lines proceed into the fourth of the passages quoted above, where the metaphors for mud—"a pustular scum, a decay, a choking/lifelessness"—as well as the rest of the statement, stress the degree of the poet's problem.

Especially, the mud is the physical form of the past, which is absolute death.

> Go down, peer among the fishes. What
> do you expect to save, muscle shells?
>
> Here's a fossil conch (a paper weight
> of sufficient quaintness) mud
> and shells baked by a near eternity
> into a melange, hard as stone, full of
> tiny shells
> —baked by endless desiccations into
> a shelly rime—turned up
> in an old pasture whose history—
> even whose partial history, is
> death itself (p. 170)

The section begins with one attempt at an answer, which I have quoted before: "Only one answer: write carelessly so that nothing that is not green will survive" (p. 155). The stress must be upon the present, not upon the dead past nor even upon a faith in the future: "Who spoke of April? Some/insane engineer. There is no recurrence" (p. 169). In the same passage Williams offers his prose "answer" in yet another way:

> . . . Let the words
> fall any way at all—that they may

> hit love aslant. It will be a rare
> visitation. (p. 169)

It is with this idea that he concludes the Section and Book III.

> The past above, the future below
> and the present pouring down: the roar,
> the roar of the present, a speech—
> is, of necessity, my sole concern .
>
> They plunged, they fell in a swoon .
> or by intention, to make an end—the
> roar, unrelenting, witnessing   .
> Neither the past nor the future
>
> Neither to stare, amnesic—forgetting.
> The language cascades into the
> invisible, beyond and above : the falls
> of which it is the visible part—
>
> Not until I have made of it a replica
> will my sins be forgiven and my
> disease cured—in wax: *la capella di S. Rocco*
> on the sandstone crest above the old
>
> copper mines—where I used to see
> the images of arms and knees
> hung on nails (de Montpellier)   .
> No meaning. And yet, unless I find a place
>
> apart from it, I am its slave,
> its sleeper, bewildered—dazzled
> by distance   .   I cannot stay here
> to spend my life looking into the past:
>
> the future's no answer. I must
> find my meaning and lay it, white,
> beside the sliding water: myself—
> comb out of the language—or succumb
>
> —whatever the complexion. Let
> me out! (Well, go!) this rhetoric
> is real! (pp. 172–73)

Again he returns to the thematic metaphors upon which *Paterson* was conceived for his final sequence, yet it is precisely this stress upon the present which now complicates the conceptual precision and simplicity. The tone of personal involvement, which culminates with the final three stanzas, is one example of the impact of the present tense upon the poem. Paterson the giant is now Paterson the poet, who is himself only a hair's breadth from Dr. William Carlos Williams. Another example is the final sentence: "this rhetoric/is real!" Thematic metaphors are perhaps the most "artificial" of any of Williams's language forms, the most rhetorical. Yet the thrust behind them is the acute urgency of the present situation as Williams perceives it, its frightening reality. This concern permeates all of *Paterson* and especially this moment of the poem, so that with "rhetoric" and "real" a new dimension is added to the familiar conjunction of idea and thing.

In summary, Paterson, in Book III, descends into his own mind to read in the Paterson Public Library. Williams is now exploring the nature of beauty, which encompasses the duality between natural and artistic form. Williams's purpose in this book is to deal directly with that single moment around which all of his other themes and observations revolve: the moment in which the poem comes into being and thereby, releases transcendent beauty from the physical form in which it is contained (the object that the poem is about). Yet this moment is realized only through destruction. Book III describes destruction from wind, fire, and water and thereby descends to earth—to "rock bottom," or mud. At the heart of the book is a description of a fire that destroys the Paterson Library, and at the heart of this description is a long metaphoric passage in which Williams renders the moment in which the poem releases beauty.

That moment is perhaps the most complex event with which Williams has to deal in all of *Paterson,* so that all of the long Book III is either a preparation for it or else comments upon and summarizes its meanings and implications. Each section of the book concentrates upon one of the natural elements involved.

Section 1 is the book of wind, Section 2 of fire, and Section 3 of water. In Book III metaphor is used primarily to identify and characterize beauty, which Williams conceives of as the "beautiful thing." Since the beautiful thing is the direct opposite of staleness, stagnation, and death, which Williams has called upon the elements to destroy, the beautiful thing is associated with the elements. In each section the metaphors indicate the relation of the beautiful thing to wind, fire, and water.

In Section 1 the wind is in books, and books (contained in libraries) are shown to be the embodiments of staleness, stagnation, and death. Nonmetaphoric descriptions of the beautiful thing in this section, primarily as the figure of a woman, indicate her quality of vitality and her association with sheer physicality, or what I have called natural form. The metaphors of the section, however, link beauty and wind, or the beautiful thing and books, or physical form and artistic form, and therefore, as is customary, conjoin these dualities. They counteract the seeming paradox by indicating a proper (and vital) function for books. The conclusion to Section 1 begins to talk about beauty at the moment of release, calling it here "the radiant gist," an image which, although soon dropped as the poem begins to speak rather in terms of flame and fire, is reintroduced in Book IV. For the first time the metaphors begin to involve active verbs, rather than the copula, as the process by which natural form becomes artistic form begins to be investigated.

In Section 2 the beautiful thing is a flame. The Section centers upon the description of an old bottle burning in the Library fire, which is the depiction of the moment of release. In this passage metaphors are primarily verbal, yet verbal forms—past and present participles—which tend to both stress action and at the same time arrest it. This is because the process of release, which involves the maximum of action—which is for Williams the ultimate act—is yet so very brief. In his attempt to fully render it, the poet—and his metaphors—must freeze its action. Because this is the single act and moment in which all dualities are dissolved and a temporary, fragile, yet total unity is achieved, metaphors are used to indicate this aspect of the event by making active passive, passive active, particular general, general particular, and so forth.

In Section 3 the metaphors for water and for mud, by not personifying them or making them in any way alive, show the degree of descent that the destruction of the preceding sections has brought about. This is the bottom. Everything about the section reinforces this fact, including its passages of garbled, inarticulate language. The only answer is to stress the present moment, the moment of writing itself, which is, for the poet, now.

V

Throughout *Paterson* love has been an essential element, or force, in all that Williams has been trying to say about language and existence, divorce and creation. It becomes the subject of Book IV, in which metaphor is used to investigate the nature of love by exploring the duality between perversion and virtue.

In the Introduction to the separate publication of Book III Williams wrote of Book IV, "The Run to the Sea":

> Book IV shows the perverse confusions that come of a failure to untangle the language and make it our own as both man and woman are carried helplessly toward the sea (of blood) which, by their failure of speech, awaits them.

As always in his comments on his poem, Williams tends to simplify—that is, to stick to describing the "theory" rather than the "design." One form taken by such simplification is that he rarely mentions the affirmative statements and actions that constantly counterbalance the negative ideas in the poem. In other words, this poem is itself like the flight of grasshoppers—going down and up, both motions being necessary to the making of poems. Most of the passages upon which I concentrate in my discussion of metaphor—such as those about the grasshoppers, the rock, the bottle, and in Book IV, radium and Madame Curie, represent the upward motion. I have quoted from Williams's description primarily because it does accurately indicate the nature of the descent in Book IV—the final descent in the poem. Especially important is his use of the word "perverse." In *I Wanted to Write a Poem* (Boston, 1958) Williams emphasizes this aspect of the Book: "With the approach to the city, international character begins to enter the innocent river and pervert it; sexual perversions, such things that every metropolis when you get to know it houses." And "when the river reaches pollution, which my river comes to face in Book Four, I had to take the characters and show them graphically" (p. 79).

In the "Idyll" of Section 1, which Sister Bernetta characterizes tersely as "a disgusting travesty of the pastoral genre,"[28] Corydon is, as "she" should be, the figure of the poet perverted. Her poem (it is a poem, and she calls attention to it much as the poet Paterson has called attention to his concept of the poem— "This is a POEM!") is a poem about perverted death, suicide, and more important, the ultimate perversion of sex—unsexing. Its metaphors, especially, make clear its function in the greater poem, *Paterson*. They have the subject matter that is characteristic of metaphors in the other books (birds and rocks, love and minds), and they use the same technique: things become "ideas" —as gulls are vortices of despair (an abstraction), while ideas become things—love, an abstraction, is personified, while the mind assumes a body. Yet they are presenting quite another point of view—a perversion of the one to which we have grown accustomed.

> The gulls, vortices of despair, circle and give
> voice to their wild responses until the thing
> is gone   .   then, ravening, having scattered
> to survive, close again upon the focus,
> the bare stones, three harbor stones, except
> for that   .   useless
>
>   unprofaned   .   (p. 191)

---

28. P. 118.

>. . . Necessity gripping the words   .   scouting
>evasion, that love is begrimed, befouled   .
>
>   begrimed
>yet lifts its head, having suffered a sea-change!
>shorn of its eyes and its hair
>its teeth kicked out   .   a bitter submersion
>in darkness   .   a gelding, not to be
>listed   .   to be made ready! fit to
>serve . . . (pp. 194–195)
>
>   predatory minds, un-
>affected
>   UNINCONVENIENCED
>   unsexed, up
>and down (without wing motion) This is how
>the money's made   .   using such plugs. (p. 195)

The final quotation, especially, is a concise travesty of the true act of creation with both its sexual and intellectual components.

This "POEM" complements the activities described in Section 1, in which the female version of Paterson, a young nurse from Paterson, encounters in New York City a lesbian poet, a married man (*Mr.* Paterson), and her drunken father. What causes Section 1 to proceed and develop into Section 2 is the fact that the nurse, exposed to every possible perversion, remains virginal—virtuous.

The metaphors in Part 2, which emphasizes, as Guimond accurately observes, "the seeds of new forms". . . "achievement despite adversity,"[29] cluster predictably around the appearances of Madame Curie, for it is she who, "divorced from neither the male nor knowledge,"[30] in that sense truly virtuous, discovers radium. Radium, as we know already, is the radiant gist—the beautiful thing, so that the passages about radium in Section 2 of Book IV are similar in form and significance to those about the beautiful thing—incarnated in the old bottle—of Book III. The metaphors

---

29. P. 195.
30. P. 196.

that accompany the appearances of Madam Curie and her discovery are devoted to an exploration of virtue, the second half of the perversion—virtue duality, even as in Section 1 they were devoted to the depiction of perversion, the first half of the duality. Pregnancy and birth is in these pages the physical manifestation of virtue. Metaphors extend the implications of pregnancy and birth to other of Williams's themes and subjects, including mind and knowledge, fire and wind, and, in the final pages of the section, money and credit.

The following, one of the earliest metaphors in the section, is a concise example of the way in which metaphors involve both ideas and things—all relevant realms of experience—in a depiction of the concept of pregnancy. In the phrase "an unhatched sun corroding her mind" "unhatched" refers to chickens, to gestation and physical birth, "sun" refers to the radiance of, among other things, the radiant gist, "corroding" refers to metal (the metal of Madame Curie's discovery) , and all of these are contained within and acting upon the mind, which is thus objectified as egg, sky, and metal, at the very least.

>   For years a nurse-girl
>   an unhatched sun corroding
>   her mind, eating away a rind
>   of impermanences, through books
>   remorseless   .
>   Curie (the movie queen) upon
>   the stage at the Sorbonne   .
>   a half mile across! walking solitary
>   as tho' in a forest, the silence
>   of a great forest (of ideas)
>   before the assembly (the
>   little Polish baby-nurse) receives
>   international acclaim (a
>   drug) (p. 202)

In the next example apposition, always useful for this particular purpose, links related "cavities," personifies and objectifies, and culminates in a birth, which is the release of the radiant gist.

—a furnace, a cavity aching
toward fission; a hollow,
a woman waiting to be filled

—a luminosity of elements, the
current leaping! (p. 206)

Other metaphors, such as the following two passages, continue
the same technique. (A complete list of these metaphors may be
found in Appendix C.) Much as in the long grasshopper sequence of Book II, Williams proceeds by using his vocabulary
of different realms in constanly shifting and illuminating combinations (interpenetrations or conjunctions). Always his technique is based upon the initial program of "no ideas but in
things."

—with ponderous belly, full
of thoughts! (p. 208)

.   knowledge, the contaminant

Uranium, the complex atom, breaking
down, a city in itself, that complex
atom, always breaking down   .
to lead.

        But giving off that, to an
exposed plate, will reveal   .

And so, with coarsened hands
                              she stirs

And love, bitterly contesting, waits
that the mind shall declare itself not
alone in dreams   . (p. 209)

The most interesting development in the use of metaphor
in this section is the process of condensation that it undergoes.
In a sense, the inclusion in *Paterson* of Madame Curie and the
radiant gist is repetitive, even superfluous, since the idea, with
a somewhat different vocabulary, mirrors with much less poetic

brilliance that of bottle and flame. Williams has already come
to the absolute crux of the matter; now he appears to be merely
going over the same ground. Yet Madame Curie is important
to his scheme of things for several reasons. First because she is
a woman, so that the element of sexuality in "invention"—present metaphorically in the bottle passage—can be reasserted in a
much more direct way through the figure of a woman who
creates both physically and intellectually. Second, from radium
he can move to money, credit, and usury—material that has
been afloat through most of the poem but has not yet been
drawn into the web of "interpenetrating realities" (a web created
with metaphor), which is the true organizing "design" of the
poem.[31]

With the introduction of the money theme in the following
passage the tone of the metaphors abruptly changes.

> MONEY : JOKE (i.e., crime
>   under the circumstances : value
>   chipped away at accelerated pace.) (p. 214)

Hammering away in these final pages of the section at his
basic idea (itself a use of metaphor in the true Aristotelian sense,
as proportion—radium is to uranium as credit is to money),
Williams relies solely on the sign of proportion itself, the colon,
to create his metaphoric transfers for him. He dispenses with
verbal means of conjunction. He is, I think, emphasizing idea
here almost to the exclusion of form. Yet the new form that
arises in the passages that follow, culminating in the final one
(which moves into Pound's own language and form—"IN/ven-
shun./O.KAY/In venshun"), is almost a shorthand version of his
concept of metaphor. The colons here stand for the transfers of
metaphor which in Williams's usual metaphors conjoin ideas

---

31. I have a feeling, too, that it is important for Williams to make the
money theme prominent if only because of Pound. It is as if he feels that *he*
may be able to communicate these ideas of Pound's, which he thinks are
basically sound, to an audience that has refused to tolerate both Pound himself and his manner of poetic expression. Williams seems here to be trying
out his own form of expressing them.

and object from separate realms; they emphasize the fact that
for Williams the metaphoric act is one of conjoining—not joining, or merging identities into one.

> Money: Uranium (bound to be lead)
> throws out the fire   .
> —the radium's the credit—the wind in
> the trees, the hurricane in the
> palm trees, the tornado that lifts
> oceans   .
> Trade winds that broached a continent
> drive the ship forward   . (p. 214)

> Defeat may steel us
> in knowledge : money : joke
> to be wiped out sooner or later at stroke
> of pen   . (p. 215)

> Money : small time
>   reciprocal action relic
> precedent to stream-lined
>   turbine; credit

> Uranium : basic thought—leadward
>   Fractured : radium : credit

> Curie : woman (of no importance) genius : radium

> THE GIST

> credit : the gist

> IN
> venshun.
> O.KAY
> In venshun (pp. 217–18)

Section 3 returns to the overriding themes of the poem—
Paterson, the falls, and the hillside—as it begins "Haven't you
forgotten your virgin purpose,/the language?" It returns, too,
to the thematic or conceptual metaphors that always "delineate"
this level of the poem:

> Shh! the old man's asleep
>
> —all but for the tides, there is no river,
> silent now, twists and turns
> in his dreams   . (p. 219)

But only for a moment. Now, in dealing with this level, some-thing different begins to happen. The movement is inner, rather than outer: it is the movement of memory, which is "a kind/of accomplishment/a sort of renewal."

> Come on, get going. The tide's in
>
> *Leise! leise! Lentement! Che va piano,*
> *va lontano!* Virtue,
> my kitten, is a complex reward in all
> languages, achieved slowly.
>
> .   which reminds me of
> an old friend, now gone   . (p. 220)

Again the theme is that of virtue and its relation to love; here it is developed in the memories that follow of girls once known.

>   —another, once gave me
> an old ash-tray, a bit of
>   porcelain inscribed
> with the legend, *La Vertue*
>   *est toute dans l'effort*
> baked into the material,
>   maroon on white, a glazed
> Venerian scallop . for
>   ashes, fit repository
> for legend, a quieting thought:
>   Virtue is wholly
> in the effort to be virtuous .
>   This takes connivance,
> takes convoluted forms, takes
>   time! A sea-shell   . (p. 221)

After these memories the poem returns to the history of the

city of Paterson. Yet here, for the first time in the poem, this history is not only recounted in prose passages but in verse. It is as if the town's history has at last become assimilated—not merely into the character's memory and consciousness, but into the poet's own consciousness. Thus it can be expressed in his poetry. What happens in Section 3 of Book IV is a subtle, tentative thing and probably understandable only in the light of *Paterson V*, which was not meant to be, and of Williams's later poetry, written after his first stroke, which he suffered in 1951, the year of the publication of Book IV and the year in which he completed his *Autobiography*. The structure of the first four books of *Paterson* rests upon the notion of "by multiplication a reduction to one"; the idea that the particular reveals the universal, and vice versa. This is the movement among the many Patersons—city, giant, man, poet doctor. Always Paterson is conceived as a character, no matter how much Williams draws upon himself in its creation. Yet almost imperceptibly even this form of poetic "objectivity" fades away, and Paterson becomes Williams. But only, as I have said, in a tentative way, and as *Paterson IV* is concluding; yet this movement is the key to the seemingly abruptly changed form of *Paterson V*.

In this way *Paterson IV* ends. The river runs into the sea, but "the sea is not our home," and the Odysseus-like figure of Paterson heads inland at the end, for reasons that Williams has explained in the prose comment quoted earlier, reasons for which the poem has prepared the reader all along. The final metaphors of the passages of conclusion (pages 234 to 238) recapitulate these reasons. They are about the sea.

> —you cannot believe
> that it can begin again, again, here
> again   .   here
> Waken from a dream, this dream of
> the whole poem . sea-bound,
>   rises, a sea of blood (p. 234)
>
> But lullaby, they say, the time sea is
> no more than sleep is . afloat

with weeds, bearing seeds . (p. 234)

You will come to it, the blood dark sea
of praise. You must come to it. Seed
of Venus, you will return . to
a girl standing upon a tilted shell, rose
pink   . (p. 236)

                    the blood dark sea!
nicked by the light alone, diamonded
by the light   . from which the sun
alone lifts undamped his wings
                              of fire! (p. 236)

The best gloss on this sea of blood is—as it should be—the Preface to *Paterson I:*

                        Rolling in, top up,
under, thrust and recoil, a great clatter:
lifted as air, boated, multicolored, a
wash of seas—
from mathematics to particulars—

                        divided as the dew,
floating mists, to be rained down and
regathered into a river that flows
and encircles:

                        shells and animalcules
generally and so to man,

                    to Paterson. (p. 13)

This sea contained "The multiple seed,/packed tight with detail, soured" that "is lost in the flux and the mind,/distracted,
floats off in the same/scum." In the Preface, coming, as it does,
first, there is no doubt as to the creative function of its sea as
the source for all kinds of life—as the generative principle itself.
This last sea is the same sea. Blood is birth as well as death. In
the series of metaphors just quoted the sea is conjoined with
blood, time, praise (art), love, and light; the seed it contains,

along with scum and wrack, is the seed of all of the kinds of creation, which are also conjoined. In the final passage the sea, too, becomes a rock—a work of art "diamonded/by the light." Here is the moment of creativity, once again, from which the sun rises on a multitude of levels. For the sun, as has been prepared for by metaphors throughout the poem, is itself a sexual organ, and even the beautiful thing. This image of the sun with wings of fire rising above the diamonded sea recalls the phoenix symbol, which Williams himself used to describe his theory of art as descent and ascent, that form which controls the movement of *Paterson*.

> The natural corrective is the salutary mutation in the expression of all truths, the continual change without which no symbol remains permanent. It must change, it must reappear in another form, to remain permanent. It is the image of the Phoenix. To stop the flames that destroy the old nest prevents the rebirth of the bird itself. All things rot and stink, nothing stinks more than an old nest, if not recreated.
>
> This is the essence of what art is expected to do and cannot live without doing.[32]

As *Paterson III* ended, Paterson had descended to the rock-bottom of existence. Yet the book nevertheless ended on a positive note: an assertion of the ongoing power of existence itself—of the present moment. In Book IV Paterson leaves the isolation of his own mind, so that his new descent is into human relations, into the nature of love. Love, like every element of Williams's world, can be both destruction and creation—perversion and virtue. This is the duality that metaphor is now used to conjoin. In Section 1 metaphors render perversion; in Section 2 they deal with virtue. Even as in Book I the green bud was the "sign" for divorce and the flower the sign for first beauty, or in Book II the flight of the grasshoppers was the physical embodiment of the process of creation, and in Book III the embrace of flame and bottle embodies the poem's release of beauty from the physical object, so in Book IV Madame Curie, as both

---

32. *The Selected Essays of William Carlos Williams*, p. 208.

woman and scientist, is the physical embodiment or sign for the creative person. In her the sexual aspects of the concept of creativity can be fully realized. Therefore, metaphors accompany her appearances and explore the implications of pregnancy and birth by conjoining many kinds of mental and physical creation. With his inclusion of the Poundian theme of money and credit in the sphere of his metaphors, Williams presents almost a shorthand version of his form and theory of metaphor.

Book IV ends with yet a new kind of descent—the descent into the "new places" of memory. Although the poem *Paterson* is ostensibly ending here, with a return to the sea of blood, time, love, light, and art with which the poem began in the Preface to Book I, the entrance into these new places provides the intrinsic need—and impetus—for further installments of *Paterson*.

VI

Throughout this essay I have been implying that a profound change comes to *Paterson* with Book V. In my discussion of Book IV I both indicated something about the nature of this change and advanced the idea that it was not so very abrupt. In a sense *Paterson V* was an inevitable sequal to *Paterson IV* (and *Paterson VI* would also have followed, inevitably). They were inevitable once Williams recognized that *Paterson* had grown to be a poem about himself.

The New Directions edition of the complete *Paterson* includes, as an "Author's Note," this justification for the existence of *Paterson V*:

> I have come to understand not only that many changes have occurred in me and the world, but I have been forced to recognize that there can be no end to such a story I have envisioned with the terms which I have laid down for myself. I had to take the world of Paterson into a new dimension if I wanted to give it imaginative validity. Yet I wanted to keep it whole, as it is to me.

Sherman Paul's study of *An Autobiography* and "The Desert

Music" clearly demonstrates and explains Williams's need, as he grew old, to turn inward rather than outward, to autobiography and to the "new places" of memory.

> Autobiography is born of time and concerns time, the time of the self, which is a vital quality of its inward experience and coherence; and one turns to it because the significance of one's life may be found within its "field," in the experiences that constitute one's relations to life. In Williams' career one begins to recognize the emergence of this impulse when time replaces space as the primary dimension in the organization of his work (as in *Paterson,* which should be compared with *The Great American Novel,* an earlier unsuccessful spatial treatment of similar materials) ; when sound replaces light as the agency of affirmation—when the poet begins to hear the music of memory and responds to the "hum of the valved voice" (as in "The Desert Music" in contrast to *A Voyage to Pagany*) ; and when the measure of his verse begins to answer to a new time, the time of memory (as in "The Descent" of *Paterson II*) .[33]

It is of great importance that Williams used "The Descent" from *Paterson II* to begin his 1954 volume of poems, *The Desert Music.* One reason, of course, was its formal pattern, for he had come to realize that its triadic line was the "new measure" for which he had been searching throughout his career. But the subject of that poem also demanded its admittance to such a position. In its new location it is much more relevant to what follows (the poems of *The Desert Music* and, by extension, those of *Journey to Love* and *Paterson V*) than it was to what followed it in *Paterson II–IV.* It introduces the themes and preoccupations of these last poems:

Memory is a kind
of accomplishment,
a sort of renewal
even
an initiation . . .

---

33. *The Music of Survival* (Urbana, 1968) , p. 27.

On the other hand, it *was* written for *Paterson II,* which indicates, as did Sherman Paul in the paragraph just quoted, that the movement into memory grew naturally out of the poetry that preceded it. This new kind of descent, into memory, into the self, brought Williams—not to new themes and forms—but to a change in emphasis upon the ones that he had previously employed. The nature of the change is clearly indicated by his use of metaphor in *Paterson V* and, even more eloquently, by his very late long poem, "Asphodel, That Greeny Flower." These two poems have much to do with one another. *Paterson V* occupies a somewhat ambivalent position, looking backward, as it does, to the rest of *Paterson,* and looking forward to a fuller realization of its themes and form in the later poetry, most especially "Asphodel." *Paterson V* is not independent of *Paterson I–IV;* it must come to terms with those books and function within their terms, even though it brings with it a "new dimension." "Asphodel" has no such restrictions upon it; it takes up where *Paterson V* leaves off.

Paterson V moves solely in the "new places" of memory. In exploring his memories Williams discovers that his true subject matter is art, in ways he had not previously understood.

<pre>
Paterson, from the air
            above the low range of its hills
                        across the river
on a rock-ridge
            has returned to the old scenes
                        to witness
What has happened
            since Soupault gave him the novel
                        the Dadaist novel
to translate—
            The Last Nights of Paris.
                        "What has happened to Paris
since that time?
            and to myself"?
</pre>

A WORLD OF ART

THAT THROUGH THE YEARS HAS

SURVIVED!

—the museum became real
             The Cloisters—
                    on its rock
casting its shadow—
                 "la réalité! la réalité!
                     la réa, la réa, la réalité!"
                                  (pp. 243–44)

Paterson V is concerned with the nature of reality itself—
with art and with the imagination. Its central image is that of
the Unicorn Tapestries in the Cloisters: its flowers, its lady who
is both virgin and whore; its unicorn, who is the artist and
Paterson. The exploration of the tapestries and of related matters and memories continues the themes of the earlier books
of the poem, yet handles them in its new way. Since the tapestry
—and especially the unicorn—is the controlling image of this
book, it is predictable that we would find the major use of metaphor in the passages that speak of it. Nevertheless, here, too,
something has changed.

Williams's old ideas about the poem as an object, about the
movement of the imagination over objects have been extended
a step further. Because art presents objects elevated by the action
of the imagination to some kind of truth unavailable to them in
their original form, art is what we mean when we use the term
reality. Reality is thus neither the inner world nor the outer
world, but a combination of both—that is, art. I have said that
metaphor is a linguistic embodiment of the imagination for
Williams; that it functions in his poetry to define relations between particulars by conjoning them, by pressing them as closely
together as is possible, by establishing, as Josephine Miles says,
both an *as* and an *if.* In this new poetic world, in which art is
shown to be reality, the content and texture of the poetry change
accordingly, and so does the function of metaphor. If the imagination is especially exalted here, then it seems reasonable to

assume that metaphor, too, would take on new proportions. Herein lies an essential difference between *Paterson V* and "Asphodel." For in *Paterson V* the role of metaphor is less pronounced than in the previous books of *Paterson* or in "Asphodel." The recognition of the reality of art seems to have offered, as a first gift, a whole new language of the literal for Williams. Such is the language of the second half of the following long sequence, which cannot, however, be extracted from it.

<pre>
Now I come to the small flowers
                that cluster about the feet
                        of my beloved

—the hunt of
                the Unicorn and
                        the god of love
    of virgin birth

                The mind is the demon
                drives us   .   well,
                would you prefer it to
                turn vegetable and

                wear no beard?

—shall we speak of love
                seen only in a mirror
                        —no replica?
    reflecting only her impalpable spirit?
                which is she whom I see
                        and not touch her flesh?

                The Unicorn roams the forest of all true
    lovers' minds. They hunt it down. Bow wow! sing hey the
    green holly!

—every married man carries in his head
                the beloved and sacred image
                        of a virgin
    whom he has whored   .
                but the living fiction
                        a tapestry
</pre>

silk and wool shot with silver threads
        a milk-white one-horned beast
                I, Paterson, the King-self
saw the lady
        through the rough woods
                outside the palace walls
among the stench of sweating horses
        and gored hounds
                yelping with pain
the heavy breathing pack
        to see the dead beast
                brought in at last
across the saddlebow
        among the oak trees.
                Paterson,
keep your pecker up
        whatever the detail!
                Anywhere is everywhere:
You can learn from poems
        that an empty head tapped on
                sounds hollow
in any language! The figures
        are of heroic size.
                The woods
are cold though it is summer
        the lady's gown is heavy
                and reaches to the grass. (pp. 271-73)

The poet, Williams, can literally be "I, Paterson, the King-self"—
the Unicorn—precisely because through his art (this poem) and
the art of the tapestry-makers he can experience the woods, the
flowers, the unicorn hunt and its reality. This is why careful
descriptions of works of art run through Book V—the tapestries
and also, as another example, the paintings of Brueghel, discussed in Section 3.

Yet to say that "the museum became real," to speak, in the
above, of "the living fiction," is not a denial of the distinction
between literal and figurative. It rather points to the notion
that *literal* is not synonymous with *real* or with *object;* that
figurative is not synonymous with *fiction* or with *idea.* Figures

are those acts of the imagination which conjoin reality and fiction, idea and thing, so that these are not antithetical.

"Asphodel," on the other hand, is a poem that is built upon the second "gift" of Williams's recognition of the reality of art: a deeper understanding of the function of metaphor and its relation to art and thought.

Nevertheless, even in *Paterson V,* which stresses the power of the literal that has been granted to the poet by his new insight— an insight derived from his descent into the spaces of memory, the "world unsuspected"—metaphor is needed, and used, in the same places where it has previously been used in the poem: where Williams is expressing the central theme of the book. Here Williams is not investigating duality but underlining unity. Earlier in the poem, the only time when the deep yearning of the divorced for unity could be realized was shown to be that ephemeral moment in which natural form became artistic form —when the poem released transcendent beauty from its imprison- ment in the physical object. In *Paterson V* Williams's new in- sight, that art is reality, is basically only an extension of that moment: that is, a discovery of a position that can extend that moment, which was intrinsic in the moment all along. In this book metaphor persists in the pattern it has been establishing all along. It accompanies references to the tapestry, the unicorn, and the virgin/whore, it is used for those moments in which Williams is trying to explain that art is reality. To do this it continues to make ideas of things and things of ideas. What changes as the poem develops is not the function of metaphor but Williams's understanding and evaluation of that function. In the early books of *Paterson* only metaphor, the linguistic embodiment of the imagination, could conjoin the elements of existing dualities—*only* in language could this take place. With his discussion of the bottle and the flame Williams proposed that there was one moment and one moment only in which dualities could truly be unified, the moment in which the poem achieved its form and "spoke." Now Williams realizes that this ability of metaphor to conjoin dualities is actually what is real; that the separation of things into dualities is what is not real; and that it is only art which can achieve this vital reality.

The metaphors of *Paterson V* continue to make things of ideas, as in the following passage, in which Death, initially personified, wandering in the woods, having no peer, then becomes a "hole," a "bag," a "cavern." The imagination, in its turn, is rendered as "a hole/in the bottom of the bag," "this hole at the bottom of the cavern/of death": "It is through this hole/we escape." The image is brilliantly explanatory.

<pre>
                    The Unicorn
     has no match
               or mate .   the artist
                       has no peer .
     Death
               has no peer:
     wandering in the woods,
               a field crowded with small flowers
     in which the wounded beast lies down to rest   .

               We shall not get to the bottom:
               death is a hole
               in which we are all buried
               Gentile and Jew.

               The flower dies down
               and rots away   .
               But there is a hole
               in the bottom of the bag.

               It is the imagination
               which cannot be fathomed.
               It is through this hole
               we escape   .   .

     So through art alone, male and female, a field of
     flowers, a tapestry, spring flowers unequaled
     in loveliness.

               Through this hole
               at the bottom of the cavern
</pre>

of death, the imagination
escapes intact.

he bears a collar round his neck
hid in the bristling hair. (pp. 246–47)

Metaphors also make things of ideas, as in the passage quoted earlier in which the mind is "the demon drives us" and the Unicorn is said to roam through "the forest of all true lovers' minds." Again, in the opening lines of the book, the mind is depicted as an eagle.

In old age
                    the mind
                            casts off
                            rebelliously
                    an eagle
          from its crag (p. 241)

Each time, and especially in a passage like the following, the conjoining function of metaphor gives form to Williams's insight—makes a thing, a work of art, of his idea. To call Pollock's blobs of paints, squeezed out pure from the tube, the world of the imagination is not only to completely reverse any duality of inner and outer, it is to destroy such an "artificial" duality. Yet the key phrase here is "with design," for it is only through art, the design, that such achievement is possible.

          —the virgin and the whore, which
          most endures? the world
          of the imagination most endures:

          Pollock's blobs of paint squeezed out
          with design!
          pure from the tube. Nothing else
          is real   .   .

          WALK in the world
                          (you can't see anything
          from a car window, still less
          from a plane, or from the moon!? Come
          off of it.)

> —a present, a "present"
> world, across three states (Ben Shahn saw it
> among its rails and wires,
> and noted it down) walked across three states
>
> for it   .   .
>   a secret world,
> a sphere, a snake with its tail in
> its mouth
>   rolls backward into the past (pp. 248-49)

Paterson V concludes with lines about "the measure" and "the dance."

> The measure intervenes, to measure is all we know,
>   a choice among the measures   .   .
>
>   the measured dance
> "unless the scent of a rose
>   startle us anew"
>
> Equally laughable
>   is to assume to know nothing, a
>   chess game
> massively, "materially," compounded!
>
>   Yo ho! ta ho!
>
> We know nothing and can know nothing   .
>   but
> the dance, to dance to a measure
> contrapuntally,
>   Satyrically, the tragic foot. (pp. 277-78)

One of the purposes—and achievements—of Book V was to demonstrate the form of Williams's new measure consonant with our day as he had finally determined it. One of J. Hillis Miller's most helpful insights is his identification of this form as

> a triumphant reconciliation of the three elements [ground, form, beauty] in a perpetual balance. Instead of moving from ground toward form to release a spark of beauty but then falling back, or holding all three separately in precarious

tension, each line or phrase of these poems gathers the elements into inextricable union. Rising and sinking are not sequential but simultaneous. Each line flows from the unfathomable ground into its unique measure and so brings beauty to light. The next does the same, and the next, and so on.[34]

Thus, he correctly argues, in *Paterson V* time has been transcended, and all the elements of the poem are there together, touching one another, interacting with one another; "all are assembled in one place, and the poem can move in a movement from one to another, for all are possessed at once" (p. 356). Yet with "possessed" Miller is referring to his central thesis in *Poets of Reality,* which he renders as follows in his discussion of *Paterson V:* "It is not, as might seem, a return to separate form, the poet bound by the surface of his body, caught in his private thought. He rises with the world contained in his body and its thoughts" (p. 355). This is a restatement of the central thesis of Miller's important book, in which he discusses Williams as a poet (also included are Yeats, Eliot, Thomas, and Stevens) who has moved out of the subjective-objective bind that characterizes Romantic and Victorian poetry by annihilating subjectivity.[35] The best answer to Miller's claim is the cen-

---

34. P. 355.
35. A more extensive explanation of Miller's position is as follows:

The act by which man turns the world inside-out into his mind leads to nihilism. This can be escaped only by a counterrevolution in which man turns himself inside-out and steps, as Wallace Stevens puts it, "barefoot into reality." This leap into the world characterizes the reversal enacted in one way or another by the five poets studied here.

To walk barefoot into reality means abandoning the independence of the ego. Instead of making everything an object for the self, the mind must efface itself before reality, or plunge into the density of an exterior world, dispersing itself in a milieu which exceeds it and which it has not made. The effacement of the ego before reality means abandoning the will to power over things. This is the most difficult of acts for a modern man to perform. It goes counter to all the penchants of our culture. To abandon its project of dominion the will must will not to will. Only through an abnegation of the will can objects begin to manifest themselves as they are, in the integrity of their presence. When man is willing to let things be then they appear in a space which is no longer that of an objective world oposed to the mind. In this new space the mind is dispersed everywhere in things and forms one with them. (pp. 7–8)

tral idea of *Paterson V*. To explain the abandonment of the independence of the ego, the "leap into the world," Miller uses Stevens's phrase "barefoot into reality." But, says Williams, art, not the world, is reality. And art, for Williams, is, as I have tried to show, a conjunction of the subjective and the objective, not a destruction of the distinction between them: a conjunction that is achieved by the power of the imagination.

6
Metaphor and Experience

For Williams, Pound, and Stevens metaphor is fundamental
to the structure of their poetry. Each poet, in writing about
experience, senses a disconnection between its elements: for
Williams, between idea and thing; for Pound, between emotion
and action; for Stevens, between abstract and concrete. These
are variations on a similar theme, the underlying, more general
dichotomy between imagination and reality.

Scholars writing about the modern period (which may go
back, for many, well into the nineteenth century) have often
commented upon this awareness of a "gap"; so have philosophers
and psychologists. This is, indeed, the "modern condition." There
have been attempts to define its origins, its symptoms, its effects.
That is, one can legitimately ask about these three poets: why
do they sense disconnection, or why, even, do they write about
experience (which is not the only possible subject matter for
art)? In this book, however, I take what they have done as a
fait accompli and am primarily interested in describing what
it is that they do do. Given the desire to write about experience,
given the accompanying sense of a dual nature to experience
(an inner and an outer, a subjective and an objective, a mind
and a body, an abstract and a concrete, a real and an imaginary,
and so on), each of these poets "solves" the "problem" with

metaphor. This is why metaphor has to be fundamental to the structure of their poetry: this is why they share so many assumptions about the nature and function of metaphor itself.

The theories of metaphor implicit and explicit in the work of Williams, Pound, and Stevens—and my own interpretations of these theories—are not at all the only ones possible. Nor are these poets' uses of metaphor the only possible uses. The list that follows indicates something of the range and emphases of theories of metaphor through the centuries. Metaphor has been seen as indicating 1) analogy or 2) identity: as 3) decoration or 4) essence; as characteristic of 5) the language of art or 6) natural or "primitive" language; as 7 a phenomenon in language or 8) a conceptual tool.[1] In terms of these categories Williams, Pound, and Stevens would all stress No. 4 (essence), No. 5 (language of art), No. 7 (phenomenon of language). Whereas both Pound and Stevens might accept No. 2 (identity), Williams, although not agreeing with No. 1 (analogy) either, might prefer a word like conjunction, which falls somewhere in between No. 1 and 2.

A very different use of metaphor results from different theories. For example, when metaphor is seen as analogy or, especially, as decoration, metaphors like this conceit from Pope's *Essay on Criticism* result.[2]

> What is this *Wit* which must our Cares employ?
> The *Owner's Wife,* that *other men* enjoy,
> Then most our *Trouble* still when most *admir'd,*
> And still the more we *give,* the more *requir'd;*

---

1. An analysis of traditional and modern theories of metaphor in terms of these categories can be found in my article "A Critical History of the Theory of Metaphor," 1972.

2. Theoretical remarks such as these from Hugh Blair's *Lectures on Rhetoric* (1762 et seq.) describe the purpose and function of such metaphors.
Simple expression just makes our ideas known to others; but Figurative Language, over and above, bestows a particular dress, upon that idea; a dress, which both makes it to be remarked, and adorns it. (p. 193)

For it is, in truth, the sentiment or passion, which lies under the figured expression, that gives it any merit. The figure is only the dress; the sentiment is the body and substance. (p. 195)

Whose Fame with *Pains* we guard, but lose with *Ease,*
Sure *some* to *vex,* but never *all* to *please;*
'Tis what the *Vicious fear,* the *Virtuous shun;*
By *Fools* 'tis *hated,* and by *Knaves undone!*[3]

For Williams, Pound, and Stevens metaphor, by its nature, conjoins dichotomies, bridges dualities, reveals true lines of relation, and so on. What, then, is its nature?

In my opening chapters I offered little in the way of a definition of metaphor, allowing the poets themselves full freedom to use metaphors in characteristic ways, so that the reader's notions about what a metaphor is might evolve from experiencing them in action. I suggested at the outset that by metaphor I meant that kind of linguistic transfer (in whatever syntactic form it occurs, such as verbal, adjectival, or nominal) which implicitly moves a literal into a nonliteral statement. I stressed metaphor's position as the most extreme of figures, in that it states the figurative as literal truth, and establishes a relation between figurative and literal within a simple statement.

The power of metaphor stems from the seeming paradox between the fact that metaphor is the most extreme of figures and the fact that it states the figurative as literal truth (it does not say "like a rose" but "is a rose" or "blooms" or "petalled"). However, these facts are paradoxical when one realizes that the difference between literal and figurative, although it may parallel the distinction between real and imaginary, is not the same as that between real and unreal. Metaphor is itself founded in the inner-outer dichotomy and the several kinds of reality thus created. Mental acts and language acts are as *real* as physical acts, but they are different and so reveal different kinds of reality. Metaphor is a linguistic act; it is the expression, in language, of a mental act. Whether it reveals acts that take place in the outer world as well is dependent upon the notions of the mind making the metaphor, upon whether or not the maker believes that

---

3. *The Poems of Alexander Pope,* ed. John Butt (New Haven, Conn., 1966), p. 159.

inner and outer can or do correspond. All of our three poets do believe so.

All of our poets also believe that metaphor is true. When Williams tells us that love is a flower, he is expecting his reader to understand, because he has given us the clue or guideline, ways in which love *can be* a flower. Here we encounter some of the strange qualities of metaphor that make it the most extraordinary, and also the most studied of figures. The reader "understands" a metaphor by means of another mental act, one that is not, as Pound's use of metaphor in particular shows, one of intellection. It is rather one of imagining, and these, as recent experiments in psychology have shown, are different.[4] Metaphor needs no carefully worked through rational process to be understood, as I have illustrated in some detail in discussing Pound. By its nature it short-circuits or by-passes such processes, which is why I have used words like clue and guideline. As Winifred Nowottny writes, "metaphor directs us to the *sense,* not to the exact terms. . . . The reader pieces out the metaphor by something supplied or constructed from his own experience, *according to the specifications given linguistically by the utterance in which the metaphor occurs.*"[5] (Italics mine) These "linguistic specifications" are contained in the metaphor itself and also in the context, both immediate and total, in which the metaphor occurs. The reader senses in what ways love can be a flower, or a woman can bloom or be petaled, because he has been reading the poem in which these metaphors occur, in which very often a consistent pattern of the metaphors has been developed. (Often in a poem that uses metaphor in a very uncontrolled manner, seemingly for the sake of being metaphoric and thus "poetic," the significance of individual metaphors becomes indeed difficult to grasp.)

Josephine Miles's observations on the act of metaphor further indicate what is implied in its transfers: "Metaphor is not so

4. Joseph Juhasz, "An Experimental Study of Imagining," *Journal of Personality* (1972) in press; Alan Paivio, "Mental Imagery in Associative Learning and Memory," *Psychological Review* 76 (1969) : 241–63.
5. *The Language Poets Use* (London, 1965) , p. 59.

simple. While image and concept present, and symbol uses image to stand for concept, metaphor, as its own reference indicates, carries across or transfers, and that action is not simple. Why not? Because qualities usually combined in one way are re-combined in another."[6] Miss Miles goes on to show how metaphor reverses ordinate and subordinate qualities, "for the sake of the metaphor's own *newly created relevance*" (p. 123). Again I italicize, to emphasize, along with Miss Miles, both the act of transfer and the power of transfer: the power to create. The following statements by Williams about art itself underline the nature of this power and also indicate the intrinsic relation that can be seen to exist between metaphor and poetry.

> You do not *copy* nature, you make something which is an *imitation* of nature—read your Aristotle again.
> That is the work of the imagination, as the late Virginia Woolf pointed out. You have to work, you have to imagine the character, you have to *be* the creator.
> Arrived at that condition, the imagination inflamed, the excitement of it is that you no longer copy but *make* a natural object. (Something comparable to nature; an other nature.) [7]

If metaphor indeed conjoins, bridges, reveals, it does so by means of the active power of the mind and of language: the power of art over nature. This is why I, and our poets, stress the importance of metaphor as transfer.

The other aspect of metaphor that must be stressed once again is, of course, relation. I have said earlier that metaphor depends for its meaning upon the perception of relation between its components. Metaphor is a language act that effects a relation between literal and figurative (reality and the imagination). Because it is language it bridges the mind and the world, for language is an act that partakes of both the acts of the mind and those of the world: it is a physical (spoken or written) expression of thoughts. Because it is figurative language it relates

---

6. *Style and Proportion: the Language of Prose and Poetry* (Boston, 1967), p. 123.
7. *Selected Essays* (New York, 1954), p. 303.

the two levels of perception itself (the act of the mind experiencing the world) by transferring truth from the literal to the figurative plane. Experience, too, as defined by each of the poets, exists as relation (as inner and outer). The task of the poet is to reveal the total or whole experience. Metaphor is thus peculiarly suited to poetry of this sort, in that it contains within itself the dual aspects of experience and can bring them together.

This approach to metaphor has been a controlling force in the development of the poetry of Williams, Pound, and Stevens. Especially, it has helped them to deal with the Imagist aesthetic, which is at the heart of their own aesthetic theories. Metaphor can reveal the dual aspects of experience while concentrating upon the object itself ("direct treatment of the 'thing'"). It has also enabled them to move beyond the confines of the short poem, which limited the range of the original Imagists, while continuing to present without explaining ("absolutely no word which does not contribute to the presentation"). Patterns of metaphor create a nondiscursive method by which to link and develop images into a complex, long work. It remains to be demonstrated how peculiarly or thoroughly "modern" this theory and practice of metaphor may be, but it is my belief that they are characteristic and central to the poetry of these three of the greatest and most influential of modern poets.

Appendix A

METAPHORS IN "ASPHODEL, THAT GREENY FLOWER"

Book I

1) Of asphodel, that greeny flower
   like a buttercup
      upon its branching stem—
 save that it's green and wooden— (p. 153)
2)   a life filled,
      if you will,
 with flowers. (p. 153)
3) that there were flowers also
   in hell. (p. 153)
4) I'm filled with the fading memory of those flowers
        (p. 153)
5)   even to this poor
 colorless thing— (p. 153)
6)   Of love, abiding love
 it will be telling
   though too weak a wash of crimson
     colors it
 to make it wholly credible. (p. 154)
7) I had a good collection.
   The asphodel,
    forebodingly,
 among them. (p. 155)
8)   I bring you,
    reawakened,

a memory of those flowers. (p. 155)
9) It is a curious odor,
        a moral odor,
                that brings me
    near to you.
            The color
                    was the first to go. (p. 155)
10) There had come to me
        a challenge,
                your dear self,
    mortal as I was,
            the lily's throat
                    to the hummingbird! (p. 155)
    Endless wealth,
            I thought,
11)   held out its arms to me.
    A thousand topics
            in an apple blossom. (p. 155)
12)   The whole world
                    became my garden! (p. 156)
13) But the sea
            which no one tends
                    is also a garden
    when the sun strikes it
            and the waves
                    are wakened.
    I have seen it
            and so have you
                    when it puts all flowers
    to shame. (p. 156)
14)   Its [love's] guerdon
                    is a fairy flower;
    a cat of twenty lives.
            If no one came to try it
                    the world
    would be the loser. (p. 157)
15) The storm unfolds . . .
            It is a flower
                    that will soon reach
    the apex of its bloom. (p. 157)
16)   those crimson petals
    spilled among the stones, (p. 158)
17) The sexual orchid that bloomed then (p. 158)

18)   and the will becomes again
                              a garden . . . (p. 159)
19)   . . . When I speak
        of flowers
                    it is to recall
                              that at one time
        we were young. (p. 159)
20)   Imagine you saw
        a field made up of women
                    all silver-white. (p. 160)
21)   Love is something else,
                              or so I thought it,
        a garden which expands,
                    though I knew you as a woman
                              and never thought otherwise,
        until the whole sea
                    has been taken up
                              and all its gardens. (p. 160)
22) I should have known
                    though I did not,
                              that the lily-of-the-valley
        is a flower makes many ill
                    who whiff it. (p. 160)
23)   Love
                              to which you too shall bow
        along with me—
                    a flower
                              a weakest flower
        shall be our trust (p. 161)
24) Of asphodel, that greeny flower,
                    I come, my sweet,
                              to sing to you! (p. 161)

Book II

1)   But if I have come from the sea
                              it is not to be
        wholly
                    fascinated by the glint of waves.
                              The free interchange
        of light over their surface
                    which I have compared
                              to a garden

should not deceive us
       or prove
                    too difficult a figure.
The poem
       if it reflects the sea
                    reflects only
its dance
       upon the profound depth
                    where
it seems to triumph.
                    The bomb puts an end
                          to all that.
I am reminded
       that the bomb
                    also
is a flower
       dedicated
                    howbeit
to our destruction. (pp. 164–65)
2) Meanwhile
       we are sick to death
                    of the bomb
and its childlike
       insistence.
                    Death is no answer,
no answer—
       to a blind old man
                    whose bones
have the movement
       of the sea,
                    a sexless old man
for whom it is a sea
       of which his verses
                    are made up.
There is no power
       so great as love
                    which is a sea,
which is a garden—
       as enduring
                    as the verses
of that blind old man
       destined
                    to live forever.

Few men believe that
        nor in the games of children.
                They believe rather
    in the bomb
        and shall die by
                the bomb. (p. 166)
3)   But Darwin
                opened our eyes
    to the gardens of the world, (p. 167)
4)   How the world opened its eyes!
                It was a flower
    upon which April
        had descended from the skies!
                How bitter
    a disappointment! (p. 167)

Book III

1) Because of this
        I have invoked the flower
                in that
    frail as it is
        after winter's harshness
                it comes again
    to delect us.
        Asphodel, the ancients believed,
                in hell's despite
    was such a flower.
        With daisies pied
                and violets blue,
    we say, the spring of the year
        comes in!
                So may it be
    with the spring of love's year
        also
                if we can but find
    the secret word
        to transform it. (pp. 169–70)
2) Fanciful or not
        it seemed to me
                a flower
    whose savor had been lost.

It was a flower
        some exotic orchid
that Herman Melville had admired
    in the
        Hawaiian jungle.
Or the lilacs
    of men who left their marks,
        by torchlight,
rituals of the hunt,
    on the walls
        of prehistoric
caves in the Pyrenees—
    what draftsmen they were—
        bison and deer.
Their women
    had big buttocks.
        But what
draftsmen they were!
    By my father's beard,
        what draftsmen.
And so, by chance,
    how should it be otherwise?
        from what came to me
in a subway train
    I build a picture
        of all men. (p. 174)

3) It is winter
    and there
        waiting for you to care for them
are your plants.
    Poor things! you say
        as you compassionately
pour at their roots
    the reviving water. (p. 175)

4)   These heads
        that stick up all around me
are, I take it,
    also proud.
        But the flowers
know at least this much,
    that it is not spring
        and will be proud only
in the proper season. (p. 176)

5)   I say to you
                    privately
that the heads of most men I see
            at meetings
                    or when I come up against them
elsewhere
            are full of cupidity.
                    Let us breed
from those others.
            They are the flowers of the race.
                    The asphodel
poor as it is
            is among them.
                    But in their pride
there come to my mind
            the daisy,
                    not the shy flower
of England but the brilliance
            that mantled
                    with white
the fields
            which we knew
                    as children.
Do you remember
            their spicy-sweet
                    odor? What abundance!
There are many other flowers.
            I could recall
                    for your pleasure:
the small yellow sweet-scented violet
            that grew
                    in marshy places!
You were like those
            though I quickly
                    correct myself
for you were a woman
            and no flower
                    and had to face
the problems which confront a woman.
            But you were for all that
                    flowerlike
and I say this to you now
            and it is the thing

which compounded
my torment
that I never
forgot it.
You have forgiven me
making me new again.
So that here
in the place
dedicated in the imagination
to memory
of the dead
I bring you
a last flower. Don't think
that because I say this
in a poem
it can be treated lightly
or that the facts will not uphold it.
Are facts not flowers
and flowers facts
or poems flowers
or all works of the imagination,
interchangable?
Which proves
that love
rules them all, for then
you will be my queen,
my queen of love
forever more. (pp. 176–78)

Appendix B

METAPHORS IN *PATERSON*

Book I, Section 2

1) —unfledged desire, irresponsible, green,
   colder to the hand than stone,
   unready—challenging our waking: (p. 28)
2) Two halfgrown girls hailing hallowed Easter,
   (an inversion of all out-of-doors) weaving
   about themselves, from under
   the heavy air, whorls of thick translucencies
   poured down, cleaving them away,
   shut from the light: bare-
   headed, their clear hair dangling—

   Two—
        disparate among the pouring
   waters of their hair in which nothing is
   molten—

   two, bound by an instinct to be the same: (p. 29)
3) upright in the air, the pouring air, (p. 29)
4)   The theme
   is as it may prove: asleep, unrecognized—
   all of a piece, alone
   in a wind that does not move the others—
   in that way: a way to spend
   a Sunday afternoon while the green bush shakes. (p. 30)
5) Thus

the first wife, with giraffish awkwardness
among thick lightnings that stab at
the mystery of a man: in sum, a sleep, a
source, a scourge . (p. 32)

6)   certainly NOT the university,
a green bud fallen upon the pavement its
sweet breath suppressed . . . (p. 32)

7)   Which is to say, though it be poorly
said, there is a first wife
and a first beauty, complex, ovate—
the woody sepals standing back under
the stress to hold it there, innate

a flower within a flower whose history
(within the mind) crouching
among the ferny rocks, laughs at the names
by which they think to trap it. Escapes!
Never by running but by lying still—

A history that has, by its den in the
rocks, bole and fangs, its own cane-brake
whence, half hid, canes and stripes
blending, it grins (beauty defied)
not for the sake of the encyclopedia.

Were we near enough its stinking breath
would fell us. The temple upon
the rock is its brother, whose majesty
lies in jungles—made to spring,
at the rifle-shot of learning: to kill

and grind those bones: (p. 33)

8) the whole din of fracturing thought
as it falls tinnily to nothing upon the streets (p. 34)

9)   Pithy philosophies of
daily exits and entrances, with books
propping up one end of the shaky table—
The vague accuracies of events dancing two
and two with language which they
forever surpass—and dawns
tangled in darkness— (p. 34)

10) and I am aware of the stream
that has no language, coursing

beneath the quiet heaven of
your eyes

      which has no speech; to
go to bed with you, to pass beyond
the moment of meeting, while the
currents float still in mid-air, to
fall—
with you from the brink, before
the crash—
      to seize the moment. (p. 35)
11) And the air lying over the water
lifts the ripples, brother
to brother, touching as the mind touches,
counter-current, upstream
brings in the fields, hot and cold
parallel but never mingling, one that whirls
backward at the brink and curls invisibly
upward, fills the hollow, whirling,
an accompaniment—but apart, observant of
the distress, sweeps down or up clearing
the spray— (p. 36)

Book I, Section 3

1) . . . What heroic
dawn of desire
is denied to his thoughts?

They are trees
from whose leaves streaming with rain
his mind drinks of desire :

Who is younger than I?
  The contemptible twig?
that I was? stale in mind
  whom the dirt

recently gave up? Weak
  to the wind.
Gracile? Taking up no place,
too narrow to be engraved
  with the maps

of a world it never knew,
   the green and
dovegrey countries of
   the mind.

a mere stick that has
   twenty leaves
against my convolutions.
   What shall it become,

Snot nose, that I have
   not been?
I enclose it and
   persist, go on.

Let it rot, at my center.
   Whose center?
I stand and surpass
   youth's leanness.

My surface is myself.
   Under which
to witness, youth is
   buried. Roots?

Everybody has roots. (pp. 42–44)
2) We go on living, we permit ourselves
   to continue—but certainly
   not for the university, what they publish
   severally or as a group: clerks
   got out of hand forgetting for the most part
   to whom they are beholden.

   spitted on fixed concepts like
   roasting hogs, sputtering, their drip sizzling
   in the fire (p. 44)
3) Moveless
   he envies the men that ran
   and could run off
   toward the peripheries—
   to other centers, direct—
   for clarity (if
   they found it)

                              loveliness and
        authority in the world—

        a sort of springtime
        toward which their minds aspired
        but which he saw,
        within himself—ice bound

        and leaped, "the body, not until
        the following spring, frozen in
        an ice cake" (p. 48)
   4) He thinks: two eyes; nothing escapes them,
        neither the convolutions of the sexual orchid
        hedged by fern and honey-smells, to
        the last hair of the consent of the dying.
        And silk spins from the hot drums to a music
        of pathetic souvenirs, a comb and nail-file
        in an imitation leather case—to
        remind him, to remind him! (p. 49)
   5)   Thought clambers up,
        snail like, upon the wet rocks
        hidden from sun and sight—
                          hedged in by the pouring torrent—

        and has its birth and death there
        in that moist chamber, shut from
        the world—and unknown to the world,
        cloak itself in mystery—

                                        And the myth
        that holds up the rock,
        that holds up the water thrives there—
        in that cavern, that profound cleft,
                                        a flickering green
        inspiring terror, watching .   .

        And standing, shrouded there, in that din,
        Earth, the chatterer, father of all
        speech .   .   .   .   (pp. 51–52)

Book IV, Section 2

   1) For years a nurse-girl

                              an unhatched sun corroding
her mind, eating away a rind
                    of impermanences, through books
remorseless   .
Curie (the movie queen) upon
                    the stage at the Sorbonne   .
a half mile across! walking solitary
                    as tho' in a forest, the silence
of a great forest (of ideas)
                    before the assembly (the
little Polish baby-nurse) receives
                    international acclaim (a
drug) (p. 202)

2) —a furnace, a cavity aching
toward fission; a hollow,
a woman waiting to be filled

—a luminosity of elements, the
current leaping! (p. 206)

3)   hydrogen
        the flame, helium the
        pregnant ash   . (p. 207)

4) Love is a kitten, a pleasant
thing, a purr and a
pounce. Chases a piece of

string, a scratch and a mew
a ball batted with a paw   .
a sheathed claw   .

Love, the sledge that smashes the atom? No, No! antagonistic
cooperation is the key, says Levy   . (pp. 207–8)

5) —with ponderous belly, full
   of thought! (p. 208)

6) .   knowledge, the contaminant

Uranium, the complex atom, breaking

down, a city in itself, that complex
atom, always breaking down   .
to lead.
        But giving off that, to an

exposed plate, will reveal   .

And so, with coarsened hands

she stirs

And love, bitterly contesting, waits
that the mind shall declare itself not
alone in dreams   . (p. 209)
7)   not half asleep
waiting for the sun to part the labia
of shabby clouds . but a man   (or
a woman) achieved

flagrant!
adept at thought, playing the words
following a table which is the synthesis
of thought, a symbol that is to him,
sun up! (p. 210)
8) Woman is the weaker vessel, but
the mind is neutral, a bead linking
continents, brow and toe (p. 211)
9) MONEY : JOKE (i.e., crime
under the circumstances : value
chipped away at accelerated pace.)   (p. 214)
10) Money: Uranium (bound to be lead)
throws out the fire   .
—the radium's the credit—the wind in
the trees, the hurricane in the
palm trees, the tornado that lifts
oceans   .
Trade winds that broached a continent
drive the ship forward   . (p. 214)
11)   Defeat may steel us
in knowledge : money : joke
to be wiped out sooner or later at stroke
of pen   . (p. 215)
12)   Money : small time
reciprocal action relic
precedent to stream-lined
turbine; credit

Uranium : basic thought—leadward
Fractured : radium : credit

Curie : woman (of no importance) genius : radium
                    THE GIST
                    credit : the gist
    IN
        venshun.
    O.KAY
        In venshun (pp. 217–18)

A Bibliography of Works Consulted

A. Metaphor, Poetic Language, and Related Subjects

a. Before 1800 (in chronological order)

Aristotle. *Poetics.*
"Longinus." *On the Sublime.*
Demetrius. *On Style.*
Faral, Edmond. *Les Arts poetiques du XIIᵉ et du XIIIᵉ siècle.* Paris, 1924.
Puttenham, George. *The Arte of English Poesie.* 1589.
Sidney, Philip. *An Apologie for Poetrie.* 1595.
Bysshe, Edward. *The Art of English Poetry.* 1702.
Blair, Hugh. *Lectures on Rhetoric and Belles Lettres, 1762 et seq.* 1813.
Kames, Henry. *Elements of Criticism.* 1762.
Campbell, George. *The Philosophy of Rhetoric.* 1770.
Scott, John. *Critical Essays on some of the poems, of several English Poets.* 1785.

b. 1800–1900 (in chronological order)

Wordsworth, William. "Preface" to the *Lyrical Ballads* (1802). *Wordsworth's Poetical Works,* edited by Thomas Hutchinson. London, 1967.
———. "Essay, Supplementary to the Preface" (1802). *Wordsworth's Poetical Works,* edited by Thomas Hutchinson, London, 1967.
———. "Preface" to the *Lyrical Ballads* (1815). *Wordsworth's Poetical Works,* edited by Thomas Hutchinson. London. 1967.
Coleridge, Samuel. *Biographia Literaria* (1817). London, 1967.

Hazlitt, William. "On Poetry in General" (1818). *Lectures on the English Poets*. London, 1910.

Shelley, Percy Bysshe. "A Defense of Poetry" (1821). *Essays and Letters of Percy Bysshe Shelley*, edited by Ernest Rhys. London, 1887.

Newman, John Henry. "Poetry, with Reference to Aristotle's 'Poetics'" (1829). *Essays Critical and Historical*. London, 1871.

Keble, John. *Keble's Lectures on Poetry* (1844). Translated by E. K. Francis. Oxford, 1912.

Mill, John Stuart. "Thoughts on Poetry and its Varieties" (1833). *Dissertations and Discussions*. vol. 1. London, 1859.

Moir, George. *Treatises on Poetry, Modern Romance, and Rhetoric; being the Articles under those Heads, Contributed to the Encyclopaedia Britannica, Seventh Edition*. Edinburgh, 1839.

Carlyle, Thomas. "The Hero as Poet. Dante: Shakespeare" (1840). *On Heroes, Hero-Worship, and the Heroic in History*. London, 1841.

Hunt, Leigh. *An Answer to the Question "What is Poetry?"* Edited by A. S. Cook. Boston, 1893.

Browning, Robert. "Introductory Essay." *Letters of Percy Bysshe Shelley, with an Introductory Essay by Robert Browning*. London, 1852.

Dallas, Eneas. *Poetics: an Essay on Poetry*. London, 1852.

Arnold, Matthew. "Preface." *Poems*. London, 1853.

Ruskin, John. *Modern Painters*. vol. 3 (1856). New York, 1885.

Bagehot, Walter. "Wordsworth, Tennyson, and Browning: or Pure, Ornate, and Grotesque Art in English Poetry" (1864). *Literary Studies*. London, 1879.

Hopkins, Gerard Manley. "Poetic Diction" (1865). *The Journals and Papers of Gerard Manley Hopkins*. Edited by Humphrey House. London, 1959.

————. "On the Origin of Beauty" (1865). *The Journals and Papers of Gerard Manley Hopkins*. Edited by Humphrey House, London, 1959.

c. Since 1900 (in alphabetical order)

Baker, William. *Syntax in English Poetry: 1870–1930*. Berkeley, 1967.

Barfield, Owen. *Poetic Diction: A Study in Meaning*. New York, 1964.

Beardsley, Monroe. *Aesthetics: Problems in the Philosophy of Criticism*. New York, 1958.

Berry, Francis. *Poets' Grammar: Person, Time, and Mood in Poetry*. London, 1958.

Black, Max. "Metaphor." *Models and Metaphors.* Ithaca, N. Y., 1962.

Brooke-Rose, Christine. *A Grammar of Metaphor.* London, 1958.

Brown, Roger. *Words and Things.* Glencoe, Ill., 1958.

Burke, Kenneth. "Four Master Tropes." *A Grammar of Motives.* New York, 1945.

———. "Lexicon Rhetoricae." *Counter-Statement.* 2nd ed. Los Altos, Calif., 1953.

———. "Perspective as Metaphor." *Permanence and Change.* New York, 1954.

Cassirer, Ernst. *Language and Myth.* New York, 1946.

Davie, Donald. *Articulate Energy.* London, 1955.

Dickey, James. *Metaphor as Pure Adventure.* Washington, 1968.

Empson, William. *The Structure of Complex Words.* London, 1951.

Fenollosa, Ernest. *The Chinese Written Character as a Medium for Poetry.* San Francisco, 1936.

Henle, Paul. "Metaphor." *Language, Thought and Culture.* Ann Arbor, Mich., 1958.

Hulme, T. E. "Notes on Language and Style." *The Criterion.* July 1925.

———. "Romanticism and Classicism." *Critiques and Essays in Criticism, 1920–1948.* Edited by Robert Stallman. New York, 1949.

Jakobson, Roman. "The Metaphoric and Metonymic Poles." *Fundamentals of Language.* The Hague, 1956.

Langer, Susanne. *Feeling and Form.* New York, 1953.

———. *Philosophy in a New Key.* New York, 1951.

Levin, Samuel. *Linguistic Structures in Poetry.* The Hague, 1962.

Miles, Josephine. *Eras and Modes in English Poetry.* 2nd ed. Berkeley, Calif., 1964.

———. *Pathetic Fallacy in the Nineteenth Century.* New York, 1965.

———. *Style and Proportion: the Language of Prose and Poetry.* Boston, 1967.

Nowottny, Winifred. *The Language Poets Use.* London, 1965.

Ohmann, Richard. "Prolegomena to the Analysis of Style." *Essays on the Language of Literature.* Edited by Seymour Chatman and Samuel R. Levin. Boston, 1967.

Ransom, John Crowe. "Poetry: A Note in Ontology." *Critiques and Essays in Criticism, 1920–1948.* Edited by Robert Stallman. New York, 1948.

Richards, I. A. *Interpretation in Teaching.* New York, 1938.

———. *The Philosophy of Rhetoric.* New York, 1936.

Stanford, W. Bedell. *Greek Metaphor.* Oxford, 1936.

Stevenson, Charles. *Ethics and Language.* New Haven, Conn., 1944.

Thomas, Owen. *Metaphor and Related Subjects.* New York, 1969.

Wheelwright, Philip. *Metaphor and Reality.* Bloomington, Ind., 1962.
Wimsatt, William. "The Substantive Level." *The Verbal Icon.* Lexington, Ky., 1954.

B. William Carlos Williams

Guimond, James. *The Art of William Carlos Williams.* Urbana, Ill., 1968.
Koch, Vivienne. *William Carlos Williams.* Norfolk, Conn., 1950.
Miller, J. Hillis. *Poets of Reality.* New York, 1969.
———, ed. *William Carlos Williams; a collection of critical essays.* Englewood Cliffs, N. J., 1966.
Paul, Sherman. *The Music of Survival.* Urbana, Ill., 1968.
Quinn, Sister M. Bernetta. *The Metamorphic Tradition in Modern Poetry.* New Brunswick, N. J., 1955.
Thirwall, John C. "William Carlos Williams' 'Paterson.'" *New Directions 17,* edited by James Laughlin, pp. 252–309. Norfolk, Conn., 1961.
Wagner, Linda. *The Poems of William Carlos Williams.* Middletown, Conn., 1964.
Williams, William Carlos. "An Approach to the Poem." *English Institute Essays, 1947.* New York, 1965, pp. 50–75.
———. *An Autobiography.* New York, 1951.
———. *Collected Earlier Poems.* New York, 1951.
———. *Collected Later Poems.* rev. ed. New York, 1963.
———. *I Wanted to Write a Poem.* Edited by Edith Heal. Boston, 1958.
———. *In the American Grain.* New York, 1956.
———. *Kora in Hell: Improvisations.* Boston, 1920.
———. *Many Loves, and Other Plays.* Norfolk, Conn., 1961.
———. *Paterson.* New York, 1963.
———. *Pictures from Brueghel, and Other Poems.* New York, 1962.
———. *Selected Essays.* New York, 1954.
———. *Selected Letters.* Edited by John C. Thirwall. New York, 1957.
———. *Spring and All.* Dijon, 1923.

C. Ezra Pound

Browning, Robert. *The Works of Robert Browning.* 10 vols. London, 1912.
Davie, Donald. *Ezra Pound: Poet as Sculptor.* New York, 1964.
Dekker, George. *The Cantos of Ezra Pound.* New York, 1963.
Edwards, John H., and Vasse, William W., *Annotated Index to the Cantos.* Berkeley and Los Angeles, 1959.

Frank, Joseph. "Spatial Form in Modern Literature." *Criticism*. Edited by Mark Schorer, Josephine Miles, and Gordon McKenzie. New York, 1958.

Kenner, Hugh. "Under the Larches of Paradise." *Gnomon*. New York, 1958.

⸻. *The Poetry of Ezra Pound*. New York, 1951.

Leary, Lewis, ed. *Motive and Method in the Cantos of Ezra Pound*. New York, 1954.

Pearce, Roy Harvey. *The Continuity of American Poetry*. Princeton, N. J., 1961.

Pound, Ezra. *ABC of Reading*. New York, 1960.

⸻. *Antheil and the Treatise on Harmony*. Chicago, 1927.

⸻. *A Draft of XVI Cantos for the Beginning of a Poem of Some Length*. Paris, 1925.

⸻. *Cavalcanti—Sonnets and Ballate*. Cambridge, Mass., 1912.

⸻. *Culture*. New York, 1938.

⸻. *Gaudier-Brzeska, a memoir*. London, 1916.

⸻. *Instigations*. New York, 1920.

⸻. *The Letters of Ezra Pound, 1907–1941*. Edited by D. D. Paige. New York, 1950.

⸻. *Literary Essays of Ezra Pound*. Edited by T. S. Eliot. New York, 1954.

⸻. *Lustra of Ezra Pound*. New York, 1917.

⸻. *Make it New*. London, 1934.

⸻. *Personae*. New York, 1926.

⸻. *Selected Poems of Ezra Pound*. New York, 1957.

⸻. *The Cantos (1–95)*. New York, 1956.

⸻. *The Spirit of Romance*. New York, 1929.

⸻. *Thrones, 96–109 de los cantares*. New York, 1959.

⸻. *Translations*. New York, 1963.

Rouse, W. H. D. *Shakespeare's Ovid, Arthur Golding's translation of the Metamorphoses*. New York, 1961.

Russel, Peter, ed. *An Examination of Ezra Pound*. London, 1950.

Sarbin, Theodore R., and Juhasz, Joseph B., "Toward a Theory of Imagination." *Journal of Personality* 38, no. 1 (March, 1970): 52–76.

Stock, Noel, ed. *Ezra Pound Perspectives*. Chicago, 1965.

⸻. *Reading the Cantos*. New York, 1966.

Slatin, Myles. "A History of Pound's Cantos I-XVI, 1915–1925," *American Literature* 35, (March 1963–January 1964): 183–95.

Sutton, Walter, ed. *Ezra Pound, A Collection of Critical Essays*. Englewood Cliffs, N. J., 1963.

Watts, Harold H. *Ezra Pound and the Cantos*. London, 1952.

Williams, William C. *The Autobiography of William Carlos Williams.* New York, 1951.

Wittemeyer, Hugh. *The Poetry of Ezra Pound. Forms and Renewals, 1908–1920.* Berkeley and Los Angeles, 1969.

D. Wallace Stevens

Baird, James. *The Dome and the Rock: Structure in the Poetry of Wallace Stevens.* Baltimore, 1968.

Borroff, Marie, ed. *Wallace Stevens: A collection of critical essays.* Englewood Cliffs, N. J., 1963.

Brown, Ashley, and Haller, Robert, eds. *The Achievement of Wallace Stevens.* Philadelphia, 1962.

Eder, Doris. "A Review of Stevens Criticism to Date," *Twentieth Century Literature* 15, no. 1 (April 1969) : 3–18.

Enck, John. *Wallace Stevens; Images and Judgements.* Carbondale, Ill., 1964.

Fuchs, Daniel. *The Comic Spirit of Wallace Stevens.* Durham, N. C., 1963.

Kermode, Frank. *Wallace Stevens.* Edinburgh, 1960.

Miller, J. Hillis. *Poets of Reality.* New York, 1969.

Nemerov, Howard. "The Poetry of Wallace Stevens," *Sewanee Review* (Winter 1957), pp. 1–14.

O'Connor, William Van. *The Shaping Spirit.* Chicago, 1950.

Pearce, Roy Harvey, and Miller, J. Hillis, eds. *The Act of the Mind.* Baltimore, 1965.

Stevens, Wallace. *Collected Poems.* New York, 1964.

———. *Letters.* Edited by Holly Stevens. New York, 1966.

———. *The Necessary Angel.* New York, 1965.

———. *Opus Posthumous.* New York, 1957.

Sukenick, Ronald. *Wallace Stevens: Musing the Obscure.* New York, 1967.

Index